THE ELIZABETHANS AT HOME

THE
ELIZABETHANS
AT HOME

BY

ELIZABETH BURTON

Illustrated by
FELIX KELLY

Longman

LONGMAN GROUP LIMITED
LONDON

*Associated companies, branches and
representatives throughout the world*

© Elizabeth Burton 1958

First published by Secker & Warburg 1958
Reissued in 1970

SBN 582 12612 6

Printed in Great Britain by
Lowe & Brydone (Printers) Ltd., London

C

1939–1954

And he will make the face of heaven so fine

ACKNOWLEDGEMENTS

I HAVE to thank His Grace the Duke of Devonshire and the Trustees of the Chatsworth Settlement for their permission to read and quote from the Family Papers and Accounts of the Cavendish Family, preserved at Chatsworth. I am also greatly indebted to Mr. T. S. Wragg, Keeper of the Devonshire Collections at Chatsworth, for his invaluable assistance.

To Mr. Felix Kelly I owe a great deal, not only for the happiest of collaborations but for his encouragement, help and enthusiasm. Indeed, this book is as much his as mine.

I am indebted to Mr. R. G. Chapman and the staff of the Bodleian Library, and to the Librarian and staff of the London Library for their courtesy and assistance; to Miss Margot Johnson of New York for her advice and encouragement; to Dr. Elizabeth Drummond and Dr. M. B. Noble for their help with Chapter VI; to Dr. Anne Hume of the Canadian Library Association for her excellent advice; and to Mr. David Farrer of Secker and Warburg —a most understanding, helpful and patient editor.

CONTENTS

CHAPTER ONE

Of Elizabethan England

SHE had come to the Tower once before. Four and a half years
ago, on Palm Sunday morning, a barge had landed her at the
water gate. The Thames, rain-pitted, high and sullen under a
leaden sky, had submerged the lower part of the landing stair.
Perhaps she slipped on the wet stone or perhaps for a moment
her courage failed—whatever the reason, she fell on her knees and
wept. The prospect of having one's head chopped off was terri-
fying enough to make one die of fear. But her mother had not
died of it. Clad in red damask* she had bared her neck with its
witch-sign—a strawberry-shaped mole—to the headsman's axe.
Being a queen had not saved her. Being a princess would not
save the twenty-year-old girl wetting her knees in dirty Thames
water and her face with salty tears.

But today, November 28th 1558, she came in purple velvet
and in triumph to the Tower. Via Cripplegate and Barbican she
rode; through narrow, filthy streets jammed with people; past
houses so brave with flags and banners, so hung with painted
cloths, silks and tapestries that they seemed to sway in the wind
like the tented pavilions of a crusading army. At the head of the
procession rode the Mayor with Garter King-at-Arms bearing
the sceptre; then the gentlemen pensioners—rich in red damask

* Some historians say that Anne Boleyn wore red, others black. She
may have worn a black mantel over a red kirtle which would account
for the seeming discrepancy of opinion.

and the bright gold of their gilded axes. After them, the heralds, gay as court cards, and the royal-cyphered footmen in crimson and silver. Directly in front of her My Lord Pembroke bore her sword; and directly behind, her new Master-of-the-Horse and ex-fellow-prisoner, Robert Dudley, followed as he was to do for the rest of his life. And as she came to the Tower, once her prison and now to be her royal residence for several weeks before she went on to her palace at Whitehall, all the Tower artillery boomed a welcome and "all the wights of the City sounded loud music" on their trumpets.[1]

What she thought, as she entered the fortress for the second time, we do not know. But what she said, turning to those who surrounded her, was this: "Some have fallen from being princes of this land to be prisoners of this place; I am raised from being a prisoner in this place to being a Prince of this land. That dejection was a work of God's justice; this advancement is a work of his mercy. . . ."

Perhaps she believed what she said, though often she said what she did not believe. But wittingly or unwittingly she spoke the truth. It was God's mercy to her—and to her country. For the country, to put it baldly, was in a mess. Its fortunes were at their lowest ebb. The new Queen inherited from her half-sister an England which, in the dozen years since her father's death, had become a third-class power—a heel-piece of Spain. Disgraced in peace and war, governed by "fools and adventurers, foreigners and fanatics",[2] it lacked financial credit, arms, men, and leaders.

In Spain, Philip, recently bereaved of his unhappy, undesired wife and his greatly desired kingdom, expressed his love for the new Queen and heard it rumoured that the canny politician Sir William Cecil—a member of the newly rising middle class of smaller gentry—was the coming man. In France, Henri II tactlessly proclaimed his daughter-in-law, Mary Stuart, Queen of England and had the Royal Arms quartered on her shield. But at home young men in a hope indistinguishable from despair, turned passionately to the third and last of Henry VIII's progeny to save them.

If there were any in the kingdom who believed, as Mary Tudor believed or pretended to believe, that Elizabeth was not a Tudor but the bastard of a court musician, Mark Smeaton, the twenty-five-year-old woman in purple velvet with a scarf around her neck was soon to disabuse their minds of this canard. She proved too like her father and her grandfather to be the by-blow of a musical groom of the bedchamber—even if her mother had been called "a stewed whore".

To be honest, even though she was her father's daughter her claim to the throne was nearly as shaky as the country's finances. From Henry she got her red hair, her imperious will, her love of finery, her talent for music, her magic touch with people, and much of the energy and ability which Henry showed before

disease had corrupted his fine brain and splendid body. From her mother, of whom she never in her whole life spoke, she drew her dark eyes and perhaps part of the temperament which had made Anne Boleyn the greatest flirt in the kingdom. But from her grandfather, pinch-faced, acquisitive Henry VII, who had laid the foundations of the Tudor dynasty so firmly that neither the extravagances of his son nor the fanaticism of his half-Spanish granddaughter could—though they brought down the edifice—shake them apart, she inherited caution, thrift, tenacity of purpose, a subtle talent for double-dealing, and a nose "rising somewhat in the middest".

Bankrupt and degraded though the country was, it had, nevertheless, reached one of those turning points in history; a crisis in affairs where, as in certain illnesses, the patient does not linger—either he gets better or he dies. At this point, desperate though the case looked to those who lived then, three important and fundamental changes had already taken place. The fever of a five-century-old desire to conquer France had at last abated. The terrible, bone-breaking, soul-shaking torments of the anti-clerical revolt were all but over, and Henry VIII had sacked the ancient, triple-mitred priest-physician with almost the same thoroughness as he had sacked the monasteries. Thus, for the first time since the Conquest, England was wholly free of Europe. She might be on her uppers but she was also on her own.

Elizabeth either saw or sensed this and she determined to keep it that way . . . and keep herself on the throne. To do so she needed two things, time and peace. Having chosen her ministers shrewdly—and the shrewdest choice was Cecil—she acted accordingly. "Mere English" was the way she described herself on her accession. It was true. She had more English blood in her veins than any sovereign since Harold. She too, like her country, was free of foreign blood and foreign entanglements. The great understatement was at once a boast and a promise.

Fortunately for her, and for England, the two great Roman Catholic Powers, France and Spain, were deadly rivals and

Elizabeth used this rivalry for years with true if obvious feminine cunning. She simply played one off against the other. When Mary Stuart and France seemed too menacing she held out hopes of marriage to several of Philip's Austrian Hapsburg cousins. When Philip—who had once proposed himself—at last saw through her, she promptly encouraged a brace of French suitors. No male monarch could have got away with it without war, but it was in this fashion that a woman gained the time she and her country so desperately needed until, at last, this small, heretic island was too strong to be invaded by any damned foreigner.

Yet this was not accomplished overnight, though it began almost immediately with an Act which proved the Queen to have inherited her grandfather's respect for money. Henry VII, called careful by those who like him and miserly by those who don't, had died leaving a large fortune. His extremely extravagant son went through this in record time, had then enjoyed the spoils of the monasteries, and had not hesitated to debase the currency when pressed to balance his budget. Mary had tried, unsuccessfully, to cope with this economic mess by issuing new coinage but, as her poverty prevented her calling in the debased coins, she merely succeeded in proving the truth of Gresham's law, "Bad money drives out good."

Elizabeth did not make this mistake. Although she was to be short of money all her life, she knew that a desperate situation needed desperate measures. She called in all mutilated currency, issued new coins of the old sterling standard of purity and stabilized money at its current value. Economic order was brought out of economic chaos. Confidence was restored and, incredible as it may seem to us, the government made a profit of £14,000 on the deal.

But she was like her father, too, in more than red hair and obstinacy. Henry with all his faults—the least of which were his matrimonial adventures—was a great man and a brilliant one. He may have been wildly extravagant but one of the good things he did was to found and maintain the Navy—building royal dockyards at Woolwich and Deptford and royal fighting ships. (He also founded the corporation of Trinity House.) Henry's Navy, under that unhealthy and wretched boy, Edward VI, and his unhappy, ill-advised half-sister Mary, had gone to wrack and ruin. It was not in King Philip's interests to have a strong English Navy. Spain, Philip thought, must be mistress of the sea. Elizabeth thought otherwise and restored the Navy which, when she began her reign, consisted of only twenty-two ships, most of them unseaworthy. Although we have no evidence that she followed her father who, as a young man when a royal ship was launched, had insisted on acting as pilot himself (dressed for the part in a sailor's coat, splendid cloth-of-gold trousers and wearing a gold chain inscribed "Dieu et Mon Droit" with a whistle attached which he blew like a trumpet), yet the Queen loved the Navy and realized, as Henry had done, its vital importance to England. It took her far longer to build up the Navy —mercantile and fighting ships—than it did to restore the currency, but she did it. Patiently and bit by bit, she built one or two ships annually until by the twenty-fourth year of her reign— six years before the Armada—a contemporary chronicler was able to say, "She (the Queen) hath likewise three notable galleys, the Speedwell, the Try Right, and the Black Galley with the sight whereof, and the rest of the navy royal it is incredible to say how greatly her grace is delighted; and not without great cause (I say) since by their means her coasts are kept quiet, and sundry foreign enemies put back which otherwise would invade us."[3]

One of these ships of the navy royal was called the *Elizabeth Jonas*, a name devised by the Queen herself "in remembrance of her own deliverance from the fury of her enemies, from which she was no less miraculously preserved than was the prophet Jonas from the belly of the whale". There seems to be just a little obscurity in these words. One would like to know what was in the Queen's mind as she named the gallant royal ship *Elizabeth Jonas*, after herself. But like so many things about this

magnificent yet strange, secret woman we shall never know who or what was meant by the whale.

There was another thing which she restored early on (in 1559), that was, the Reformation in its Anglican form. This was done by passing the Act of Supremacy and the Act of Uniformity. The first abolished the papal power . . . the power which Mary had looked to. The second made the Prayer Book the only form of legal worship. Yet it is significant that she restrained the zeal of the House of Commons by refusing to adopt the title of Supreme Head of the Church, although she did become its Supreme Governor and, as such, among other and less pleasant things, levied a fine of 12d. on those who did not attend church on Sundays. This meant everyone, no matter what his persuasion—

Roman Catholic, Puritan, Calvinist or Anabaptist. A certain Cornishman, a Roman Catholic, who preferred to attend church rather than pay the fine, managed to bear up under the reading of the lessons and the "Geneva Jig" (the scornful name given to the Psalms sung to Sternhold and Hopkins' setting), but when it came to the sermon he could bear it no longer and invariably stumped out of the church calling out loudly to the parson in the pulpit, "When thou hast said what thou hast to say come and dine with me."[4] The Anglican compromise had begun to do its work. By the end of the reign the "new religion" had become an old religion, a family religion, and the dreary Puritan Sunday of the next century was on its way.

On the way too were the persecutions of the Roman Catholics which took place during the plot-ridden eighties. These, in fairness, it must be said, were far fewer than those suffered by Protestants under Mary Tudor. By the Acts of Supremacy and Uniformity Elizabeth sought a *via media* for her people. Canterbury, not Rome—or Geneva—was to be England's path. John Knox, who detested women in general and Elizabeth in particular, called her "neither good Protestant nor resolute Papist". But she, herself, said, "I desire to open a window on no man's conscience." An unusually tolerant statement for a sixteenth-century ruler.

Yet, in the end, she was forced to it. Her reasons were national and political not religious or personal. In the forty-five years of her reign eight different Pontiffs occupied the Papal throne and every one of them—with the possible exception of Sixtus V and three short-lived Popes, Urban VII, Gregory XIV and Innocent IX—were against Elizabeth. Even Sixtus V who is said to have admired her, supported the Armada. It was Sixtus who said, "It is a pity Elizabeth and I cannot marry, our children would master the world."[5]

Paul IV, who was Pope on her accession, regarded England as a Papal fief and, while casting aspersions on the Queen's legitimacy, required that she should submit her claims to him. There could hardly have been a better way to ensure that England would never return to Rome. Pius IV who, with great realism, saw that

Of Elizabethan England

England and Germany were lost to the papacy and France on the verge of civil war, did what he had to do—he supported Spain. But Pius V issued the famous Papal Bull of 1570 which excommunicated Elizabeth and declared her to be a usurper.

This put English Roman Catholics in an impossible position. Loyalty to the Queen meant disloyalty to their Faith, and vice versa. They were thus laid open to a charge of treason. So the Papal Bull, not surprisingly, gave the Puritan faction the whip hand. When such extremes meet, they clash. Gregory XIII did not assist matters when he incited attacks on England via Ireland, and although Clement VIII, who was a great reconciler, hoped—through James I—to recover England when Elizabeth died (he outlived her by two years) he was too late by half a century.

It should also be remembered that Calvinists, too, were against the Anglican compromise and held that the new Prayer Book was "culled and picked out of that Popish dunghill, the Mas Book"[6] (much of their language on the subject is far too offensive to be repeated here). They believed that man could be saved neither by faith nor by grace but, rather, that God had predestined all human beings either to eternal salvation or eternal damnation. According to some terrible and arbitrary system which was the Will of God, sheep and goats were fore-ordained. Serene in the knowledge that they were of the "elect", convinced that they alone were the possessors of truth, the Calvinists sought to persuade or force others into a way of life which, although these others could not gain salvation by it, would at least not offend God, or His "chosen". Roman Catholics were guilty of treason. Calvinists were guilty of heresy. Both were persecuted. But the present-day division of English religion into three main streams, Anglican, Nonconformist and Roman Catholic, began here.

Yet safe behind a wooden wall of ships, possessed of a sound sterling, free of the fear of foreign domination and internal anarchy, England—and that peculiar thing which can only be called Englishness—emerged quite clearly for the first time in our history. And Englishness, in its broadest and most general

sense, was compounded of an intense nationalism, extreme indivi-
dualism, and superb if not insolent insularity. These qualities—
which we today are painfully trying to get rid of—gave the age
its greatness, its flavour and its vivid colour but, naturally, did
not make for popularity abroad. By other nations the Elizabethans were envied, feared, hated and mistrusted. Our ancestors were, however, totally unembarrassed by envy, flattered
by being feared, didn't care a jot about being hated, hated back
with enormous spirit, and thought foreigners even more un-
trustworthy than foreigners thought them.

The English, according to Paul Hentzner, a foreign visitor of
the day, were "good sailors and better pirates; cunning, treacher-
ous and thievish. They are powerful in the field, successful against
their enemies, impatient of anything like slavery, vastly fond of
noises that fill the ear, such as the firing of cannon, drums and
the ringing of bells. . . . If they see a foreigner very well made or
particularly handsome they will say 'it is a pity he's not an
Englishman'."⁷* This rather unattractive picture of the English

---

* This was by no means a new accusation: in 1558 Maister Etienne
Perlin was even ruder about us. "These villains", he says, "hate all sorts
of Foreigners and although they have a good country they are constantly wicked. . . ." He cites the English as being "proud, seditious,

with bad consciences and faithless to their
word". Even earlier, in 1497, Andrea Trevisano,
the Venetian Ambassador, described us as having
"an antipathy to foreigners" and of imagining
that foreigners "never come into these islands
but to make themselves masters of it and to
usurp their goods". Paolo Giovio, writing in
1548, is of the same opinion. "The English are
commonly destitute of good breeding and are
despisers of foreigners, since they esteem him a
wretched being and but half a man who may be
born elsewhere but in Britain, and far more
miserable him whose fate it should be to leave
his breath and his bones in a foreign land."

character seems, at least to me, to indicate that the Elizabethans were far too active and busy to bother their heads very much about what outsiders thought.

And they were extremely busy. They were, it is perfectly true, energetically and enthusiastically becoming first-rate seamen, pirates, freebooters and merchant adventurers. As such they laid the foundation of our own modern capitalist economy. Commerce was not looked down upon as it was in the eighteenth century, it was looked up to as a dangerous, exciting adventure, romantic and rewarding. Commerce was, in fact, the triune goddess of warfare, exploration and fortune.

Never before had England's banners been seen in the Caspian Sea, nor her envoys at the Courts of the Emperor of Persia or the Grand Signor of Constantinople. Her consuls and agents were newly in Tripoli, Aleppo, Babylon, Bakara and Goa. Her ships—some were the lean low swift ones, newly designed by Hawkins—anchored in the River Plate, passing and re-passing the formidable Straits of Magellan to range the coasts of Chile, Peru and "all the backside of Nova Hispania,"[8] to the amazement and rage of the Spanish.

They, at first, could not comprehend how the English ships had got to the west coast of South America. Spain built many of her ships to carry back the tribute of the Americas in her own territories there.

But for the English the world was, at last, round. It could be girdled. East and West were linked no longer in imagination but in fact. They were there to be explored and exploited. The Americas no less than Russia.

China as well as the Levant, and the cold coasts of Newfoundland. The risks were enormous but so were the prizes.

Richard Chancellor, back in 1553, had by mistake discovered Russia instead of India when searching for the North-East Passage and was well received by Ivan, not then "the terrible". So the first of the great trading companies, the Muscovy Company, came into being and the pattern of other great trading companies set. Relations with Russia were, oddly enough, so good in the beginning that Ivan greatly desired to marry Elizabeth. Elizabeth refused the kind offer—and one cannot but think that it was just as well that she did, as all of Ivan's seven wives died in mysterious circumstances. Relations between the two countries remained fairly amicable however even though Ivan, irked by refusal, wrote to the Queen upbraiding her for her "maidenly estate".

Relations between Spain and England were decidedly less happy. The English harassed and looted Spanish ships on the high seas, usually in the Caribbean or south of the Line, even though Philip had protected the Queen's accession and continued to protect her for years. And Spanish ships were well worth looting. A visiting merchant of Ulm[9] reported breathlessly home (1585) that news of a Spanish ship captured by Drake had just been received and the booty was said to consist of two millions of uncoined gold and silver in ingots, fifty thousand crowns coined in "reals", seven thousand hides, and four chests of pearls—each containing two bushels—and some sacks of cochineal. The whole was valued at twenty-five barrels of gold and was alleged to be the one and a half years' tribute of Peru. The report was exaggerated—perhaps not greatly. But Elizabeth did not plunder her people. She thought it more profitable to let her seamen plunder her enemies—which indeed it was, as a share in the plunder augmented her insufficient income.*

* The first Elizabethans were proud of being the lowest-taxed people in the world. The second seem to take a melancholy and bitter pride in being the highest.

"Drake!" she exclaimed when Walsingham had secretly persuaded her to take shares in Drake's expedition to circum-
navigate the globe—an expedition of piracy which has no parallel
in history—"Drake! so it is, that I would gladly be revenged on
the King of Spain for divers injuries I have received." She had
found the right man for the job and he the right mistress.

At home the world had become round, too—or if not round at
least less stratified. People were no less busy on land than on the
sea. Out of a defeudalized society a new gentry arose to replace
the old nobility and to build up a strong middle class. For the
Tudors were rather on the upstart side themselves and the old
nobility was to be feared. All the great servants of the Tudors—
even Wolsey, the son of an Ipswich butcher—were of humble
birth, while Cecil came of yeoman stock (his enemies said his
father had been a tavern-keeper). Class distinctions were thus
no longer rigid or even hereditary. There was a freedom of move-
ment within and between the classes. This meant that private

enterprise and individual initiative, from any quarter, were the keys which could open all doors.

Greatness was not defined as we define it. It applied neither to character nor to ability. It was not a moral quality and it had nothing to do with stature. Greatness was purely a material thing. The great man was the rich man and he showed his greatness by the style and manner in which he lived. The Joneses weren't there to be lived up to. They were there to be ostentatiously surpassed. To be *nouveau riche* was not to be despised, it was an admirable state—a goal which now could be achieved by almost any man nimble-witted, vigorous, enthusiastic and lucky.

So the new gentry, small squires, and landowners put their sons into trade and commerce, or apprenticed them to merchants and traders, or sent them to sea to try their luck at freebooting— to the horror of foreign nobles who, wrong as usual, thought this showed a lamentable want of family feeling and affection. It did nothing of the sort. It showed a shrewd realization of the fact that trade—which means path—was the highroad to riches and "greatness". The rise of the merchant classes was phenomenal. We became known as a nation of merchants as later we were to become known as a nation of shopkeepers.

So the Elizabethans were busy making money. Those who made it spent it—and were allowed to do so. The result was a boom—and continuing inflation. Yet, as in all boom times, there was prosperity. More and more people acquired land, built and furnished houses, great and small; begat children and founded families. But the go-getting Elizabethans, exuberant and bent on material success as they were, expressed themselves in other ways too. They expressed themselves in magnificent music and poetry, if less well in prose and painting. They ate enormously and dressed fantastically, yet had conscience enough to introduce a Parish Poor Rate (this is where we inherit our own rates), which had its faults but was far in advance of anything existing in contemporary Europe. They were also fanatical

about freedom. They welcomed *emigrés* fleeing from the persecutions in France and the Lowlands, yet they burned four heretics,
tortured Jesuits, were beastly to the Irish and traded in slaves—
the Queen herself had shares in a slave-trading ship called, most
inappropriately, *Jesus.* They believed firmly in God but also in
magic, astrology, alchemy, divination, witches and sorcerers.
The Queen had even insisted that Dr. Dee, her pet astrologer and
alchemist, should pick an auspicious day for her Coronation. He
chose January 15th.

Viewing them from this safe distance in time it seems to us
to be an age of splendour full of great names and great deeds
which, if only for a moment, transform the sad, sober stuff of
history into cloth-of-gold. Yet it was also an age of squalor and
misery, of treachery and sudden death. Of beggars, vagabonds,
criminals and thieves; of the ragged poor and the unemployable.
It is an age dominated by Elizabeth and a handful of men—though
a good-sized handful—who surrounded her and made up her
Court. But it is also an age when England was still predominantly
rural. Yet somehow, the glitter of the Court and the spirit of the
times penetrated the almost primeval forests which still enclosed
the fat fields; the farms; the towns and villages, where four to
five million Englishmen lived. If the Queen was England's
Elizabeth, the country was no less Elizabeth's England—and the
England of Elizabeth the First was at one and the same time
astonishingly like and unlike the England of Elizabeth the Second.

England, topographically, seemed to one unhappy foreign
visitor to be nothing but "one continued forest",[10] through which
vile roads, little better than cart tracks, straggled. There were
vast stretches of uncharted marshy waste and moorland and wild,
dangerous hills. Yet in forest clearings—and one can see this in
miniature in what remains of Wychwood forest today—lay the
villages and farms, the manors and the estates, the "champion"
fields as well as those newly enclosed by park paling or hedge. It
was here, and in a belt of arable land which stretched across the

Midlands from the Wash to Bristol, that the Golden Fleece of England and the "abundance of necessaries" were produced. In those days England could feed herself—and well. Apart from such accessories as spices, cane-sugar, wines, semi-tropical fruit, and oil (olive) which she imported, she produced so much that there was a very comfortable margin for export.

This made the English the envy of almost any foreigner brave enough to venture upon the roads at all. If he stuck to the four great Roman roads and their subsidiaries, still the best in the land, he might be all right. When he took to the purely English roads he may have travelled hopefully but he often failed to arrive at all. Or he may have arrived minus all his valuables for the country was full of highwaymen.

Roads, in fact, were not built. They happened. No one travelled for pleasure, he travelled only on business or because it was necessary to get from one place to another. And, curiously enough, the bad condition of the roads which had been fairly good in medieval times was due to the decay of the manorial system and the break with Rome. The manor no longer kept up the non-Roman roads and by-paths of its territory, while pilgrims no longer visited the shrines and holy places in such numbers as to make a thoroughly beaten track from one part of the country to another. Elizabethan roads were "very noisome and tedious to travel in, and dangerous to all passengers and carriages", as a statute of 1555 to amend the highways described them. Fifty years later the complaint was much the same and the lack of good roads was "the daily continual great grief and heartbreaking of man and beast; with charges, hindrances, wearing and tiring of them, and sometimes to the great and imminent danger of their lives".

This has a modern ring about it. It seems to be the unchanged and unchanging cry which echoes plaintively down the centuries from Elizabethan to neo-Elizabethan. Yet we are, in a way, better off. We at least have maps and signposts, they hadn't. Even royalty got lost.

Of Elizabethan England

Once when Elizabeth was young—in fact it was on the occasion when Mary had refrained from beheading her, but had instead released her from close captivity in the Tower and sent her to a less irksome confinement at Woodstock—she, in a shabby old litter with Sir Henry Beddingfield as her "keeper", and guarded by a hundred blue-coated men armed with pikes, guns and bows, had had to make her way from London to Oxfordshire. Naturally, and without apparent effort, the journey became almost a royal progress. At Eton the boys crowded out to see her and all along the way the country-folk rushed out to look at "my lady Elizabeth" and to make her presents of bread, cakes, honey and nosegays plucked from cottage gardens—for it was May. When they reached Woburn in Buckinghamshire, not one member of the party knew how to get from there to Woodstock. Fortunately, just outside the town, they found a farmer who had come to catch sight of this "jolly, liberal dame and nothing like so unthankful as her sister",[11] so they took him along with them to point out the way. How he got back home we don't know but it is safe to assume that when—and if—he did get back he lived off the story for the rest of his life, an object of wonder and veneration to his neighbours.

Even as late as 1592 the pompous Frederick, Duke of Württemberg, who journeyed from Oxford to Cambridge (fens covered about 75,000 acres then, and sometimes the floods reached Cambridge), gives us an astonishing picture of the difficulties of travel and the wildness of the country. "We passed", he says—or rather his secretary, Jacob Rathgeb, says it for him—"through a villainous, boggy and wild country and several times missed our way because the countryside thereabouts is very little inhabited and is nearly a waste, and there is one spot in particular where the mud is so deep that it would scarcely be possible to pass with a coach in winter or in rainy weather."

In truth, villages in winter unless they lay on a navigable river were practically isolated and the villagers simply "holed up", like groundhogs, until better weather came, which it sometimes, even then, did. But the surprising thing to us, brought up on all the modern and almost instantaneous means of communications, is how news travelled. How news—and rumour—managed to penetrate so quickly a land so ill served by roads, so densely covered by trees, so thinly populated. Yet it did. Each traveller had something to relate either of his own corner of England or of the world beyond. News of how St. Paul's steeple had been consumed to ashes by lightning on June 4th 1560, and an earthquake had been felt in London due, some thought, to witchcraft and sorcery. News of the latest Spanish prize taken, or the latest Spanish insult received. Rumour that the Queen intended to marry her "creature" Robert Dudley—and a very unpopular idea it was with the people who believed Dudley had murdered, or been a party to the murder of, his wife Amy Robsart even though the coroner's jury found no presumption of evil. There would be tales of strange happenings and portents in remote parts of the country. News of the border raids; how the Mosstroopers carried off cattle; and how the Duke of Norfolk, England's only Duke and the Queen's cousin, had been sent to the Tower for plotting with Mary of Scotland.

News, views, rumour and gossip would also be exchanged on market days and at country fairs where itinerant pedlars, like Autolycus, brought their wares along with the latest broadsheets and popular ballads. There were hundreds of these printed, for the most part, on a single sheet illustrated with a woodcut, and selling for a halfpenny or a penny. Many of them were grossly libellous and even obscene but in an age without newspapers, magazines, or tabloids they were gobbled up. The character of a ballad-monger or Pot-Poet as "the dregs of wit, yet mingled with good drink may have some relish"[12] is probably perfectly accurate. As to his work! "His frequentest works go out in single sheets and are chanted from market to market to a vile tune and a worse throat; whilst the poor country wench melts like butter to hear them; and these are the stories of some men of Tyburn, or a strange monster out of Germany; or, sitting in a bawdy house he writes God's judgment. . . ."[13]

We cannot fail to recognize here a familiar picture of mass appeal and mass reaction. So news travelled. In some curious way by an almost jungle grape-vine it was spread from market-places throughout the country . . . and speedily too. It may have become exaggerated in the retelling—as the tale of Drake's prize was enlarged—but it was generally based on fact even if the facts were distorted. News of England and of the new round world was somehow blown through the forests, across the wastes of marshland and moor, up or down the lonely limestone escarpment from Lincolnshire to Wiltshire inhabited by solitary shepherds and their flocks, to end up in the hall of an isolated Norfolk squire or the kitchen of a wattle and daub cottage on the wild border of Wales.

And if the country seems to present at once a familiar and unfamiliar picture so, too, do the cities. London, the capital with a

population which had already reached between 100,000 and 150,000 people, was one of the greatest cities of Europe, though not architecturally. But it was growing so fast that to feed and house its swarms, to maintain order and to check plague, which quite often brought the death rate level with the birth rate, became one of the major anxieties of the authorities. The great highway which served London was the river. Most of the streets were so filthy, so narrow, so crooked, so ill-paved and at night so danger-ous that the tenants of great houses such as Norfolk, Arundel, Essex House, Baynards Castle and Durham Place which were built on the Thames, used the river exclusively as a road. Robert Dudley, Earl of Leicester, however built his new house in the fields and suburbs where Leicester Square now stands. But Dudley was ever brilliant, and adventurous—if unsavoury.

But the Thames was also a royal thoroughfare, on its banks nearly all the royal palaces were sited. Greenwich where the Queen had been born and which was her favourite palace; Whitehall of which we know very little as it was destroyed in the succeeding century; Syon House where Lady Jane Grey had accepted the crown; Hampton Court taken over from Wolsey and added to by Henry VIII; Richmond built by Henry VII, and Windsor Castle. The Tower, the Mint, the Royal Arsenal, the Houses of Parliament were also on the Thames and when the Court was in London gaily painted and coloured barges moved up and down the river "shooting the rapids" under London Bridge bent on the Queen's business.

Often the Queen, herself, could be seen on the river in the royal barge. One of her earliest recorded appearances as Queen was on St. George's Day, 1559, when she went by water to Baynards Castle to have supper with the Earl of Pembroke. After supper, "she took a boat and was rowed up and down in the river Thames; hundreds of boats and barges rowing about her; and thousands of people thronging the water-side to look upon her Majesty; rejoicing to see her and partaking of the music and sights on the Thames; for the trumpets blew, drums beat, flutes played, guns were discharged, squibs hurled up into the air as the Queen moved from place to place. And this continued until ten o'clock at night when the Queen departed home. By these means showing herself so freely and condescendingly unto her people, she made herself dear and acceptable unto them."[14]

But the river was also a playground. There water festivals were held, and pageants where floats ingeniously devised startled or overshadowed the thousands of swans who also claimed the river as their own. On other occasions great firework displays burst upon the river, paling the stars and, for a brief moment, reflected and duplicated themselves in all their glittering and transient brilliance in the dark, shining strip below. Or there would be music. Music coming across the water to fall upon and delight the ear of those who belonged to a country known abroad as the most musical nation in the world. And once or twice during the famous frosts of the reign, ice carnivals were held with feasting and floats, music, dancing and fireworks.

What is not so easy for us to imagine about London, is the extraordinary transformation which took place when the Court was there. Most of the time, populous though it was, London had all the characteristics of a provincial town married not too unhappily to a seaport. But when Elizabeth took up residence there it became invested with a strange magic and importance. It burst into the same dazzling if transient brilliance as the fireworks over the Thames. Only this brilliance was reflected and touched the whole of the City, Westminster, and the surrounding countryside.

Much of this was due to the Queen's personality, her flair for publicity but, equally, a great deal was to do with the prevailing idea of what royalty meant. We may differ in our opinions of Elizabeth. We may think her admirable or base, according to which histories or biographies we have read, but the fact remains that whatever she may have been—and wherever she was—she captured the imagination and fitted men's picture of what royalty should be. As one of her ministers put it, when rebuking opposition to her will, "She is our God on earth." This was not flattery, it was a simple statement of belief. We may feel it smacks of idolatry, nevertheless, the anointed sovereign was both human and divine. It was an ideal which the Tudors found very useful and which they maintained. It was a unifying force turning regional loyalties into national loyalty. A man no longer felt that he owed his first allegiance to his lord, his town, or his guild but to his Queen—and his country. Shakespeare's historical plays are full of this feeling that the King was the Lord's anointed and that because of this his person was sacred:

> Let not the heavens hear these tell tale women
> Rail on the Lord's anointed,

Richard Crookback cries, ordering a flourish of trumpets and drums to drown out the accusations of his mother and his sister-in-law.

Richard II, on his return from Ireland, puts it even more strongly:

> Not all the water in the rough rude sea
> Can wash the balm from an anointed king,
> The breath of worldly men cannot depose
> The deputy elected of the Lord.

Yet Bolingbroke did depose him, and Carlisle's speech after the event gives us a very clear indication of how "black and heinous" a deed it was to depose

> God's captain, steward, deputy elect,
> Anointed, crowned, planted many years.

Carlisle, or Shakespeare, voiced the spirit of the time in its attitude towards kings. He spoke for the Elizabethans and for Tudor policy.

On the human aspect of the reigning demi-goddess, Sir John Hayward gives us a picture of the Queen which is both moving and beautiful. "All her faculties", he writes, "were in motion, and every motion seemed a well guided action; her eye was set upon one, her ear listened to another, her judgment ran upon a third, to a fourth she addressed her speech; her spirit seemed to be everywhere and yet so entire in herself, as it seemed to be nowhere else. Some she pitied, some she commended, some she thanked, at others she pleasantly and wittily jested, condemning no person, neglecting no office and distributing her smiles, looks and graces, so artificially, that thereupon the people again redoubled the testimonies of their joys; and afterwards raising everything to the highest strain, filled the ears of men with immoderate extolling of their Prince."[15] Yet this Prince hatedto be crossed, swore roundly, often boxed ears, and flung her slipper at Walsingham after an argument, crying "Point de guerre. Point de Guerre" as she let fly. Small wonder that this spirit, which seemed to be everywhere but so entire in herself, enlivened London and any place where the Queen was.

And where the Queen was, there, too, was the Court. The Court was not only the mortal household of this half-divinity, it was the centre of nearly all the major activities of the State. Those who managed the Queen's domestic affairs also managed the affairs of the kingdom; separately when it came to the sovereign, collectively, as her privy council, when it came to the kingdom. Through them the Queen determined and carried out her policies and it is staggering to realize that for forty-five years she acted as her own Prime Minister without rest or respite. Her Lord High Treasurer, who was the chief political minister, the Lord Chamberlain, the Vice-Chamberlain, the Lord High Admiral, and a host of other officials were members of her household. Where she was, they were. If the whole of our modern Cabinet, plus the heads of the three services and many of the top officials of the Civil Service were to move into Buckingham Palace and follow the Queen to Sandringham, Balmoral, Windsor, Holyrood or wherever Her Majesty went in the dual capacity of household and state officials, we should have some idea of what

the Elizabethan Court meant to whatever part of the country the first Elizabeth betook herself.

But this busyness was not the sole significance of the Court. Elizabeth may have been a child of the Reformation but, like her father, she was a Renaissance Prince.* And it was the fashion in those days for Princes to be brilliant, learned, accomplished and magnificent. Elizabeth was no exception. The Court had to live up to the Queen. In doing so it summed up the cultural aspirations of her subjects.

Man, too, was many-sided. He was not a flat piece of painted

* Prince was the term used for a ruling sovereign.

Of Elizabethan England

board or a narrow specialist, blinkered by his speciality. A courtier had to have brains—and wit—but he must also be a sportsman, poet, soldier, linguist, nimble-footed in dancing, and able to play a stringed instrument. The Queen was neither soldier nor much of a poet but she possessed all the other qualities in abundance. She was an uncommonly good linguist and told a visiting French Ambassador that when she had come to the Crown she spoke six languages better than her own. When the Ambassador remarked this to be a great virtue in a Princess, she replied that "it was no marvel to teach a woman to talk; it were far harder to teach her to hold her tongue."[16] This may be one of the reasons why wives of courtiers were certainly not encouraged to live within the Court but there were necessarily a number of women who attended the Queen. These were the model for female excellence . . . an excellence to be imitated by all women throughout the country. The Queen's maids were well read, knew modern languages as well as Latin and Greek. They were supposed to be skilled at a number of "delicate dishes of their own devising" as well as in surgery. The young and able-bodied were supposed to be as keen on sports as the men, and all were expected to be tolerably good in needlework, distilling, and music. The younger women, in particular, went in "much for lutes, citherns, pricksongs and all kinds of music when not in attendance on the Queen".

And the Queen, knowing the predilection of Satan for idle hands, kept her women and servants busy. She would tolerate no nonsense. As one of the popular ballads, written to lament her death, puts it:

A wiser Queen never was to be seen,
For a woman, or yet a stouter;
For if anything vexed her, with that which came next her
O how she would lay about her.[17]

They were proud of her, her people. They understood her and she understood them, though it was a constant source of wonder and amazement to them that a woman—even a demi-goddess—could do what she did. And what she did and said rayed out from the golden circle of the Court, wherein she was the central sun, to warm and illuminate the country.

For London might be the largest city but there were other important centres too. Despite the dreadful roads she visited them all. York, the capital of the north; Norwich, a great centre of the cloth trade; Bristol with a prosperous mercantile and inland trade, all boasting a population of about 20,000 while lesser provincial towns were large at 5,000.* Sooner or later the manners, the fashions, the ways of the Court arrived "in person", so to speak, or in other ways reached these centres; were adopted and imitated and spread out from there to affect the ordinary domestic life of the average Elizabethan.

And here we come up against a problem. Much as we know of the Queen and the great men of her time, about the others—the less great and the small—we know maddeningly little. What were they like, these other Elizabethans? The You, the I of the time. They didn't all eat roast peacock. They didn't all build great new houses of brick or imported Caen and West Country stone. They weren't all courtiers like the doubtful Leicester, admirals like Drake, financial wizards like Gresham, statesmen like Cecil, dramatists like Shakespeare, poets like Spenser, scholars like Bacon, musicians like John Bull or limners like Nicholas Hillyard. They were, it is true, living in the same golden age as the lordly ones—and the rascals—who made it famous. But was it a golden age for them?

Unfortunately for us we cannot eavesdrop on their time as we can on later ages and discover what they really thought and felt about life or even who they were. They did not commit themselves in writing. They left, or rather some of them did, household accounts which tell us the price of oranges and white herring, of children's shoes and a peach-coloured beaver hat

* Elizabeth never went much farther north than York nor did she ever visit Wales.

trimmed with silver lace which cost £2, but they made no comment on themselves or on their daily life.

There are few intimate touches anywhere. Not even in the infrequent diaries of the time. They were, perhaps, too busy living to record the details as Sam Pepys did in the next century —though he was busy too. As for letters, there seems to be no Elizabethan equivalent of Margaret Paston who a hundred years before wrote to her husband, "I pray you heartily that you will send me a pot of treacle, in haste." Sir Henry Wotton's letters are dull, orotund and aloof in an age which was none of these things. Francis Bacon deals magnificently but formally with matters of State, minus gossip. And the real John Donne is not to be found in his letters. Donne the man lies in his poetry and also in his metaphysical sermons.

Yet ordinary, domestic, everyday life there certainly was and it was bound to be influenced by the extraordinary spirit of the time if for no reason other than that the extraordinary becomes ordinary if you live with it long enough and Elizabeth reigned for nearly half a century. So the small squires, the well-to-do middle classes, and the country-folk must have followed, after various lapses of time, the lead given by a peripatetic Court— since this happens in every age. Yet on small points as well as on larger ones the Elizabethans are mute. Like the swan they have no voice. We do not know what they felt or what they said, these ordinary English men and women. And here is where they completely elude us as, indeed, the Queen, no matter how much we know about her, eludes us. There is little recorded conversation to reveal or hide their thoughts. They do not comment on life, death, wet boots or the cook's temper.

All we can do if we wish to find them is to seek them in the things which surrounded them, in the houses, the furniture, the ornaments and utensils they used. As Egyptologists interpreted a civilization by the artifacts found in tombs, so the Elizabethans speak to us of human everyday things mainly through inanimate objects and through the food they ate, the games they played, the sicknesses they suffered, the things which pleased or displeased them. This book is about such things. It is about the minor matters, the domestic details, the lighter side of daily life. And in daily life the first Elizabeth, by her love for her people and their love for her, plays an important part.

CHAPTER TWO

Of Houses, Prodigy and Otherwise

WILLIAM HARRISON was a year younger than the Queen. She was born in the Virgin Chamber at Greenwich Palace on the Eve of the Virgin's Nativity 1533; he in a house next to "The Holy Lamb" in Cordwainer Street "otherwise called Bow Lane" on the morning of April 18th 1534. During the turbulent twenty-five years while she was being educated—and even more, was educating herself—for the great, unsuspected destiny which awaited her, he was at St. Paul's school, then at Westminster and subsequently up at Oxford reading for his M.A. The year of her Coronation when she came into her inheritance, he came into the living of Radwinter in Essex, a living in the gift of his patron, Sir William Brooke, Lord Cobham—a friend of the new Queen. And while she and her Court were busy creating and expressing an era, he was busy observing and recording it.

Or rather, a part of it. He did not concern himself with high politics or the great events of history, he set down facts about the changing England in which he lived. Facts about natural resources, birds and beasts, soil and air, armaments and the navy, people and laws, palaces and houses; a monster compendium, a *Description of England*, an introduction to Holinshed's Chronicle. And Harrison is one of the very few Elizabethans who *do* comment. The asides of this sturdy Cockney and country parson often tell us as much, if not more, than the matter which he compiled with such "exquisite diligence". It is through the asides that we learn he thought all lawyers rascals, collected

39

Roman coins, was a keen gardener, kept a mastiff, was married
to a wife (half French) who brewed his beer, had three or more
children and admired the Queen.

It is a sincere and honest admiration, free of the gross courtier-
flattery common to the age. Perhaps he first saw and admired
her on the initial Royal Progress of the reign. That was in July
1559 when she went to visit his patron, Lord Cobham, at Cobham
in Kent.

In any event, years later, he was to write of these Progresses—
"When it pleases her in the summer season to re-create herself
abroad, and view the estate of the country and hear the complaints
of her poor commons injured by her unjust officers, or their
substitutes, every nobleman's house is her palace where she
continueth during pleasure and till she return again to one of her
own, in which she remaineth as long as she pleases."

Here, Harrison tells us the real reason for most of the Prodigy
Houses of the time. The Queen, as we have seen, from the very
beginning of her reign, sometimes on horseback, sometimes in
a litter, later in a new-fangled carriage—though she complained
carriage travel made her black and blue—made a yearly progress
through some part of her realm. Though she certainly heard the
grievances of her poor commoners and undoubtedly re-created
herself by these journeys, yet there were two other motives
behind these royal tours. First, by showing herself to her people
she increased her popularity until it reached fantastic proportions.
Second, she saved money.

Elizabeth's reputation for public thrift and private parsimony
we now accept without question, but we forget that she knew
her people would not bear taxation—and forbore to tax them.
The year after the Armada her total revenue amounted to less
than £400,000. In addition to ordinary, recurring expenses she
had to maintain the fleet out of the permanent sources of royal
revenue (imposts, customs levies, crown lands, etc.). The
whole sum obtained throughout her reign by extraordinary
Parliamentary taxation—and the operative word is extraordinary

—amounted to around three and a half million pounds and this was spread over more than forty years. It is hardly surprising, then, that on her progresses Elizabeth stayed with select and selected hosts and from these she expected, and received, lavish and more than royal hospitality. This cost the host a fortune. Sometimes it even ruined him.

But such hosts had generally made money out of the Queen or, more accurately, by aid of the Queen since she had little money to give away. There were honours, titles, and lands to come by her hand, and certain monopolies to be granted which made those who received them very unpopular since their rake-off added to the traders' difficulties and the consumers' costs. Robert

Dudley made a fortune out of his licensed imposition on barrel staves, sweet wines, oils, currants, and velvets. Yet he died in almost unassessable debt. On Kenilworth alone he spent £60,000 in turning a small insignificant property into a Prodigy House and he had houses at Denbigh, London and Wanstead as well. All made fit for a queen, should she come that way—which she did. But those who built Prodigy Houses built them not only because the Queen was coming but also as a memorial to her visit.

The host, of course, received more than just the Queen and a personal servant or two. He had to house and feed her large retinue, the members of her household and her own servants. He also had to find and provide stabling and fodder for her horses. As Elizabeth, despite the awful roads, usually travelled with a train of some three hundred strong carts, each drawn by five or six horses (Harrison says 400 carewares* and 2,400 horses) only a Prodigy House could provide the necessary accommodation.

The long-vanished Theobalds, in Hertfordshire, was or became such a house. It belonged to William Cecil, later Lord Burghley, who began it in 1566 in what he claims was a "modest fashion". He explains in a letter to an unknown friend dated August 14th 1585, how it grew into something quite other than he intended.

"My house at Theobald's", he says, "was begun by me with a mean measure but increased by occasion of Her Majesty's often coming, whom to please I never would omit to strain myself to more charges than building it. And yet not without some special direction of Her Majesty. Upon fault found with the small measure of her chamber (which was in good measure for me) I was forced to enlarge a room for a larger chamber; which need not be envied of any for riches in it. . . ."

It would be interesting to know just what the Queen said about

* Carewares—two-wheeled carts. Rathgeb says: "In England besides coaches, they use no waggons for the goods but have only two wheeled carts which, however, are so large that they carry quite as much as waggons and as many as five or six strong horses to draw them."

Of Houses, Prodigy and Otherwise

the poky little room first allotted to her; a room which was good enough for Cecil—or so he says with perhaps just a touch of disingenuity. But of the subsequent alterations which transformed the house into one of the sights of the times the Queen must have approved as she visited her Lord Treasurer on at least a dozen occasions during her reign and each visit cost him around three thousand pounds.

Sir Thomas Gresham, the financial wizard, also did not escape criticism but for the opposite reason. The Queen had given him Osterley Park, once owned by an Abbess of Syon. Here Gresham built a magnificent house and when it was completed in 1577 the Queen came to see what it was like. The house apparently met with her approval but the courtyard, she thought, was far too big and would be greatly improved if divided by a wall. Having said this she supped and went off to bed. What does Sir Thomas do? "In the night time sends for workmen to London who so speedily and silently apply their business"[1] that next morning the court was double which the night before was single. Thus, says the commentator, "money commands all things". Elizabeth must have been a sound sleeper, or the house may have been so vast that the royal apartment lay miles from the courtyard. Otherwise it is hard to believe she wouldn't have heard the workmen—and cursed them roundly. But the Queen was pleased with the house and the divided courtyard and stayed several days. Gresham entertained her sumptuously. There were rides in the new park which had been made by enclosing Hounslow Heath, there was the heronry to be admired and the ornamental ponds. There was a great banquet and a play was performed before her. But one unfortunate incident happened—some of the local inhabitants who resented the enclosure of Hounslow Heath set fire to Gresham's new park palings. This so annoyed the Queen that she clapped four men into prison for it. She might object to a feature of Osterley, herself, but no one else could—and get away with it.

What Lord Burghley and Gresham did, other men did too,

vying with each other in producing enormous, elaborate and fantastic houses—that is why so many houses can claim, quite rightly, "Queen Elizabeth slept here." (It is also why some village blacksmiths' shops display, with perhaps not quite so much validity, horseshoes cast from one of the innumerable horses in her train.)

Building was not confined solely to members of the aristocracy nor to the extremely rich. Two things are necessary for building in any age—land and money—and in Elizabeth's time land and wealth were no longer concentrated in a few hands. Land had been freed by the decline and fall of feudalism no less than by the confiscation of the monastic estates. The first was gradual,

the second, sudden, both happened before 1558. As for money, some Elizabethans inherited it, some stole it, many made it.

But not for them the building of churches and cathedrals. Not only had the medieval period amply supplied them with these, but very probably the Ecclesiastical compromise had left them uncertain as to just what a non-Roman Catholic church should look like. Nor did they build castles, fortified palaces or walled manors. There was peace at home and, besides, gunpowder had fully come into its own. Walls which had been difficult to scale were fatally easy to breach with cannon. Walls, battlements and turrets no longer spelled security. They were pointless save as ornament. So the Elizabethans built houses—quantities of them. And the richer they grew the more splendid, ornate, fantastic and even eccentric their houses became. Motivated by a perfectly simple and uninhibited desire to stun the eye with splendour, Prodigy Houses were often their owners' exuberant boast of greatness translated into brick and stone.

The new gentry, the smaller squires and wealthy tradesmen went in for the manor or country mansion type of house, while many landowners and yeoman farmers put up new farmhouses and cottages. The wool trade was no longer so prosperous as it had been so the Queen, very wisely, encouraged farmers to change over from sheep-grazing to arable farming. This meant that more labour was required on the land and, as a result, more small farmhouses and cottages. Although at the beginning of the century tenant farmers had little more than a few shillings in ready cash, by the end of the century, despite increasing rents, they were prosperous and could build and furnish well.

Elizabethan architecture, however, did not arise *de novo*. It was the child of an uneasy *mésalliance* between the debased Gothic and earlier Tudor styles and an ill-understood and coarsened Classical, which had arrived from Italy where the Renaissance was now dying, via France and the Low Countries, suffering greatly in the process. This *mésalliance* produced, in the main, some perfectly dreadful architectural and decorative

offspring. Furthermore, building—particularly of great houses—
often proceeded in such a leisurely fashion that a house changed
character during the building, if not in plan at least in detail.
Longleat took about thirty years to build while Kyre Park, a
relatively unprodigious house begun in 1588, was not completed
when the owner-builder, Sir Edward Pytts, died in 1617. He
left two thousand pounds for its completion in his will.

Scale plans were certainly known and used but there were no
architects in the modern sense of the word. Sometimes a "platt"
or a "platt and upright" were bought from a Court Surveyor but
more often plans were provided by the master mason himself.
It was the master mason and his workmen, at an average wage of
sevenpence a day, who built the shell of the house. Internal
details, ceilings, walls, staircases came under a master carpenter
and his men. The masters, as well as the owner, would contri-
bute new ideas as building progressed—Cecil and Pytts each
made certain drawings for their own houses. This made for
individuality and startling, not to say exotic, effects which delighted the Elizabethans, but it poses problems for the amateur
who tries to date any Elizabethan house.

Take, for example, Longleat in Wiltshire and Hardwick Hall
in Derbyshire. Both are Elizabethan, yet they are very different.
Longleat was begun in 1554, completed in 1567 and badly burnt
in the same year. It was begun again in 1568 and by 1575 Elizabeth stayed there, even though the prodigy was still probably
without its top storey. Longleat is perhaps the most beautiful
example of the very brief High Renaissance of Tudor building.
It is a house which suggests adult composure, not adolescent
exuberance or elderly eccentricity. It has neither the crude
exhibitionism of the former nor the debased rhodomontade of
the latter. It is symmetrical, coherent and reserved. Outwardly,
it is a four-sided palace without the extruded corners; but the
flat façade is given light and shade by carefully spaced bays. It
appears to be nearly all windows and glitters with splendour. Yet
nothing disturbs the tranquillity of its outward look as all stair-

Of Houses, Prodigy and Otherwise

towers and chimney stacks rise from two inner courts. These courts may be what was left of the house of 1567 after the fire. Longleat in its restraint and beauty is exceptional among Elizabethan Prodigy Houses.

Hardwick Hall, on the other hand, took only seven years to run up (1590–97). And it was built by a woman, Bess of Hardwick, who was born fifteen years before Elizabeth and outlived her by five years. More to the point is the fact that she also outlived four husbands which is probably why she could afford to build as she did:

> Four times the nuptial bed she warmed
> And every time so well performed
> That when death spoiled each husband's billing
> He left his widow every shilling.

Bess was no cosy character—no Elizabethan was. She was rather horrid, being "proud, furious, selfish and unfeeling; a builder, a buyer, and seller of estates, a moneylender, a farmer, a merchant of lead, coals and timber". Her income was around £60,000 a year—and there was no income tax or surtax to eat up most of it.

Bess had a passion for building and built Oldscotes, Worksop, Bolsover and an earlier Chatsworth (pulled down in 1688) but Hardwick Hall is the greatest surviving memorial to this old woman who was certainly disagreeable and bossy, insensitive and malicious, bad-tempered and shrewd, but somehow magnificent in a revolting sort of way. Hardwick Hall is, like its mistress, unusual. It has many windows—like Longleat—but of such size and quantity that the jingle "Hardwick Hall more glass than wall" seems at first glance to say all that is needed. The walls in fact are built of a wonderful veined golden stone, and it is a romantic and imaginative-looking building in many ways. It has not the Longleat "palace" look. Square towers, which are very exaggerated bays, rise a storey above the main mass, so that the silhouette has a rather castle-like appearance. But it is a castle that has decided to give up being a rather dumpy fortress and become slim and elegant with more than a touch of dramatic hauteur to go with its new look.

Here, there is no inner court, in fact the house is long and narrow for its length. Oblong rather than square—and its interior, as in most great Elizabethan houses, bears little relation to its exterior.

Nevertheless, speaking very broadly, the chief feature of Elizabethan external architecture is a certain symmetry of façade. Doing away with fortified walls led to the extrusion of the corners

Of Houses, Prodigy and Otherwise

of the house and the now familiar E and H plan came into being; though, of course, Tudor courtyard houses were still built, probably by the more conservative. The siting of a house was no less important than the house itself. Andrew Boorde, the physician whom Parson Harrison couldn't abide, had earlier on in the century given some sensible suggestions as to the siting of a house. He advises strongly against building near stinking ponds, ditches or channels. The house should have an outer Quadrangle for servants' privies and the stabling of riding horses. The Gate House should be opposite—but not directly opposite—the Hall Door. While stables for work horses, slaughter-house, milking-sheds and brew-house should be located a half a mile away from the house. The moat—if any—should be fresh, cleaned frequently and not used as a dump for kitchen waste and worse. And the house should have gardens, an orchard, a park, a pair of Butts and a Bowling Alley. The great house was almost a self-contained village or a miniature city but that was no reason why it should imitate London in matters of filth and refuse!

Francis Bacon, concerned less with hygiene than with the nature of man, says sagely, "He that builds a fair house upon an ill seat committeth himself to prison." And an ill seat in Bacon's view was a matter of unwholesome air, bad access to the place, bad markets, bad neighbours, lack of wood, water, shade, shelter and fruitfulness. A poor prospect; too near or too far from the sea or great cities, an absence of facilities for hunting, hawking and racing, these too made for an ill seat. Without such things a man might as well be incarcerated in the Fleet or the Clink—where poor Andrew Boorde had indeed been confined for a spell.

William Harrison is far less exacting. He marvels at the quantity of new houses being built, but is conservative enough to deplore their quality. These modern houses were nothing like so good as those built during the reign of Henry VIII, whom he regards, rather mystifyingly, as "the only Phoenix of his time for fine and curious masonrie".

The Elizabethans at Home

Shaking his head as he contrasts the good old days of sturdy building with what, for him, was the Elizabethan equivalent of jerry building, he comments sadly, " . . . albeit in these days there be many goodly houses erected in sundry quarters of this Island; yet they are curious to the eye, like paper work, than substantial for continuance; whereas such as he [Henry] did set up, excel in both, and therefore may justly be preferred far above all the rest".

Many of these new "paper work" houses must have been fiendishly cold as they were built facing north-east. The Elizabethans believed firmly that "the south wind doth corrupt and make for evil vapours".[2] Cottages and farmhouses, however, were built by those who were not handicapped by this new hygienic idea and so, happily, continued to be warmed and corrupted by a southern aspect. But Renaissance features, first exhibited in Prodigy Houses, gradually filtered down to the minor manor and then to the farmhouse and even to the cottage.

The minor manor, the country house of the well-to-do town merchant, the seat of the local squire, the new house of the yeoman—many yeomen were far better off than the small gentry of the time—were built by people who were not likely to entertain the Queen but were apt to have large families and frequent guests. These gave to rural England much of its characteristic architecture, but they, too, varied in size and appearance to an astonishing degree. Chastleton House, in Oxfordshire, is an almost perfect example of the late Elizabethan style which carried over well into the Jacobean. It is a great house in miniature, with an interior courtyard, and was built by a prosperous farmer. Not too far away there is its much earlier opposite; tiny, grey Owlpen in Gloucestershire, walled in by enormous yews, a small, secret house. And bearing no resemblance to either of these—although in roughly the same area—Compton Wynyates, just over the border in Warwickshire, rambles about in a confused fashion without much design at all. It has been added to, here and there, from 1525 on. England is fortunately peppered, or

Of Houses, Prodigy and Otherwise

rather, jewelled, with minor manors and small houses. Many are famous or well known but there are just as many tucked away in or near small villages, off the main roads and tourist trails, or reached by a lane so narrow, so twisted, so rutted, so boggy in winter that a returning first Elizabethan—or first Elizabeth—would recognize both road and house without a moment's hesitation.

Of course, one couldn't be all that sure that the Queen *wouldn't* turn up unannounced. One Saturday night, in 1572, Mrs. Thomas Fisher who lived near Kenilworth was at supper when suddenly, and quite unexpectedly, Elizabeth arrived, *en suite*. She had decided to drop in, on the spur of the moment, on her way back from Kenilworth to Warwick. The Queen and her party joined Mrs. Fisher at supper and afterwards Elizabeth went to see poor Mr. Fisher who was "grievously vexed with the gout".[3] Mr. Fisher was brought out into the gallery and would have knelt "or rather fallen down" but the Queen wouldn't permit it. She "with the most gracious words comforted him". These gracious words, or the shock of seeing the Queen so unexpectedly, seem to have had a wonderful effect on Mr. Fisher's gout for on the Monday he mounted his horse, joined the Queen and rode back with her when she returned from Warwick to Kenilworth. We are told that he repented of this action later—but we aren't told why. Repentance had nothing to do with a recurrence of gout because our commentator says darkly, that "Mr. Fisher's character was no great secret"[4] and maddeningly leaves it at that.

Mrs. Fisher obviously had a large house. The gallery, and all those people fed on the spur of the moment, indicate this, and Mr. Fisher was doubtless a "great" man in the Elizabethan meaning of the word. But the farmer, too, built houses or had houses built for him. No longer tied by the manorial system which had obliged him to supply food only for his own lord and his own family—in that order—he now marketed his produce in the large towns and prospered. Agriculture became an industry and in

51

good years there was a boom in farm building. In bad years, building stopped and, worse, thousands went hungry.

What gives the Elizabethan farmhouse its character and complexity—at least for us—is that local materials were invariably used in construction. The great houses, wherever they stood, were built in dressed stone, imported or otherwise, or in brick; but farmhouses and, to a lesser extent, cottages spoke not only of the prosperity of the owner but of the nature of the country in which they stood. In eastern counties, rich in timber and flint and with a chalky subsoil, houses were half timber with clay between the timbers and then plastered or parged over. Sometimes the timbers were left exposed, sometimes they too were parged. Plastering, which really came into its own in the sixteenth century, kept out the weather and improved the appearance of the house. Old wattle and daub cottages were now increasingly plastered over with lime plaster. Good, long-lasting stuff mixed with hair or cow's dung. Yet these farmhouses of the eastern and north-eastern counties bear as little resemblance to the "black and white" houses of Chester as Norfolk flint houses resemble those of mountain limestone found in the northern counties. In Sussex it was timber-framed stone or brick, set in a herringbone pattern. In parts of Essex, Middlesex, and Herefordshire, weather-boarding was the principal material used. Later on, a pocket of Pilgrim Fathers originating in these parts took the idea to New England and built there the enchanting and beautiful houses and churches which have, indeed, weathered several centuries.

In places where wood was lacking and stone plentiful, farmhouses, farm-buildings and walls were almost entirely of stone. Black granite, so gloomy, so difficult to work, gave Cornwall its dark, secret look. Golden, grey, and rosy limestone gave and still gives the Cotswolds their enchanting houses. In Devon, however, they were in a fix. There was neither an abundance of timber nor of stone. So they built of cob; another name for mud. Strictly, cob—or clem—was a mixture of marl, gravel and straw.

Well thatched and with overhanging eaves, like fierce lowered eyebrows, and standing upon a stone course, cob lasted for generations.

So Elizabethan farmhouses made up in variety of material anything they may have lacked in individuality of planning. And farmhouse planning was certainly not notably individual. Farmhouses were usually but one room thick and this accounts for the narrow span of the high-pitched roofs, particularly in the Cotswolds. Downstairs, the house was divided into two, possibly three, rooms while upstairs the farmer and his wife occupied a bedroom strategically placed at the head of the stairs. Daughters and maidservants were allotted a bedroom on one side, sons and menservants on the other. Partitions were of wood and all rooms were intercommunicating. If there was an attic floor where the hired hands (male) slept, there was often an outside staircase leading to it.

In towns where space is valuable far fewer houses survive. In fact there is not one purely Elizabethan house left in London. The mansion of one period is the shop of the next and ends as a slum dwelling before it is finally demolished either by fire, bombs, or demolition squads. If it survives such hazards long enough, time will restore it to its original importance while taxation will make it possible for you and me to see it—on payment of a shilling.

The population of Elizabethan London doubled in less than half a century. In Elizabeth's reign the old walled city had become the stronghold and centre of mercantile and civic communities—but there were still small open spaces with gardens, trees, courtyards and stables within the city walls. These enclosed an irregular crescent-shaped area which stretched from the Tower on the east to the muddy Fleet River on the west. Boats plied busily up, down and across the river for there was only one bridge linking the north and south side. It had nineteen arches (when the river was high no boat could get through the arches), a drawbridge and a gatehouse at its southern end. Above the gatehouse the heads of executed criminals were displayed on pikes, like cocktail cherries on toothpicks.

The City with its mayor, citizens and strong militia was, in effect, a state within a state. Neither Elizabeth nor the aristocracy had any power there, though they often borrowed money from it. (Even today the second Elizabeth, as sovereign, cannot enter the City unless the Lord Mayor permits her to.) It had welcomed with relief, after the turmoil of the Barons' War, the first Tudor. It had stood by Mary during Wyatt's rebellion and it supported Elizabeth. The City and the Tudors in fact got on well together.

The City contained the great markets of West and East Chepe, with Poultry, Newgate Street, Cornhill, Leadenhall, and Gracechurch Street—and in its northern end the industrial quarter lay. Between West and East Chepe were the houses of the nobles and merchants—but even before Elizabeth the nobles were moving out of the medieval city (leaving it to merchants and industry) and building new mansions nearer to the Court and Westminster and in the surrounding fields beyond, while London spread itself in a narrow strip along the river from beyond Shadwell in the east to Westminster Abbey in the west. It was growing out northward, too, beyond the City walls into those lands which had once been monastic, and south, across the river at Bankside. Chelsea, Battersea, and Brompton were country villages surrounded by agricultural land, so were Mary le bone, Paddington, Islington and Hoxton.

It is true, Sir Thomas Gresham preferred to build his new house within the City walls, in Bishopsgate, where, returning one evening in 1579, he had a stroke in the kitchen and shortly after died. But the Earl of Leicester built his own town house near Whitehall, in Leicester Fields, and William Cecil put his new town house near the river on the north side of the Strand. It was "a very fair house raised with brick proportionately adorned with turrets and beautified inside with curious and rare devices". Both houses were on much the same plan as the country houses of the period, though smaller.

The typical dwelling of the average Londoner was, however, very different. It followed a simple plan which dated back to the Middle Ages. A very narrow frontage on the street, rooms back and front on each floor, and a long garden or court at the back. It wasn't very different from many London houses of today.

Most of such London houses had a cellar, a shop and kitchen on the ground floor, two or three floors above, and a garret in the gable. Many houses were shockingly overcrowded, dark, insanitary, flea- and rat-ridden slums. Some had narrow alleyways down one side where vagrants and thieves lurked at night, and children played by day amid the heaps of kitchen waste and excrement.

As space was limited then, as now, even new houses followed this pattern. The well-to-do middle-class merchant—as opposed to the merchant prince—would build a house which looked exactly like these narrow houses outside. The difference was that such a house which looked like two or three houses was really one house—despite two or three gables and two or three front doors. They were spacious inside and had fine gardens at the back yet they fronted the street like twins or triplets. Whether this was due to lack of imagination or a sneaking desire for regimentation, or a canny fear of being thought too rich, it is difficult to say. But there are no surviving examples of this kind of Elizabethan house in neo-Elizabethan London. The only house illustrative of this type at all, is the range of timbered houses at Staple Inn, Holborn. It is true that they were built between 1545 and 1589 but they have been so altered and restored that they cannot be said to be Elizabethan.

But Sherar's Mansion in Shrewsbury was a perfect example of this type of Elizabethan house. It looked like three houses but was, in fact, one. It was three storeys high, each top storey rose into a gable, and the top storeys jutted out over the street—the higher the farther—while shallow bay windows carry them even farther out. In houses with such "jettied" floors, the top room was the largest and was usually the principal or "reception room". The house was really Gothic in style and construction, but consols which appeared to—but did not—support the "jetties" were carved in the Renaissance manner and so date the house. Shrewsbury is rich in real Elizabethan houses. The Tudors had established law and order in the Marches which brought Shrewsbury and the surrounding area great prosperity. There was trade with the Welsh in wool and flax and, as the Severn was navigable for about forty miles, there was also a vast amount of business carried on with Gloucester and Bristol. So Shrewsbury became wealthy and expressed itself in building a fine new Drapers' Hall, a stone market and quantities of half-timbered houses. They tell us more about an Elizabethan town than great and powerful London ever can.

But in houses of any size or consequence in the country the shape, both outside and in, changed considerably during the reign. The Great Hall—a medieval and Tudor feature—lost much of its importance as a communal dining-room and living-room. Sometimes "ceiled" (panelled) halfway up, it became the entrance hall where a great staircase with carved balustrades and newel posts often picked out in colour led to the upper regions. Here, on the upper floor, was the long gallery which, as the Great Hall declined in function and importance, became the chief room of the house.

The Elizabethans at Home

Lighted generally on one side only, the long gallery is a characteristic of Elizabethan houses in the second half of the sixteenth century. The "only Phoenix" had had one added to Hampton Court (later pulled down by Wren) which had eleven windows, three of them bays, along its eastern wall. The windows were filled with painted heraldic glass while above was a fretwork frieze and cornice, painted and gilded, joining a richly embossed ceiling bearing "1256 balls of burnished gold with leaves of gilt".[5] Was it here, perhaps, that Henry danced—dressed all in yellow with a white feather in his cap—the day after Catherine of Aragon's death? He wore yellow, he said, as mourning—and as he danced he joggled the red-haired infant, Elizabeth, in his arms. She crowed and gurgled with pleasure.

In any event, galleries were not usual in Henry's reign, and a Venetian Ambassador to Henry's Court thought them such a new thing that he describes them in a despatch to the Lords of the Signory. "Galleries", he writes—the Venetians were very observant of detail—"are long porticoes or halls without chambers, with windows on each side, looking on gardens or rivers, the ceilings being marvellously wrought in stone with gold; and the wainscote of carved wood representing a thousand beautiful figures." By figures he meant not the human form but various designs.

This new conception, the gallery, gave the Elizabethans a chance for a lavish display of riches. The longer the gallery the better. But a gallery, despite the brilliance and richness of ceiling, walls and windows, was enormous and difficult to heat, so in addition to one or more fireplaces, braziers which could be carried about and huddled over were used in winter. In wet weather, the gallery became what modern Americans would call a "rumpus room". What an Elizabethan rumpus was like is probably a little difficult for our own rather seedy age to imagine. But the long gallery was much used for mummery, games, dancing and music, exercising with foils or even with the broadsword. It was also used as a promenade in winter while the rain beat against windows, a sneaping wind howled about the chimneys, and the inadequate braziers gave out less heat than fumes.

The Great Hall and the Gallery were, thus, more or less public rooms (for the great Elizabethan lived and enjoyed a very public life) but private apartments or "lodgings" for members of the family and guests, private dining-rooms, and parlours, all became more or less a standard part of the plan.

"Make your parlour at the top of the hall", Andrew Boorde advises even before 1558.[6] And he recommends putting pantry and buttery at the bottom, kitchens next to pantry or buttery, and pastryhouse and larder adjoining. Thus the parlour could be private and relatively quiet. The kitchen end of the hall was cut off by a screen, which made a passage known as the screens, and hid the doors which led to kitchens and pantries.

As for private lodgings—that is a bedroom and an ante-room—the house would indeed have to be huge to provide these for the family, which included members of the owner's household just as the Court contained members of the Queen's household. Lodgings were usually built round a courtyard. At Theobalds there were thirty persons in the family who might all have private "lodgings" there. There was also a hall without pillars about sixty feet long and thirty feet wide and in it stood "a very high rock of all colours made of real stones, out of which gushes a splendid fountain that falls into a large circular bowl or basin supported by two savages".[7] On each side, either of this hall or another, were six artificial trees with leaves, natural bark, birds, and fruit so real as to be "indistinguishable from natural trees".

But Theobalds was one of the greatest palaces ever built in England and none of it survives. We know it had towers and five courtyards through which one passed to get to the house from the London road. The inner or fountain court was the last to be built. Each other court had "lodgings" surrounding it sufficient to accommodate the Queen's household. For the Queen received Ambassadors at Theobalds or "Tibbals" as she spelled it. And always, wherever she went, there were crowds of petitioners whom she saw herself. It is said that although she often used her household badly, hit people, lost her temper and flew into a rage, yet always to the people, whoever they were, wherever they were, she behaved with the greatest gentleness and consideration. She smiled, she listened, she reassured—and stole their hearts.

There is on record a description of Theobalds given in a report by the Court Surveyor in the year 1650—during the Protectorate when it was destroyed. Theobalds had changed hands years before when Cecil's son, Lord Salisbury, traded it with James I for Hatfield House and Manor which were crown property. The house had probably been greatly altered by then, but the report gives details of two principal quadrangles, a dial court, a buttery court and a dove-house court. The fountain court it states was eighty-six feet square with "cloisters" on the east side. On the ground floor of this court was a great hall with an arched and timbered roof "curiously carved". On the same floor were principal apartments, a council chamber and a waiting-room. The floor above had a Presence Chamber. Near were withdrawing rooms, the privy chamber, the king's bedroom and a

gallery 123 feet long. The floor above had lodgings and apartments with terraces and walks on the leads. Other courts had similar apartments and great rooms off them. And there seems to have been, in addition to the four towers, a large turret "over in the middle" made "in the fashion of a lantern curiously wrought with divers pinnacles at each corner, wherein hangeth 12 bells for chiming and a clock with chimes and sundry work". This report was made some ninety years after the house was built and it is not possible to say how well the description fits the Theobalds built by Lord Burghley who "never would omit to strain himself in building to please his sovereign". It obviously did not please Cromwell. Cecil, like Bess of Hardwick, always seems to have had some building in hand. Burghley House (Northants) was an old house which he altered greatly but, as he writes to a friend, he "set his wall" on the old foundations yet left one side "as my father left it to me". It looks a more conservative or traditional house than Theobalds sounds, with its great entrance façade and towers at each end. It, too, has a great tower topped by an obelisk-ornamented clock stage and this is overtopped by a much larger obelisk.

Obelisks were used in great profusion not only as architectural ornament but as fitting decoration for those no less ornate but infinitely smaller edifices built to house greater—and lesser— Elizabethans after death had husked soul from body. Cecil, one imagines, preferred Burghley to his other houses because he hoped that after his death his son, Thomas, "will be able to maintain it, considering there are in that shire a dozen larger, of men under my degree". Burghley House is a Prodigy and this statement that there were a dozen even greater Prodigy Houses in Northants gives us an indication of the size and quantity of such houses built at the time—and by lesser men than the Lord Treasurer.

Less richly and less extensively housed was the Archbishop of Canterbury, and when Elizabeth paid him a visit in 1574 at his summer palace at Croydon there seems to have been absolute chaos before her arrival as the Archbishop's household scurried about trying to fit in her large retinue. Appended to the list of the illustrious visitors there is a frantic little note on the problem of accommodation. It is signed J. Bowyer (an official of the Queen's household). "For the Queen's waiters," he writes, "I cannot find any convenient rooms to place them in, but I will do the best I can to place them elsewhere." Things were in such a muddle, one gathers, that unless other arrangements could be made the grooms of the privy chamber, and Mr. Drury, wouldn't be able to reach their quarters except by passing through Lady Oxford's rooms. As for Mr. Hatton (Christopher Hatton of whom it is said it took him twenty years to dance himself into the Queen's favour), J. Bowyer didn't know where to put him at all. Poor Lady Carewe couldn't be found a room "with a chimney" so she, too, couldn't be lodged in the Palace but had to sleep out "by Mrs. A. Parry and [curiously] the rest of the privy chamber". As for Mrs. Shelton, goodness knows where she ended. Mr. Bowyer was going to try to find her a room somewhere in Croydon. "Here is as much as I am able to do in this house", the note ends despairingly.

In addition to lodgings, the Prodigy House had to have a Presence Chamber or State Apartments for the Queen. At the beginning of the reign—and before competitive prodigy building began—such rooms were small and often sparsely furnished, or the Sovereign made do with the Great Hall, but by the last quarter of the reign they had become vast, magnificent and often over-ornate.

Despite all this showy magnificence, plumbing was not the strong point of the first Elizabethans any more than it is of the second. Water was supplied by cisterns and wells and in great houses by fountains. In the country water supply was less of a problem than in towns. In London and other cities, water was carried by hand, for the most part, from conduits and cisterns. Narrow-topped, broad-based wooden buckets, hooped with iron, were used and water-carrying was one of the occupations of the time. Water-carriers, or "Cobs", were paid by those who could afford it to supply their houses with water. Those who couldn't, lugged the buckets through the streets themselves.

Even more dire than water supply was sanitation. In the older moated castles, manor houses, or buildings which stood near a river or stream, moat, river or stream functioned as an open sewer. Those terrible little tower rooms with a hole in the floor and a draughty drop to the moat or a connecting ditch below were

Of Houses, Prodigy and Otherwise

the medieval equivalent of the W.C. But in the newly built houses of the era it seems to have been the bucket brigade again, though a separate room or rooms were set aside for the buckets. Servants in large houses used a collective latrine.

"I will tread this unbolted villain into mortar and daub the walls of a jakes with him", Kent says to Oswald in *King Lear*. Jakes was the good old English and Shakespearean word for privy, and the men who manned the bucket brigade were known as laystall or laystow men. A laystow was a common dungheap—which tells us where the buckets were emptied when they weren't emptied outside the front door as they were often in London despite laws against it.

Curiously enough, the water-closet was invented in 1596 and by none other than Sir John Harington, "that saucy poet, my godson" as the Queen called him.

Harington announced his invention in what a prudish Victorian called "an indescribable cloacine satire". The title of the satire was really *The Metamorphosis of Ajax*, plus other pamphlets such as *Ulysses upon Ajax*. This was a punning reference to "Jakes". Harington was a witty man and a charming one and though he often incurred the Queen's displeasure, he was fond of his godmother and she of him. He must have been well ahead of his era in ideas of sanitation and thoroughly disgusted by the primitive arrangements of the time, for he even went so far as to have a diagram drawn of his invention—with costs! In the overhead tank, just to show it was filled with water, several fish swim . . . and he works out the costs with care: a cistern of brick or stone—at eight and six; the pipe from it "with a stopple to the washer" three and six; a waste pipe one shilling; the "stem of the great stopple with a key to it" one and sixpence. The "stool pit" of stone cost as much as the cistern while the most expensive part of the lot was the great brass sluice "to which is three inches current to send it to gallop into the jax". This cost ten shillings. The seat, we are informed, was made with a "peak devant for elbow room". The whole cost thirty-three shillings—but the inventor's secretary tells us that "a mason of my master's was offered thirty pounds for the like".

The Queen, fortunately, was so little offended by this "cloacine satire" that she had the newly metamorphosed ajax installed at Richmond Palace.

Nevertheless, this revolutionary change in sanitation certainly did not come into common use and was not perfected until 182 years later. So even in the sixteenth century, the characteristic English suspicion of innovations, particularly of anything in the plumbing and heating line, was already well established. (In all fairness, it must be said that the French were even more backward. The interior, dry privy common here in the sixteenth century was not known in France until the eighteenth century when it was introduced as an "English novelty".) Still, one is a little startled to learn that gentlemen were advised against using the chimney as a urinal, not because it was bad-mannered but because it made for unsavoury air!

As for that common domestic utensil of the bedchamber, it was called a Jordan and rather grand ones were made of pewter.

Heating, too, was just as backward. Even though Andrew Boorde recommends a fire in the bedroom, many bedrooms must have been damp as he warns against the dangers of lying in old rooms already occupied by rats, mice—and snails. Open fires, then as now, frizzled the front while the back froze. But rich men were beginning to install stove rooms in their houses (there were two at Windsor Castle). These were not "to work and feed in, as in Germany and elsewhere, but to sweat in", as William Harrison informs us. Still, one of the first suggestions for steam heating comes in this century. Sir Hugh Platt had the notion of conveying heat by means of pipes from a steam boiler in the kitchen. The heat—again with characteristic Englishness—was not for the purpose of warming the house but was to be piped to various growing plants so that they could flourish no matter what the weather.

Lack of adequate heating was, to a certain extent, offset by

summer and winter parlours, the latter built to catch the sun, the former to remain cool and shaded. Francis Bacon even recommends "rooms from the sun both for fore noon and afternoon".[8] He also favours a few "inbowed windows" as "pretty retiring places for conference" and then adds, oddly enough, "besides they keep both the wind and sun off". Bacon's ideas of a perfect palace—one in which to entertain a Prince—seem to be a mixture of Roman, Renaissance and Oriental; one side for feasts and triumphs, the other for dwelling; a "stately tower" in front, a gallery forty feet high, a cellar sunk in the ground, courts, a hall, chambers, bedchambers with adjoining anticamera and re-camera and even an infirmary—"if the Prince or any Special Person be sick". He also recommends two small rooms with "rich cupolas". These are to be "daintily paved, richly hanged and glazed with crystalline glass".

Glass by this time had become so cheap and plentiful that it had entirely supplanted oiled linen, canvas, panels of horn, or, as Harrison observes, lattice "made of wicker or fine rifts of oak chequerwise". Windows, consequently, became larger and larger and although it is not unusual to find Gothic windows in houses of the earlier Elizabethan period, the simple grid—vertical transoms, horizontal mullions with square or diamond-shaped leaded panes between—is characteristically Elizabethan. These windows, rectangular in shape and surmounted by a Gothic dripstone or classical moulding added to the symmetry of the exterior and the light of the interior.

Coal, too, came into domestic and industrial use at this time and so influenced the internal and external details of the house. Chimneys which on the great houses of the preceding period looked like fantastic clusters of giant corkscrews became rectangular and often resembled classical columns. They were now grouped in conversational twos or threes rather than in more conspiratorial numbers, and shared the sky-line with the new balustered or lattice-work parapets, curved and notched gables, ornamental obelisks and turrets. In fact, fantastic gables, parapets, columned and entablatured fronts lent an exotic, not to say bizarre, look to many a new house.

In humbler dwellings the hole in the roof no longer sufficed to draw off the sooty smoke and poisonous fumes, or to carry away the sparks which often ignited thatched roofs although, by law, these were roughly fire-proofed with lime washed over the thatch. So forests of chimneys now began to rise in the towns. And whereas "formerly each one made his fire against a reredos in the hall where he dined and dressed his meat"[9] there were now recessed fireplaces in many rooms.

Harrison, as might be expected, did not approve of this sudden multiplication of fireplaces and chimneys. Doubtless the rectory at Radwinter was cold and beastly but he thought it healthy. He regarded too many of these fireplaces as a threat to the health if not to the morale of the nation. "Now have we many chimnies," he writes, "and yet our tenderlings complain of rheumes, catarrhs and poses." And, harking back no doubt to the time of the "onlie Phoenix", he adds, "Then had we none but reredoses; and our heads did never ache. For as the smoke in those days was supposed to be a sufficient hardening for the timbers of the house, so it was reputed to be a far better medicine to keep the goodman and his family from the quack."

A good thick smoke filling a room, it seems, not only wonderfully preserved timbers and cured headaches, but must have so kippered the goodman and his family that no decent cold or influenza germ could find a foothold on the smoke-dried membranes of nose and throat.

Yet careless of these warnings and heedless of the dangers of contracting rheumes and runny noses, the Elizabethans saw in these newer and more numerous fireplaces yet another glorious opportunity for ornamentation. Chimney-pieces became a most important feature of a room—often a very personal one, for they were apt to be decorated with the owners' initials and medallion head. The unfortunate Sir Edward Pytts, who spent twenty-seven years building his house and died before it was finished,

ordered two carved chimney-pieces for his grander fireplaces. One was to portray the story of Susanna, the other to depict some incident between Mars and Venus. The latter cost him fifteen pounds.

Of Houses, Prodigy and Otherwise

All this happened because the old-fashioned Tudor fireplace—a flattened four-centred stone arch—had given way to the rectangular opening. So the chimney-piece, which no longer projected awkwardly into the room, was yet another free space to be occupied often by structures which, sometimes rising in three tiers, looked more like the front elevation of a fantastic gatehouse or a riotous Sicilian tomb than anything else. Columns or caryatids or both might support an entablature and an upper stage where panels of plaster or wood were carved, painted and gilded; above this there was frequently yet another stage filled with carved panels and topped with terminal figures.

Religious subjects were no less popular than classical—and a carved panel over the fireplace at Great Fulford House shows the temptation scene from the story of Adam and Eve. Surrounded by some excessively odd animals, the unhappy couple stand under a tree which looks like a lighthouse topped by a curly cabbage, and they are so hopelessly and haplessly enmeshed in the coils of several large snakes that they look like twin Laöcoons.

Such grand new fireplaces needed new furnishings to match. So firebacks of iron, from the newly established ironworks of the Sussex Weald, were required. They had moulded edges and were ornamented with birds or flowers, cable twist or pilasters, and were often dated and initialled. Andirons, too, did not escape. The simple and beautiful andirons of the Middle Ages with a vertical standard bent into a scroll were no longer enough for the elaborate Elizabethans. So this standard now very often took the form of a column standing on badly bowed legs. The column was, of course, ornamented or fluted and so were the bowed legs. Sometimes an ornamented shield placed, I can only say like a sporran, was used to join legs to standard. But sometimes the standard took the form of a terminal figure. Some of these are quite loathsome and look like squashed-down caryatids who are unfortunately mongolian idiots as well.

Imported coloured marbles were also much fancied for decorating fireplaces, while black and white marble chessboard floors

E

were favoured in the halls of the wealthy. Farmhouses had deep stone fireplaces with the beam above occasionally carved with the owner's initials and date, and stone-slab floors laid directly on the earth. Cottages, more often than not, dispensed with the stone.

Interior walls were now usually panelled in oak or, if made of stone, were decorated with panels of moulded plaster or embossed leather. But both external and internal walls were lavishly decorated. Fat columns of extremely dubious ancestry appear along with pillars and pilasters of classical design. Gothic heraldry, plump cupids, and grotesques were inextricably and intemperately mixed with strap work. This latter, a favourite ornament of the period, originated in the light decorative motifs of Renaissance Italy but paused far too long in Antwerp before crossing the Channel. As an applied design—which was its original purpose—it could be beautiful, gay and delicate. But when coarsened by Germanic minds and carved in English or, more usually, imported Scandinavian oak, or patterned in red brick, or cut from stone and used externally and internally everywhere and upon everything with unlimited enthusiasm, it became both fantastically illogical and extremely ugly.

Fantastic, too, were some of the symbolic houses built during the reign. These were sheer extravaganzas. Some of them existed on paper only—such as John Thorpe's design for a house based on a plan of his own initials. It is a most inconvenient-looking house and would have been even more impossible had John spelled his Christian name with a "J" instead of using the Latin "I".

Longford Castle in Wiltshire built by Sir Thomas Gorges in 1580 was a symbol of the Trinity—triangular in shape with a tower at each corner. The towers, Pater, Filius, and Sanctus Spiritus, were joined by three centre blocks incorporating and repeating "non est". Repetition of "est" led to a central "Deus".

Sir Thomas Tresham—not to be confused with Sir Thomas Gresham—was another Elizabethan with a passion for symbolism in architecture. His Market House at Rothwall is a positive monument of the arms borne by him and his friends. He, too, built a Lodge of unparalleled Trinitarian complexity. The triangular shape is surmounted on each of its three sides by triangular gables. From the roof a triangular chimney emerges. The doorhead is a trefoil and all windows are either trefoils or built up of trefoils. The Lodge was completed in 1596, and in the same year the indefatigable Tresham began Hawkfield Lodge. This has not survived but we know that it was a twelve-sided building with four projections giving it a cruciform look. Although no explanation is offered or known for this particular symbol, one might hazard a guess—and perhaps such a guess has often been hazarded —that the twelve sides represent the Apostles, and the projections the four Evangelists of the Gospels. Both men are expressing something very personal, extremely individual, and thoroughly untraditional in this kind of architecture. In doing so they underline for us the whole Elizabethan approach to life.

CHAPTER THREE

Of Furniture and Furnishings

THERE was nothing the sixteenth-century Englishman liked
better than shows, spectacles, masques and pageants of all kinds,
and the more filled with allegorical, mythological, historical and
biblical figures, the better! The day of Elizabeth's Coronation
procession through the city of London gave her enthusiastic
subjects a marvellous opportunity to put on a show and transform the whole of the city into a stage.*

The star of the pageant—who appears to have been just as keen
on shows as everyone else—was Elizabeth herself. She was
letter perfect in her part. She rode through the transformed
streets in a chariot preceded by trumpeters and heralds in coat
armour, accompanied by gentlemen, barons, the nobility, and a
train of ladies on horseback all of whom—including the horses—
were dressed or caparisoned in crimson velvet. Over her head
was a rich canopy held by various knights; one was her half-
brother, Sir John Perrot, a natural son of Henry VIII.

Of course, all houses and buildings along the route were
splendidly decorated and hung with silks, velvets, tapestries,
carpets and bedspreads, but the really big effect, the overriding
theme, which displayed the uncommon virtues of the new Queen,
was expressed in gigantic, tiered, triumphal arches which spanned
various streets.

* The pageants for Elizabeth's Coronation were designed by Sir
Thomas Cawarden, Master of the Revels. He died the following year.

Of Furniture and Furnishings

The first arch, at the end of Gracechurch Street, was built—like a court cupboard—in three tiers. On the bottom shelf were two gigantic roses—one red, one white. Henry VII emerged from the centre of the red rose; Elizabeth of York, after whom the Queen was named, centred the white. From these, a single branch shot up to the second shelf where Henry VIII splendidly ornamented the centre of a striped red and white rose. Anne Boleyn was with him, her wedding ring prominently displayed. Again, a stem shot up to the top shelf where a figure in royal robes represented the new Queen in solitary and magnificent splendour.

Having safely and tactfully indicated the parentage and legitimacy of their new sovereign by this first arch, the second proclaimed, by means of a text in Latin and English, "The Seat of a Worthy Governance". Again the Queen occupied the top tier; below the seven cardinal virtues made short work of the seven deadly sins, among which Ignorance and Superstition were included, less perhaps for their own sake than for the sake of getting one back at her late Majesty, Mary Tudor.

In the arch above Soper's Lane, children personified the eight Beatitudes, all of which were satisfactorily attributed to Elizabeth. How they got round the meek one is a little difficult to see. Perhaps the child who sat on every arch and declaimed its significance in verse helped with the lines:

Thou hast been eight times blessed, oh Queen of worthy fame,
By meekness of thy sprite, when care did thee beset. . . .

But there could be no mistaking the meaning of the arch spanning Little Conduit in Cheapside. Here a decayed (the past) and a prosperous (the present and future) Commonwealth were displayed. Below, on the bottom shelf, was a dark cavern. As the Queen approached Time emerged from the cave together with his daughter, Truth, who held in her hand a Bible—in English—which, as the Queen halted under the arch, she lowered on a silk cord into the Queen's chariot.

73

The Elizabethans at Home

The Queen did not disappoint the wildly cheering crowds who lined the way and who continually stopped her chariot for a word with her or to press upon her little nosegays and branches of rosemary. She took the Bible, suspended like a spider on its string, kissed it, rolled her eyes heavenward, pressed the Book to her breast and then thanked the city "more for this gift than for all the cost bestowed" on her.

And so the procession proceeded. Deborah—who was a judge in Israel—rather oddly clad in English Parliamentary robes and bearing a sceptre, appeared at one point and the City Companies at another. They enlivened the rather grave morality expressed in the arches by giving the Queen a purse containing a thousand gold marks accompanied by a speech. The Queen received both most graciously and answered the speech "marvellously pithily".

At last Temple Bar was reached where it was discovered that the two tutelary dieties of the City, Gog and Magog (or, as some held, Gogmagog the Albion and Corineus the Briton), had forsaken their headquarters at the Guildhall to station themselves on either side of Temple Bar. They bore aloft a great text which in Latin verse explained, yet once more to the Queen, the sense of all the pageants she had just seen.

It cannot be that they feared her Majesty incapable of understanding what had been so clearly and so showily displayed, since every single arch had borne a text explaining its significance and, in addition, had had a child within who declaimed its meaning in extravagantly dull verse. It was just that in the matter of shows and pageants the Elizabethans weren't very subtle. On the contrary they were given to rather boring and endless repetition; to an over-emphasis which, in time, became a gross and ugly distortion. It was naïveté gone wild.

This trait, this great and excessive love for masques, pageants, spectacles and shows of all kinds, strongly influenced the decorative taste and design of the period. Not only in their chimney-pieces, but in much else, many of the prodigy and great houses of the day displayed in their interior décor what has been aptly called "pageants in woodwork, stone, and plaster."[1] Once simple furniture now began to show a tedious and endless repetition of flamboyant ornamentation, an over-emphasis of functional parts, so that, in the end, it galloped merrily downhill on fearful, dropsical legs into a positive morass of distortion. Had Elizabethan houses been as crammed and overloaded as late Victorian houses, we would feel, no doubt, that it was the ugliest period for furniture of all. Survival, as usual, has been only of the fittest.

Unfortunately, the fittest is what can only be termed the over-ornamented elephantine.

The fact must be faced that the Elizabethans for all their qualities and virtues, for all the delicacy of their poetry and music, had more money than taste. The austere Gothic, the subtle Perpendicular, the restrained ornamentation of the Decorated were considered *démodé*. The vigour and beauty of thirteenth to fifteenth century carving which so enchants us to-day had degenerated to the crude and blunt. To a new, exuberant, money-making generation the formalized beauty of linen-fold panelling, the curving and flowing of the traditional vine pattern must have seemed *vieux jeu*. So, plain basic shapes were inflated and relentlessly carved with acanthus leaves, scrolls, rosettes, crude versions of classical gods, mythological figures and mis-cegenated columns. The Elizabethans never really understood or mastered the five orders—Ionic, Doric, Corinthian, Tuscan and Composite—as a system of architecture; they regarded them simply as material for decoration. Perhaps they didn't care. Perhaps they didn't want to understand. Perhaps they were in too much of a hurry to get on with things or too eager to startle and stun with the bizarre and grotesque, but the result is mainly deplorable. Bloated and contorted variations of the five orders disfigure nearly everything from chair-legs to bed-heads. The Italian style, coarsened by Flemish minds and applied with a heavy hand to sturdy—not English but Danish—oak, was the delight of the fashionable and rich Elizabethan.

This taste in furniture was, in a minor way, a true reflection of the spirit and mood of the age. In politics the Queen, herself, combined English aims with Italian ideas and methods, and the current jingle "An Englishman Italianate is a Devil incarnate" though meant as a stricture on policy might equally well be applied to furniture. Happily for us, country districts remained, to a greater or lesser extent, uncorrupted by the fashionable notions of the time. The country carpenter and joiner, the candlestick-maker and pewter-worker still turned out wares of

Of Furniture and Furnishings

fine proportion and beautiful design. "Base kinds of furniture", as Harrison calls it, was still to be found, "in Bedfordshire and elsewhere further off from our southern parts".

Harrison was obviously all for the flamboyant in furniture although he deplored it in dress. He says, "The furniture of our houses also exceedeth and is grown in a manner even to passing delicacy; and here I do not speak of the nobility and gentry only but like-wise of the lowest sort—I do rejoice to see how God hath blessed us with his good gifts and whilst I behold that, in a time when all things are grown to most excessive price—we do yet find the means to obtain and achieve such furniture as hath heretofore been unpossible."

But there can have been few houses, other than the great ones, completely furnished in the new "unpossible" style until the last quarter of the century. The completely period room must have been rare. Furniture, which had always been scanty and built to last, was handed down from generation to generation and left in wills to various members of a family, as Shakespeare willed his "second best bed" with furniture (furnishings) to his wife. Shakespeare certainly seems to have been as furniture and clothes conscious as any ordinary Elizabethan. His plays are full of wonderfully observed detail about both, and his will gives us

an indication of his property both real and personal. But his will was signed on March 25th 1616, thirteen years after Elizabeth's death and by then furniture had become much less scanty and much more hideous. Only thirty-five years before, in 1580, at Arundel Castle which was held to be richly furnished, the "King's Chamber" had in it nothing but a bed, a table

77

and a chair. Even as late as 1585 that visiting merchant of Ulm, Samuel Keichel reported that "the royal treasures and tapestries are kept only in that place in which, for the time being, the Queen resides; when she removes to another everything is taken away and only bare walls remain standing". No wonder Elizabeth travelled with 400 carewares and 2,400 horses!

Just as late Elizabethan furniture melts or writhes into the Jacobean so early Elizabethan furniture shows the influence of previous ages. Thus the typical Tudor box—or coffer-seat chair—solid backed, solid armed and with a cupboard beneath the seat—was still in use. It was unlikely to be moved or thrown away since it was so heavy that it took two or more men to lift it. This weighty inheritance probably stood in the Great Hall or in what had become the

Entrance Hall. But such a chair, though grand, was an obvious handicap, particularly when the first floor gallery became the important room, so the design was modified. Solid arm-supports were removed, the cupboard disappeared in favour of legs, the back remained straight and was uncomfortably carved. This "streamlined" box-chair, which could be dragged across a room by one person, or even lugged upstairs by a brace or more of servants, was the parent of the frame chair.

Of Furniture and Furnishings

Upholstered and leathered chairs were certainly not unheard of at the time. Antonio Moro's portrait of Mary Tudor* shows her sitting bolt upright in an upholstered or leather-covered chair, as do his wonderful portraits of Sir Thomas and Lady Gresham.† But such chairs were not common and were owned only by the rich. There were also turned chairs, insane-looking bobbin-frame chairs, and the long-known X-shaped or Glastonbury chair, as well as settles and forms.

But chairs, as such, did not become plentiful until the end of the reign. Traditionally they were for important people and had been, originally, ecclesiastical furniture reserved especially for the bishop. So when the chair crept out of the exclusive cathedral into the inclusive home, it still retained much of its special aura and was reserved for the head of the house or for a very superior sort of guest. Thus, the Queen sat in a chair wherever she went but her courtiers occupied stools. These, Sir John Harington complained, were extremely hard and uncomfortable. He even suggested that the court might well provide lined or quilted forms and stools for lords and ladies to sit on—a fashion which had long since been taken up by rich merchants. Great plank forms and "wainscot" stools he says, plaintively and with feeling, are so hard that "since great breeches were laid aside men can scarce endure to sit upon (them)".

* Now at Castle Ashby, the seat of the Marquis of Northampton.

† In the Rijksmuseum, Amsterdam.

The Elizabethans at Home

When families were gathered together for meals, either in the Hall or in the newer dining-rooms, and sat around the table or "board", as it was more usually called, the head of the house or host occupied a chair. The rest of the family, guests and retainers sat on forms, chests or stools. The host was, in actual fact, the "chairman" of the board and the importance of this position is still recognized today in our very different use of the phrase.

As for the infrequent stuffed upholstered chair which arrived late in the reign—it was a development of the frame chair and was made by nailing leather across back and seat. This type of chair really did not come into its own until the next century and its sixteenth-century origins were very simple. A cushion or "bagge" was tacked to the frame above the leather seat. Later, leather was replaced by webbing or sacking, still later the back was stuffed. Very few examples of such chairs remain since the moth has corrupted the bagge and the worm invaded and destroyed the frame—generally a beech wood one.

It may be that the sixteenth century also saw the introduction or invention of the chair with the movable back which could be raised or lowered at will. Certainly Elizabeth had one, and

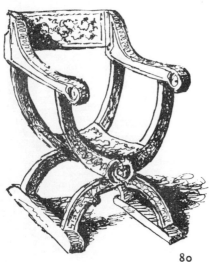

very early in her reign too. In 1560–61 there is mention of payment being made to John Grene "for one great stool of wall-nutre with one large pillow covered with cloth of gold and ffrenged with silk and gold, with one staie for the back of the Queen covered with cloth of gold with staies, springes and staples of iron to set the same higher and lower with a pillow of down".

Of Furniture and Furnishings

The rather chaotic description sounds very like a couch or a chaise-longue with an adjustable back, or it may have been something resembling a Knole sofa. Nor must we forget that "lewd day-bed" mentioned in Shakespeare's *Richard III* which may have been the same sort of thing. On this, according to Buckingham, the good Richard, unlike his wicked and voluptuous brother Edward IV, was NOT lolling.

Stools and chests, many of them of Tudor and earlier designs, were still indispensable (the box chair was a development of the chest) and constituted the main articles of furniture in humbler homes. The chest had been for centuries an all-purpose piece. It was used for storage, for sitting on, for eating from and even, with a straw pallet, for sleeping on. It was also the usual trunk of the time (although leather-covered trunks were coming in) which is another reason why Elizabeth's luggage was so heavy and cumbersome. But this plain piece of standard furniture did not escape the passion for ornamentation; heavily carved in a much-favoured chequered or lozenge pattern, with rails and styles inlaid, the chest certainly lost its pure monastic look.

Great noblemen often imported wonderful chests from Italy, like the "fair flat Venetian" one of walnut carved, gilded, and furnished with locks and keys which was part of Leicester's furniture at Kenilworth. Spruce or "Dansk" chests were also imported, to say nothing of cypress or cedar wood chests. The latter were used to protect winter woollens and furs from the ravages of the moth.*

* Indeed, this custom persisted across the Atlantic right up until the invention of the new anti-moth

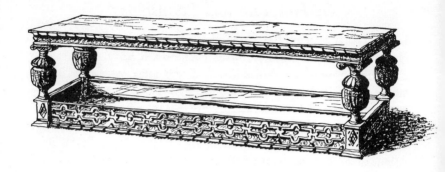

Then, towards the end of the century, some nameless genius appeared and added a single range of drawers beneath the box. In time this chest *with* drawers became a chest *of* drawers though by then the original chest part had entirely vanished.

The heavy trestle table of earlier eras was also still in use but just around the time Elizabeth became Queen the top became fixed to the trestle or to legs framed by a joiner. Often people turned an old table into a new one by nailing the removable top firmly to the trestles. These tables varied greatly in size and in number of legs but were made chiefly in oak, ash, elm or walnut; the latter was extremely rare and much valued. It is interesting to note that deal, which we so much despise, was considered to be a rare and precious wood. Henry VIII had a room at his fabulous palace of Nonsuch panelled in deal which he "prized exceedingly".

Another invention of the period was the draw-top table—an elaboration of the trestle table. Two leaves which lay beneath the centreboard on raking bearers were drawn out and allowed the centre to fall by its own weight so that it became flush with the ends.

There is a fantastic draw table at Hardwick, the top supported

---

aerosol sprays. When I was a child no well-run Canadian or American home was complete without its cedar chest or cedar-lined closet used for exactly the same purpose as those chests imported into England in Elizabethan times.

by four "sea dogges". At least these beasts have rather doggy faces with spaniel-type, leafy ears, but their bodies are extremely confusing. They have wings, women's breasts, paws ending in leaves (or perhaps seaweed) and fishes' tails. Each is garlanded round the neck with a sort of lei of fruit and flowers, and the support upon which these extraordinary creatures sit is, itself, supported by four turtles. It is an unbelievable table, a nightmare of a table, yet it has a sort of hideous beauty of its own. Hardwick also boasts of one of the most beautiful home-made framed tables in the world. Produced on the estate by the estate carpenters, its top is inlaid with Elizabethan musical instruments and pieces of music in various woods. The top is in three pieces and to hide the joins the designer, or maker, has inserted wood so that the three pieces look as if they were laced together with leather.

Such heavy tables needed stalwart legs but as time went on plain legs gave way to legs bulbous as onions. The "cup and cover" leg (or melon bulb leg) gadrooned and carved with jewel ornament, and frequently surmounted by an extremely dubious Ionic capital, was a great favourite. Feet, which were tied with stretchers, were less amenable to torture, or perhaps they were just less noticeable so they quite often remained four square.

Smaller tables, including the gate-legged, made increasingly frequent appearances during the period, probably as developments of the joined stool, still often used as a small table. There was a red-marble table streaked with white in the Queen's bedroom at Windsor, while Jacob Rathgeb, secretary to the Duke of Württemberg, noted at Theobald's a number of tables inlaid with various coloured marbles, including one of black touch-stone "fourteen spans long, seven wide and one thick".[2] This black-basalt or

jasper table which must have been ten and a half feet long and more than eight feet wide stood in a summer-house in the garden.

There were oval and round tables—like the one Falstaff sat at, in the Dolphin chamber of Mistress Quickly's Inn. There were tables with tip-up tops, and the very occasional octagonal table and pedestal tables with, often, a chess-board top. On these smaller tables, towards the end of the century, obese, bulbous legs were sometimes mercifully slimmed down and fluted. This ultimately led to the far more graceful and beautiful column leg.

Other innovations—or near innovations—were the press and the small court or short cupboard. The latter was probably used for the display of plate and as a service table, as it was open and built in three tiers or stages. Presses were closed and were larger and wider. Built in two or three stages, the upper part was often recessed, making it necessary to support the carved frieze with columns—usually bulbous. The lower part was also enclosed by hinged doors which, like the upper part, were panelled and carved.

There were, of course, side "boards"; massive and heavily carved, and a sort of chest, often on legs with doors in front, known as a hutch. Those used as food cupboards had perforated doors.

And then there was the wardrobe. Originally the wardrobe had been a separate room where clothes and valuables were stored in chests. The Queen's wardrobe, for example, was a

sort of third treasury, and wardrobe officials were those who dealt with the treasure. But now the wardrobe as a piece of furniture appeared. In my opinion this is the unforgivable crime of Elizabethan furniture. The massive, hideous wardrobe which has disfigured every English bedroom for centuries began here. That monstrosity which we accept and which many architects still love, since it absolves them from the necessity of designing decent built-in clothes closets, we owe to the first Elizabethans.

Now we come to beds. As the Elizabethan Age progressed, beds were developing apace. The traditional, uncurtained stump-bed remained in common use in farmhouses, cottages and hospitals, a bed without posts or tester, with a head of nailed boards. As this was plain it offered an inviting surface for carving. But Parson Harrison tells us that even in farmhouses straw pallets were being replaced by feather-beds, and that no one now used a log of wood as a pillow. There were also "trussing" beds, none of which seems to have survived, but as they were supposed to accompany the owner on his travels they can't have been too weighty and were perhaps made to come apart in sections, while

F

a field bed—in the sense of a camp bed—is mentioned in *Romeo and Juliet*. There were also truckle or trundle beds for servants. These were very low and were made to be pushed under the great beds when not in use.

The great beds of the day were of enormous size, weight and importance; the head-boards were often as elaborately carved as a choir screen and frequently arcaded or compartmented with recesses for candles. The foot-posts, with heavy bulbs, were supported on massive pedestals or plinths, sometimes joined to the bed itself, sometimes separated from it but always supporting the tester which, in this century, was no longer suspended from the ceiling. Every bit of woodwork from tester to toe was carved within an inch of its life.

Bed-springs were unknown. Stuffed woollen mattresses were placed on top of bed-boards or on interwoven strips of leather. On top of this went the feather-bed, usually imported from the Continent. Then came enormous sheets, so difficult to launder in bad weather that they often remained unwashed for months on end; then blankets of fustian or wool, down pillows and the coverlet. This varied from the simple to the gloriously ornate depending on the means of the owner.

But all bed coverings must have been considered of great value and were probably not too plentiful. Women often lent each other their lying-in sheets with apologies for their un-cleanness which, no doubt, partly explains the infant and maternal mortality rate of the time.

Andrew Boorde, that "Lewd and ungracious priest" as Harrison rather unfairly calls him, who died some nine years be-fore Elizabeth came to the

Of Furniture and Furnishings

throne, bequeathed his soul to God and his feather-bed, a bolster, a pair of sheets and a coverlet, to his friend Edward Hudson. Hangings and curtains which enclosed these great beds became richer, fuller, and more varied in design and could cost hundreds or even thousands of pounds. Massive and hideous and no doubt fairly uncomfortable (but handily private and warm which bed-rooms weren't) the great beds-stood in the new big houses like the funeral monuments of the later, debased Roman senators. The astonished eye of the visiting Paul Hentzner noted various Royal beds at Windsor Castle which he toured in September 1598. Those of Henry VII and his Queen; Edward VI; Henry VIII and Anne Boleyn were eleven feet square and furnished with hangings which glittered with gold and silver. Queen Elizabeth's bed was neither so long nor so large as these but it had "curious coverings of embroidery".

As might be expected, everything which could be and many things which shouldn't have been were embroidered. Stom-achers, clothes, coifs, night-caps, pillow beres (pillow cases about thirty-five inches long by twenty inches wide), gloves, ruffs, mantles, scarves, cases, and caskets were embellished with em-broidery of various kinds. Black work, found often in conjunc-tion with gold thread; stump work—that is raised embroidery padded out to give a three-dimensional effect—which had also, like the chair, crept out of the church and entered private homes; petit point; applied work—this particularly on bed-covers and hangings—and turkey work, were all extremely popular. In-deed, more fabrics were used in furnishing than ever before in history and they were embroidered with the same lavishness and enthusiasm with which furniture was carved.

Even book covers were made of velvet and beautifully em-broidered. The books in Elizabeth's library at Whitehall were bound in coloured velvets, chiefly red. They bore her cypher and had clasps of gold and silver. Pearls and precious stones were set in the binding. But there was one book which never found its way to the Queen's library at Whitehall or any other palace,

The Elizabethans at Home

for the simple reason that it was stolen before she had a chance to read it. The thief was William Cecil, Lord Burghley.

The incident which turned the great statesman into a petty thief was this; a certain Mr. Fuller, a Puritan, asked leave to present the Queen, through a lady-in-waiting, with a book he had written. The Queen, accustomed to paeans of praise written in her honour, graciously consented. It is almost certain that she could not have opened the book when the lady-in-waiting gave it to her for, after stating bluntly that God's commandments against swearing were abundantly clear, tactful Mr. Fuller went on to elaborate his thesis in these words:

". . . yet notwithstanding your Grace's Majesty in anger hath used to swear sometimes by that abomination the Mass, and often grievously by God and Christ and by many parts of His glorified body, and by saints, faith, troth and other forbidden things; and by your Majesty' evil example and sufferance, the most part of your subjects and people of every degree do commonly swear and blaspheme to God's unspeakable dishonour . . . without any punishment."

Mr. Fuller also complained that the Queen had been much too lax about the execution of murderers (i.e. Mary Stuart) and about punishing adultery and fornication.

Fortunately for Mr. Fuller, the Queen left the book on her chair and Lord Burghley, who must have been aware of its contents or who had perhaps idly picked it up to look at, quietly purloined it. Mr. Fuller, of course, could not present the book in person to the Queen because, by her language and laxness in putting down sin in her subjects, she had put herself beyond God's pale. Mr. Fuller was not going to risk contamination even by association. And Lord Burghley wasn't going to risk a row with the Puritans over what the Queen would do if she read Mr. Fuller's book. He was extremely evasive when the Queen asked what had become of it, hoping that she'd forget about it . . . which, fortunately, she did. No doubt she cursed Burghley roundly for mislaying it—though Mr.

Of Furniture and Furnishings

Fuller's book can hardly have had a handsome and embroidered cover.

Needlework of the period was a not inconsiderable art, and most women prided themselves on their ability to further ornament their already elaborate clothing with coloured or silver and gold threads. The Queen, herself, when younger, had been a fine needlewoman. At the age of six she had presented her infant half-brother, Prince Edward, with a cambric shirt as a New Year's gift. It was very possibly of her own making as in the following year she gave him a piece of needlework which she certainly had made herself. Elizabeth's maids-of-honour were reputed to be highly accomplished in this art and we may be sure that Elizabeth herself saw to it that they were, and that they occupied themselves with needlework at fixed hours or in their spare time. We can also be reasonably sure that she inspected their handiwork, praising the good and being sarcastic about the bad. As one who knew not only how the job should be done but who could do it "excellently well" herself, it is easy to imagine how, with an oath (alas, Mr. Fuller was right, the Queen did swear terribly), she would snatch away a bit of work being carelessly or incompetently done by some unfortunate thumb-fingered maid, and show her exactly and impatiently how she should set about the task.

Mary of Scotland was also a very fine needlewoman and on New Year's Day 1575, she presented an olive-branch to her cousin, Elizabeth, in the shape of an elegant head-dress of network together with collars, cuffs and other little pieces which she had made herself. This peace-offering was presented by the French Ambassador, La Mothe.* Elizabeth received the gift amiably and admired the fine work prodigiously. Later on, in the spring, La Mothe sought to consolidate the peace, as it were, by presenting the Queen with three caps made by Mary. This time Elizabeth demurred, "great commotions and jealousies have taken

* More correctly, La Motte Fénèlon.

place in the privy council", she told La Mothe—because she had accepted the gift of the Queen of Scots!

But, Privy Council or no, Elizabeth could not long hold out against a gift, particularly of something to wear and one so beautifully embroidered. Finally, she gave in, accepted the caps, saying to the Ambassador as she did so, "Tell the Queen of Scots that I am older than she is and when people arrive at my age they take all they can get with both hands and only give with their little finger." She was, at the time, forty-two, but had anyone else remarked on her age she would have found it difficult to forgive them.

She was always particularly delighted with gifts of clothing and was probably the most clothes-conscious woman in the then known world. Yet during the time her half-sister was on the throne (and Mary too, was addicted to finery) Elizabeth, had for the most part, affected the simple, sober dress of the Puritan which was, in turn, based on the dress of the country folk. Here, I fear, she was influenced by what was politically expedient for her future rather than by any religious scruple.

She was a Protestant Princess, Mary a Roman Catholic one. It was therefore prudent for Elizabeth to dress the part. She might be forced to attend Mass to save not her soul but her neck, but she attended wearing a dress that even John Knox couldn't have disapproved of—much! The contrast between a Protestant Princess who dressed in simple country and Puritan fashion, and the magnificent and splendid vestments of the Roman priests showed more strongly—and more safely—than any words where Elizabeth's sympathies lay, and from what quarter she expected support if Mary should die childless.

But once she became Queen she could dress for that part— and it was far more to her liking. This must have been appreciated by her court and members of her household very early on in the reign. Gifts of money as New Year's gifts certainly predominate in 1561, yet in that year we find she received at least eleven pairs of sleeves, several smocks and some very fancy

Of Furniture and Furnishings

handkerchiefs, six of them edged with gold lace and others made of black and red silk. One smock, embroidered with the favourite black silk, was a present from the Earl of Warwick. It was probably a day-smock or chemise-smock with a standing collar.

Sleeves, which sound a curious present to us, were detachable, and green was a favourite colour—as the song "Greensleeves" indicates.

Mr. Adams, "schoolmaster" couldn't afford to give the Queen sleeves but he did give her "a patron (pattern) for a peir of sleeves" and was rewarded with forty, no doubt badly needed, shillings. At this New Year Elizabeth also received a present which must have delighted her nearly as much as money or clothes—"two greyhounds, a fallow and a black pyed" were presented by Sir James Strumpe.

By 1578, when boom times were under way, the clothes presented to the Queen were far more numerous and far more splendidly embroidered. There was a "tawny tapheta hat" embroidered with gold scorpions and having a border garnished with seed pearls, given by Ralph Bowes. There was a handsome waistcoat of quilted white sarsanet embroidered with gold and silver lace, given by Philip Sidney. Smythe, the dustman, uncertain of his taste in clothing fit for a Queen, took no chances and presented two bolts of "cameryck" while a certain Mrs. Dale, if she kept a diary would have noted down with satisfaction that she had presented the Queen with "doublet and forepart of cloth of gold with passamayne of gold".[3]

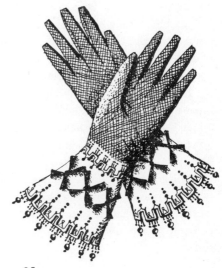

The Elizabethans at Home

The Countess of Shrewsbury, better known as Bess of Hard-wick, the richest woman in the kingdom, gave a "mantel" of "tawney" satin lined with white taffeta, faced with white satin and bordered with Venice gold and silver. Sir Francis Walsingham, Principal Secretary, a sober-dressing Puritan, presented his sovereign with a magnificent night-gown. It, too, was of tawny satin faced with "heare" coloured satin and was "embrawdered" all over.

A night-gown may sound a rather odd present for a Principal Secretary to give a Queen, but night-gowns in those days weren't something you slept in; they were what you put on when you got up. Women slept in night-smocks and on rising put the night-gown on over the smock. Both men and women wore such night-gowns as morning dress—as women today wear house-coats. But in the sixteenth century ordinary dress for going out in, was so complicated, so elaborate, and consisted of so many pieces that a night-gown was an absolute necessity for an early rising and extremely busy Queen.

Fashionable women of the day rose late and could spend hours dressing. Indeed they had to. A complete outfit consisted of a chemise-smock, then a petticoat which, as it was often exposed, had to be of rich material. Next a laced bodice with "busks". Sometimes the busks were of iron and curved out like a cuirasse of armour; often they were carved. Next a skirt, perhaps a Spanish hooped one or a French one padded and stiffened round the hips in a "bumrawle". Then the kirtle, in two parts, like our separates, a bodice and a skirt. The bodice was often made like a man's doublet but it had a long point in front. Then came the gown which fell from shoulder to heel and was entirely open. Over the gown, often instead of it, went a cloak or mantle and in addition there were major accessories like sleeves and ruffs which at one time grew so large that special long-handled spoons were made so that the wearer could eat. There were also collars, cuffs, foreparts and stomachers or placards as they were often called.

Of Furniture and Furnishings

Knitted stockings came in. Mrs. Montague, the Queen's silk woman, gave her a pair of black silk stockings in 1561 which the Queen "liked so well that she never wore cloth hose again".[4] In 1588 a Mrs. Vaughan gave the Queen a pair of stockings and garters of white cypress and by the time Harrison started to write his book he tells us that "knit hosen" had become so common that even countrywomen wore them—and dyed them black with alder bark. The stocking-knitting frame was an invention of the time, its inventor—a Nottingham clergyman. It was the parent of all future inventions of knitting and lace-making machines.

Women wore low-cut slippers in the house and probably looked rather sluttish in them as our word slipshod derives from this custom. They also wore court-shoes, or pumps as they were called and are still called across the Atlantic today. There were also shoes with high cork soles and overshoes with cloth uppers to go over court-shoes.

Hats were elaborate—as richly ornamented and embroidered as that of the Quangle Wangle.* Married women wore them on the street and at home, unmarried women didn't. Men wore hats indoors too, and uncovered when the Queen entered or left a room. Early Elizabethan hats were tall steeple hats or conical "copintakes" and the low-crowned wide-brimmed or unbrimmed hat was also very popular. The brimmed type was, in the next century, adopted by the Cavaliers. Hats were made of velvet, silk, felt, taffeta, beaver and ermine. Coifs, hoods, cauls, and caps were also worn.

A statute passed in 1571, made it compulsory for everyone over the age of seven, unless the head of the family had an income of over twenty marks a year from land, to wear a cap made of "woll knitte, thicked and dressed in England" on the Sabbath and other holy days. The penalty for non-observance was 3s. 3d. The law was passed to provide cappers with a livelihood and to

* According to Edward Lear the Quangle Wangle's hat was of beaver. It was 102 feet wide with "ribbons and bibbons on every side".

The Elizabethans at Home

prevent them begging and "raunging and gadding through the realm, in practicing and exercising sundry kinds of lewdness". The thought of hundreds of lewd, mad cappers ranging and gadding about the country is indeed a sobering one. But the statute must have been either effective or have ultimately become unenforceable as it was repealed in 1597.

Men no less than women went in for elaborate and complicated dress and often wore a fortune on their backs. The whole point of the Ralegh story is that a man's cloak was frequently the most valuable part of his wardrobe, costing hundreds of pounds. As the punning reference to Ralegh's piece of gallantry has it—"by spreading his cloak he gained many good suits".

Another gentleman, Robert Sidney, in a letter to John Harington towards the end of the reign describes the dress he wore the day Elizabeth visited him. The Queen, he says, wore "a marvellous suit of velvet", his own wife was in a purple kirtle fringed with gold. So much for the women! When he describes his own dress he is full of detail and delight. He was clad, he says, "in a rich band and collar of needlework, a dress of rich stuff and bravest-cut and fashioned with an underbody of silver and loops". Even though the Queen was so tired she had to use a stick to help her up the stair and was so much wearied

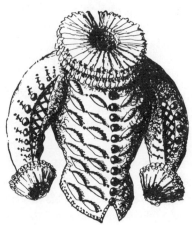

walking about the house that she ate only "two morsels of rich comfit çake and drank a small cordial out of a golden cup", she was so pleased with the attire of Robert and his wife (so he says) that she commended them on it.

Perhaps she did, perhaps she didn't. What emerges most clearly from the letter is, that Robert was positively delighted with himself and his fine clothes.

Of Furniture and Furnishings

It is more than likely that the Queen enjoyed her visit to Sir Julius Caesar far more, because Sir Julius gave her some beautiful clothes to mark the occasion. The visit took place on September 12th 1590 five days after her fifty-seventh birthday. To use his own words, Sir Julius presented her with "a gown of cloth of silver, richly embroidered, a black net work mantel with pure gold, a taffeta hat, white with several flowers and a jewel of gold". The cost of the whole visit which was only overnight, including food provided for Her Majesty, was, he says, some £700. The Earl of Leicester was, of course, always gorgeously dressed and spent a fabulous amount on clothes. But old Burghley, like Walsingham, stuck to sober grey and black. Children dressed as their elders. Today the reverse is true.

Did the Queen ever embroider bits and pieces for her Court favourites to wear or present them with hand-worked cushion cloths? Very probably she did, as these were very popular gifts of the era. It is known that she worked a scarf for the Duke of Anjou. Cushions were plentiful and necessary—even though the Queen didn't provide them for her Court to sit on. There was, at Windsor, "a cushion most curiously wrought by the Queen's own hand".[5] There was also a famous tapestry which, Hentzner tells us, "the English had taken or stolen from France when they were masters there". This showed Clovis receiving the fleur-de-lis from an angel; the emblem which, on a blue field, became the arms of France. This angelic intervention banished for ever the three toads which had hitherto been borne upon the shields of the French kings.

What the Elizabethan home lacked in hard furniture—and the operative word is hard—it made up in the brilliance, novelty, variety and abundance of "soft furnishings". In those ages where people cover themselves with rich and complicated attire they also cover their furniture and their walls. So in Elizabeth's time walls, beds and windows were richly hung. Carpets covered tables—as they still do in the Netherlands—cupboards and very much later on, floors. "Bankers" disguised forms and settles, while cushions were strewn about everywhere. In fact the Elizabethans were really very like the Victorians in their passion for draping everything with something else—though of course their reasons were pleasure and ostentation, not prudery. Even that silly twin, Antipholus of Ephesus, in Shakespeare's *The Comedy of Errors* kept his ducats in a desk "covered o'er with turkish tapestry".

In the homes of the rich, cushions, bankers, table and cupboard carpets, were of tapestry, silk or velvet. The less rich made do with painted cloths or leather, and even the poorest homes were not without a threadbare table-cloth.

Harrison, still full of wonder and admiration, says: "The walls of our houses on the inner sides . . . be either hanged with tapestries or Arras work or painted cloths, wherein either diverse histories or herbs, or beasts, knots and such like are stained; or else they are ceiled with oak of our own, or wainscote brought out of the east countries whereby the rooms are . . . made warm and much more close than otherwise they would be."

Plaster walls were often painted with a running design or with figure subjects rather crudely if colourfully executed. A good example was discovered about thirty years ago at Stratford on Avon.* It shows the Story of Tobit, complete with explanatory notes, the odd, in-between spaces being filled with strange fruits, flowers and foliage in the manner of William Morris. All the characters in this apocryphal Old Testament story are handsomely dressed in early Elizabethan clothes, while fluted Italianate pilasters separate the scenes which have little more perspective than Chinese painting. Colour was also used on wainscotted walls and to pick out ornamental details. The framework of wainscotting was often painted a brilliant red with touches of blue and gold while the panels were often decorated with designs and sometimes landscapes; or, instead, pictures were pasted in the panels and then painted.† It was an age of such colour that

* At the White Swan Inn. It is still there under glass, in the lounge.
† As in the Great High Chamber at Hardwick.

Of Furniture and Furnishings

we, accustomed now to subtler tones, are positively assaulted by it when we see a bit restored to its original brilliance.

Jewel-like colours were also introduced into new houses through the big new windows which had such enormous areas for glazing that small panels of coloured glass were often let in. The arms of the family, scrolls, grotesques, Morris dancers, the inevitable strap-work, flowers, herbs and, loyally, the Royal Arms with supporters were often made up in coloured glass. There was some enamel-painting on glass too, while ventilation was afforded by ventilating squares of lead of a rather more restrained and geometric design; indeed, some of the clear-glass glazing-patterns were also almost reticent.

Rathgeb was absolutely stunned by the splendour and richness of the hangings at Hampton Court. On behalf of his master the Duke of Württemberg—a rather tedious little man whose one ambition in life was to be given the Order of the Garter—he writes in his diary, "All apartments and rooms in this immensely large structure are hung with rich tapestry of pure gold and fine

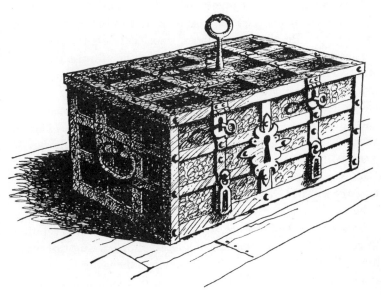

The Elizabethans at Home

silks, so exceedingly beautiful and royally ornamented that it would hardly be possible to find more magnificent things of the kind in any other place. In particular, there is one apartment belonging to the Queen, in which she is accustomed to sit in state, costly beyond everything; the tapestries are garnished with gold, pearls and precious stones, one table-cover alone is valued at above fifty thousand crowns—not to mention the royal throne studded with very large diamonds, rubies, sapphires and the like that glitter among other precious stones and pearls as the sun among the stars."

Hentzner takes it more quietly. He was a jurist by profession and obviously less swayed by emotional appeal . . . but even he admits that in one chamber there were "several excessively rich tapestries which are hung up when the Queen gives audience to foreign ambassadors". There were also numbers of cushions ornamented with gold and silver, many counterpanes and coverlets—or coverlids—for beds lined with ermine, while all the walls of the palace "shone with gold and silver".

Both Rathgeb and Hentzner were late reign visitors and by then rich noblemen and merchants were furnishing with great ostentation. By then the Queen, too, had acquired, by one means or another, a great deal of furniture and furnishings. She went in for magnificence and splendour as did all Renaissance princes. She hung her palaces with pictures by the best artists. She collected jewels, pearls and all sorts of precious stones, gold and silver plate, rich beds, fine couches and chariots. Persian and Indian carpets, statues and medals "which she would buy at great cost". She covered her walls with rich tapestries and, at Hampton Court, she had her naval victories worked in fine tapestry and laid them up among the richest pieces in her wardrobe.

Tapestries, like furniture, were handed down from generation to generation, but the impetus in house-building meant that many more were now imported. In fact, much of the materials, decorations, ornaments and furniture for the Elizabethan home came

direct from the great Mart at
Antwerp. All the materials for
the new "Burse"—the Royal
Exchange—built by Sir Thomas
Gresham were shipped from
Antwerp at his own direction
right down, or up, to the statute
of the Queen herself. And, with
the great and prosperous con-
nexion between London and the
Lowlands, merchants great and
small were able to furnish their
homes in town or country with
imported articles. Some tapestries were certainly made in
England, but the supply could
not possibly keep up with the
enormously increased demand.

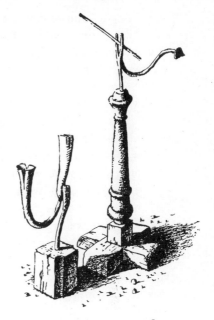

William Sheldon's tapestry-weaving works had been started in
Warwick some fifty years before Elizabeth came to the throne.
Wall-hangings and perhaps carpets were made at this works.
Designs on the whole were usually oriental, sometimes incon-
gruously mixed with heraldic devices. (Carpets too, came into
the country from the Continent, from Turkey and the Levant.)

The portrait of the Queen by an unknown artist, known as
the Ditchley portrait, now in the National Gallery, shows her
standing upon a tapestry map of Oxfordshire which was made at
Sheldon's works. Her feet cover Ditchley, the house belonging
to Sir Henry Lee,* where the Queen stayed when she visited
Oxford in 1592.

> Happy hour, happy day
> That Eliza came this way.

* He was personal champion to the Queen; Master of the Ordnance;
and a great builder and sheep-farmer.

The Elizabethans at Home

was a jingle composed and chanted on this occasion. After all the poetry, some good and some incredibly bad, written in her honour this small bit of doggerel may seem too plain, too unvarnished. But to the subtle, silent woman in a red wig, it must have been a gratifying form of "Mere English" calypso.

Nevertheless, though carpets and tapestries and even cloaks were spread for the Queen, floor-coverings as such were not in general use. Floors in farmhouses and cottages were strewn with rushes, reeds and straw mixed with lavender and rosemary clippings. The same was true of Prodigy Houses, though even greater quantities of sweet-smelling herbs were used there. At Greenwich palace the floors were strewn with bay.

Ceilings, however, made up for the lack of floor decoration. There was a famous ceiling at Theobalds which contained the signs of the Zodiac. At night the stars proper to each sign appeared and looked down upon the room. Whether an astrologer was kept to interpret these glittering signs as an entertainment for guests I cannot say, but in the daytime the stars evidently disappeared for we are told by Rathgeb that "the sun traversed the heavens".[6] So even the planetarium is not original to our own time. It wasn't original to the Elizabethan era either. There was a famous prototype in Antioch in the fourth century A.D.*

The output of plaster-work (a great deal of this was English) must have been prodigious—though again time has consumed much of it. Yet Diana, her attendants and dogs still hunt stags, elephants and lions in a forest of trees in the magnificent plaster frieze of the High Great Chamber of Hardwick. And various rather clumsy-looking people "ride the Skimmington" in a plaster panel at Montacute House.

* Ammianus Marcellinus mentions a building in Antioch, closed by the Emperor Constantius II and reopened by Julian the Apostate. It was known variously as the House of the Moon, the Chamber of Perseus or the Planetarium. It had been used for divination purposes and under Julian housed the School of Astrologers.

Of Furniture and Furnishings

Less fantastic ceilings were embossed and pendative—the Elizabethans had taken to Italian stucco-work with the same enthusiasm they brought to strap-work. But the brilliant colours typical of the age were those of the Americas rather than of Europe.

Shakespeare who wrote for the people of his own age, and who was always wise enough to write what was wanted, lets Gremio in *The Taming of the Shrew* describe the desired interior of the time when he catalogues his possessions in suing for Bianca's hand. Gremio's house was in Padua, but from the description it might have been any rich house in England

> ". . . my house within the city
> Is richly furnished with plate and gold;
> Basins and ewers to lave her dainty hands;
> My hangings all of Tyrian tapestry;
> In ivory coffers I have stuffed my crowns;
> In Cypress chests my arras counterpoints,
> Costly apparel, tents and canopies,
> Fine linen, Turkey cushions boss'd with pearls,
> Valance of Venice gold in needlework,
> Pewter and brass and all things that belong
> To house or housekeeping . . ."

G

CHAPTER FOUR

Of Silver and Curious Ornaments

THE "golden" age of Elizabeth was also an age of silver which, in the sixteenth century suddenly poured into Europe from the New World. At least, the silver was destined for Europe but often large quantities of it got side-tracked and ended up in England, along with cochineal, spices, gold, church plate, hides, and pearls. One of the chief side-trackers was "El cosario Ingles, Francisco Draques" as the Spanish called him—better known at home as Admiral, Sir Francis Drake circumnavigator of the globe.

Thomas Cavendish, the third person to girdle the world, did even better—though he shot his bolt in a single adventure. Nevertheless, Cavendish "brought home the richest prize that ever was brought at one time to England".[1] Part of the booty consisted of treasure taken from the Galleon *Great Ste. Anne* which, among others, he captured off the southernmost tip of California. Cavendish, as theatrical as the times in which he lived, put on a tremendous show for his countrymen on his return. It caused the wildest excitement in London when his ship *The Desire*, sailed up the Thames and it was seen that "all his mariners and sailors were clothed in silk, his sails were of damask, and his topmasts, cloth-of-gold".[2] Thus, part of the "tribute" of Peru exacted by the King of Spain, fetched up in England to the intense pleasure of all those who had helped finance such enterprises and who received an enormous return in proportion to the amount invested.

Of Silver and Curious Ornaments

Goldsmiths, silversmiths and jewellers were no less delighted with the booty. They were kept busy beating ingots of captured gold and silver into plain or elaborate shapes, garnishing them with precious and semi-precious stones, engraving and enamelling them; copying exuberant German designs, altering the old and traditional, creating the new and sometimes preposterous; selling their wares to courtiers as gifts for the Queen, to noblemen, to merchant princes, to newly rich tradesmen and prosperous farmers.

The Rector of Radwinter, who had many correspondents in "sundry places and shires" all over the country, notes the sudden increase in rich furnishings and silver plate with mingled pride and astonishment. In noblemen's houses, he says (and his patron was a nobleman), it had never been rare to see "silver vessels and so much other plate as may furnish sundry cupboards to the sum oftentimes of a thousand or two thousand pounds". But nowadays even knights, gentlemen, merchants and other wealthy citizens could afford "costly cupboards of plate worth five or six hundred or even a thousand pounds". To understand what this represents in today's money, one would have to multiply by at least fifteen.*

As for farmers, even in the Rector's own village there were old men, and they probably weren't particularly old judged by our standards, who had seen how greatly things had changed for them within their own lifetime. Why, in a good and frugal farmer's house when they were lads there had never been more than four pieces of pewter—and one of them a salt. Now, many farmers were doing so well that they too "garnished their cupboards with plate".

All over the land trenchers of silver and pewter rapidly

---

* To arrive at the equivalent in terms of the pound sterling today is not easy. It has been variously estimated that one should multiply by a figure of from 15 to 30. A. L. Rowse gives the latter figure, while the American historian Denis Meadows gives 15. The discrepancy can be accounted for by the fact that prices rose by 100 per cent between 1545 and 1645.

displaced the thick pieces of bread or wooden trenchers formerly used, although these must still have been common in cottages. The Ancaster accounts show that in the early '60's a dozen new silver-plate trenchers cost £26 (6s. 8d. was contributed towards the repair of St. Paul's steeple demolished by lightning and fire in 1560). In smart new houses the old leather-jug or blackjack was relegated to the kitchen and silver or pewter jugs took its place. Silver spoons, formerly owned only by the few, now became the property of many, and together with Cornish-mined tin spoons ousted those made of wood or horn. The design changed as well. The bowl became fig-shaped, the stem broader and flatter than in earlier times and ended in a knop or finial. Knop designs became much more varied. The plain seal, pricked with a monogram or date; nimbus headed apostles; the "lyon sejant guardant"; the woodwose, a wild man with a club ("wood" is Old English for wild or lunatic); the "maden head", an often quite unrecognizable representation of the Virgin—all these became increasingly popular. But spoons, though becoming more common, were still so highly valued that they were kept in specially made leather-cases. They were a recognized gift at christenings (hence the phrase to be born with a silver spoon in one's mouth) and they were also handed down. Among the things willed to her son, Edward, by "that lofty lady, relect of the Great Duke of Somerset"[3] were a gold spoon and three or four other spoons, "gilt antick fashion". She also left him a basin and ewer of silver gilt, a pair of silver-gilt pots, two flagons and two silver-gilt bowls with covers.

Forks were not known in England until near the end of the reign when this refinement was brought back by travellers who had visited Italy. The Countess of Lincoln once presented the Queen with a fork, knife, and spoon of crystal ornamented with gold and set with "sparks of garnets" but that wasn't until 1581. Seven years later, the Countess of Warwick gave Elizabeth a similar gift—a fork accompanied only by a spoon. Both were of gold but the spoon had a coral handle while the fork, with less coral, was ornamented with two rubies and two pearls.*

Knives with pointed or wedge-shaped ends and hafts of agate or red and yellow amber, though rarely of silver, were now common. Men no longer cut their meat with the dagger which hung from their waists, and the old custom which required guests to bring their own knives to a feast died out.

During what must have been an excessively tedious masque given in honour of the Queen's visit to Norwich, classical gods and goddesses stepped forward, recited bad verse of interminable

length, and presented gifts which indicated the nature of the giver. Venus, of course, presented a white dove which, when loosed, went straight to the Queen and sat on a table beside her "as quietly as if it had been tied". But Mars, as befitting a war lord, presented a fine pair of knives engraved and inscribed with the following stupefying doggerel:

> To meet your foe and help your friend
> These knives were made unto that end.
> Both blunt and sharp you shall us find
> As pleaseth best your princely mind.

* Thomas Coryat is reputed to have introduced forks into England during the reign of James I. This is probably untrue. Forks were certainly known but only to the "great" prior to the latter half of the sixteenth century. Yet it is on record that Eleanor of Castille, first wife of Edward I, had among her own plate a crystal-handled fork and a pair of knives in silver sheaths.

The Elizabethans at Home

The Earl of Leicester had a splendid knife case—a St. George on horseback slaying the dragon. It was carved in wood, painted and gilded, and must have been of considerable size since the case which held the knives was in the horse's tail while in the breast of the writhing dragon there was another case for oyster knives. But at the new, bulbous legged side-boards, carvers cut beef, sliced mutton, unlatched curlew, thighed woodcock, chined salmon, tranched sturgeon, unlaced coney or tamed crab before offering it round in silver or pewter plates or plate-trenchers which grew deeper as time went on.

Silver or gold goblets, the lid often used as a tasting-cup, now supplanted leather or pewter in great homes, the cup-cover lavishly decorated with floral scroll work, the handle "S" shaped and the thumb-piece ornamented. There were also fantastic cups shaped like birds, animals or figures. Some were fitted with a clockwork mechanism which propelled them along the table. Such cups were probably imported from Germany, a country noted even then for the perfection of clockwork mechanism.

A cup and cover was the quite usual gift made to the Queen by the mayor and aldermen of any of the cities or towns which she visited on a Royal Progress (with a gift of greatly appreciated money tucked inside). There were other cups, too, made of alabaster or quartz. These were often elaborately shaped and decorated. Elizabeth had a crystal cup shaped like a slipper—a curiously Victorian touch, this—with a white-enamelled falcon on top. She also had a cup of gold fretted with pearls which had been given her on her christening by the Duke of Norfolk. And when Henry Frederick, first son of James VI of Scotland (and later I of England) was christened the Queen's gift was "a fair cupboard of silver, overgilt, cunningly wrought and some cups of massy gold". Other cups of massy gold were presented to the royal infant by various foreign ambassadors—two were so heavy that Sir James Melvil who was present and recorded the event could hardly lift them. This great weight did not remain a handicap for very long. Gold was of more use to King James than cups

Of Silver and Curious Ornaments

were to a princeling, so they were soon broken up and melted down.

More English were silver tankards; cylindrical and tapering down from lip to base like the older horn drinking-vessels. They were often chased and were frequently ornamented with the inevitable strap-work. Tankards of horn were still with us, though they too were now banded with silver at neck, rim and centre. Most tankards were six to seven inches high and held a pint. Near the end of the century they grew taller and thinner in imitation of Danish tankards. They, too, became more fantastic in design and, like cups, were made of other substances. Lady Cobham once gave the Queen an unusual tankard carved in alabaster. It was mounted in gold and silver gilt and the cover was a woman's head. Then there were wine-tasters, used less now for the purpose of discovering poison and more to try the taste of the wine. These were shallow bowls, plain or fluted, with a loop handle and small enough to be carried about in the pocket. There were mazers, flagons, voiding-bowls for the removal of food, while rosewater basins and ewers were held in particular veneration.

Inventories listing the contents of the great houses of the time are full of basins and ewers used always to wash the hands before and after a meal. They are also full of covered bowls of silver, silver gilt and even of crystal. Handsome, debonair Sir John Harington—who was never a very rich man—once presented his tart, if Royal, godmother, with a crystal bowl. The description of it reads rather pathetically "a crystal bowl, not round; without a cover; *slightly* garnished with gold and . . . *broken*".

On the other hand, Sir John had more than a broken bowl to offer the Queen. When royal displeasure, or dunning creditors made him take refuge at his house in the depths of the country, near Bath, he jots in his diary, "I am to send a good store of news from the country for Her Highness's entertainment . . . Her Highness loveth merry tales."

One tale of quite another order had been a bit too merry.

The Elizabethans at Home

Harington, like all Renaissance gentlemen and courtiers, knew several languages and translated—or Englished—foreign works as we would do crossword puzzles. He also rather liked to shock his contemporaries and as they were practically shock-proof, this was quite a feat. Curly-haired Sir John accomplished it thoroughly with his translation of the Giocondo story from Ariosto's *Orlando Furioso* and circulated his translation, in manuscript, at the Court. It is doubtful if Elizabeth was shocked but she was very strict about the conduct, manners and morals of her young ladies-in-waiting, and this particular episode was not at all the sort of thing these girls should read. It did not improve their minds, it merely led to sniggering in corners. She was exceedingly cross with the "saucy poet"* and banished him from Court. She did not send him to the tower, though he feared she would, she sent him home to the country. He was not to return to London, she told him, until he had translated the WHOLE of Ariosto's poem.

But the really great piece of gold, silver, or silver gilt in all families of consequence was the salt or salter. Salt, the most important adjunct to every meal had been for centuries both ceremonial and symbolic, and salt-containers were of almost ritualistic importance. In lesser homes they were plain enough, cylindrical, square or hour-glass in shape, made in pewter or silver, but the great ceremonial salts of the day were magnificent and often fantastic architectural pieces. Some of them seem almost to forecast, in miniature, the excesses of the Albert Memorial. Queen Elizabeth's great salt, now at Windsor Castle is, fortunately, not in this class. It is a beautiful cylinder with a domed top surmounted by an urn upon which a knight in armour stands. The body, ornamented with three medallions in low repoussé work, stands upon feet which are cast in the likeness of a sphinx with forepaws. A later addition was the three dolphins, which now hold the cover above the body of the salt. The salt,

* Elizabeth referred to Harington as "that saucy poet, my godson", and sometimes as "that merry poet".

itself, was held in a shallow dish in the upper part of the body.

Leicester, not to be outdone in magnificence by any save the Queen, had his great salt made of mother-of-pearl and shaped like a ship or Nef. It was "garnished with silver and diverse warlike engines and ornaments; with sixteen pieces of ordinance whereof two (are) on wheels; two anchors in the forepart; and on the stern an image of Dame Fortune standing on a globe with a flag in her hand".[4] Dame Fortune, who sounds rather like an early version of Britannia, might well have been cast in the image  of the Queen since it was to her that perennial favourite, Dudley, owed his vast estates, his riches and his titles.

Another and lesser salt, owned by the Queen, was a globe of gold enamelled green. It was embellished with two naked "personages" enamelled in white and the cover bore a royal lion. Yet another of her salts represented a turkey-cock carved in agate, picked out with gold, and studded with pearls and other stones.

It was in front of the ceremonial salt that grace was said and it is tempting to imagine that this custom accounted for the typically and peculiarly English "steeple salt" original to the period. But the Elizabethans were mad on four-sided steeples as well as on obelisks and put them everywhere from tombs to clock-towers. Ceremonial salts, architectural, bell-shaped, or steeple, were generally three-tiered, and the highest tier with a perforated cover was often a pepper-caster, although separate pepper-casters came in at this period.

Highly spiced foods, which became extremely fashionable at

the time, gave rise to a variety of spice-boxes. Elizabeth had a personal spice-box for table use . . . so did all the great ones. Hers was of silver gilt and the cover was splendidly adorned with amethysts, rubies, garnets and turquoises. Whether the jewels were carefully selected more for their virtue than their value is not easy to say. Amethysts prevented intoxication—and wine was heavily spiced—though Elizabeth was very temperate. The ruby was an antidote to poison, even though every dish set before the Queen was first tasted for poison by a yeoman of the guard. The garnet signified constancy and the turquoise meant prosperity. With spices the price they were one, indeed, had to be very prosperous to afford them in the large quantities needed to gratify the taste of the time. Even as early in the reign as 1560, before inflation really got heavily under way, mace cost 14s. a pound; cloves 11s.; cinnamon 10s. 6d.; and ginger around 3s. 8d. In our money that would be the equivalent of about per pound £14; £11; £10 5s. and £3 13s. 6d. respectively.*

American spices were held to be more pungent than Indian or Malayan spices. Some sixty-five years before Elizabeth came to the throne, Columbus had, himself, brought back to Europe "a new pepper, more fiery than the black peppercorn from beyond the Caucasus".[5] This was, undoubtedly, capsicum from which paprika is made.

Another highly popular ornament, usually in silver or silver gilt, was the Nef or galleon. With all sails set and pennants flying it ornamented the dining-tables in houses prodigy and otherwise. Although none with an Elizabethan hall-mark survive there is evidence that some were made in this country and exported to Spain (the best Nefs came from Nuremburg). Nefs were not new, they had been known for several centuries; but now as a symbol of power (and later as a wine service) they passed from the exclusive province of kings and princes into the hands of merchant adventurers. Made with a scrupulous and exact eye

* See note on p. 103.

for detail, the owner, his family, and immediate entourage moulded in silver could be seen on deck with a navigator at the helm and sailors among the rigging. The Nef, with its movable deck, was placed before the host and often contained in its hull salt-cellars (as Leicester's did), boxes of condiments, knives or spoons and, occasionally, napkins. Very often it was used as a perfuming-pan with a mixture of "forget-me-not, sweet perfumes of rosewater, cloves, mace and vinegar" concealed inside. Indeed, every room of importance in a well-ordered house had its silver or latten (a brass-like metal) perfuming-pan. Perfuming-pans and pomanders were not only the Elizabethan equivalent of chlorophyl—this was merely incidental—the real purpose was to ward off disease.

Pomanders, the Anglicized version of *pomme d'embre*, had been known and used for many years for this purpose but the original pomander—an aromatic orange hollowed-out and filled with spices—was now thought to be too strong, particularly for feminine noses, and was replaced by the silver pomander and the pouncet-box which soon captured the wayward fancy of both men and women. The pomander, a perforated sphere opening horizontally or segmentally like an orange, was about one inch

in diameter usually filigreed, and often enamelled and jewelled. Pomanders were also often made into ornamental necklaces and girdles. Anne, Duchess of Somerset, had a splendid chain of "pomander beads", each bead separated either by á pearl or a true-love's knot of mother-of-pearl and with a little acorn as a pendant. Cheaper pomanders were made in hardwood with silver mountings.

Of Silver and Curious Ornaments

The pouncet-box—shallow, circular, or square, with a domed and perforated lid—could, like the pomander, be carried in the pocket, worn at the waist or round the neck. Staves or wands of office were often crowned with pouncet-boxes or pomanders and were carried not only by court officials to indicate function and status, but by doctors, clergymen and others who were likely to visit disease-ridden areas.

Silver candlesticks and wall sconces replaced brass and iron in rich houses, though the poor still used the open flame lamp and the rush-candles which they had used for centuries, and which they continued to use down to the time of George I.

Old halls and new galleries were also lighted by a corona of wood or iron suspended from the ceiling. Although there are records of silver chandeliers, or "branches" as they were called, none seem to have survived. Henry VIII had a "branch" of silver "parcel gilt" but what it was like we don't know as most of the royal plate was melted down during the Commonwealth. The Queen had one of silver gilt given to her by William Cornwallis; it is described as a "hanging candlestick" so it may or may not have been a "branch".

A State Lottery held in 1567, lists among its prizes a pair of silver candlesticks with solid sockets, short stems with grease-pans, and spreading-bases. Nevertheless, at the beginning of the reign the simple pricket candlestick with a conical spike which would support a candle of any size was most commonly used. This usually had a tripod foot and a turned stem ending in a conical spike or pricket. Between stem and spike a very large, very necessary, but largely ineffective wax-pan was fitted. Later on, came the low-bowl type with shaped base inverted to make the socket and to support a tubular candleholder.

Owing to the difficulty of getting melted wax and sticky wick out of the sockets, this type of candlestick was rarely in silver. Roughly treated by careless servants the soft silver could be so marked and distorted by the cleaning process that the candlestick would be ruined. Socket candlesticks of silver did, however, come in with a rush in the early '70's and this was entirely due to a vast improvement in candles. Candles had always been of two kinds, wax or tallow, wax being much more expensive. But we made very fine wax-candles indeed. They were noted far and wide for their brightness and fragrance. Contrary to popular belief wax-candles were not moulded, they were rolled into shape. A wick of Turkey cotton was laid along a flat slab of wax, the wax was folded over the wick and rolled into candle shape. You could startle and astonish your friends by inserting a thin wire along with the wick, before rolling; letting the wire protrude a good length beyond the wick. You then suspended the candle from a beam by the wire, lit the wick, and the candles floated in air as if by magic. Amazement must have soon been superseded by dismay, as hot wax dropped on hair and clothing.

Tallow-candles dating from the mid-sixteenth century must have been perfectly ghastly. It was all due to our new trade agreement with Russia. From Muscovy we imported quantities of bullock's fat with which to make candles. These unlit gave off an offensive odour and a positively horrifying one when lighted. The revolting smell was due to specks of flesh in the tallow and, worse, the specks made the tallow melt more quickly than the wick could consume it. Hence these candles gutted in streams into wax-pans and overflowed in rivulets on to tables or down walls. The mess was then cleaned up and reconverted into candles once more . . . by dipping. Tallow-candles were much less rigid than wax, and when warm bent alarmingly and dripped in torrents.

Tallow was eventually improved and purified by melting it in copper pans, where it was kept liquid until all the flesh bits floated to the surface. These were skimmed off and fed to the dog. The purified tallow was then mixed with an equal part of sheep's tallow and made into candles which were further improved by a spun or twisted wick. Tallow-candles then gave a brighter light than wax, the smell was reduced, and they were a good deal firmer. Such candles could now be used—even on the table—in socket candlesticks without fear that the candlesticks would end up as the hard core to a mass of congealed fat.

Candles, with their thick wicks curling over until the hot charred end dipped into the melted wax of the gutter, needed constant care and attention and a servant or several servants were employed whose sole duty was to see to the candles. The implements of the service were often of silver or silver gilt. Snuffers— the blades of which when closed looked like a Valentine heart— to cut off the snuff or charred wick were often enamelled, chased or jewelled. In time, the lower blade became flattened and dished to hold the snuff and later on a box was added for this purpose. Coats of arms, scenes from the loves of the gods taken from Homer and Virgil, and a hundred other conceits and fancies embroidered the little box. Gradually, the lower blade of the snuffer was extended into a spike to make the lifting and cutting of the wick easier. Candle shears of iron were also used in farmhouses and were made, as were most clocks of the early period, by the local blacksmith.

These clocks, mural, weight-driven, and with coarse wheelwork, were gradually displaced by the framed clock with a bell and the first really individual type of English chamber clock—the lantern clock—was evolved. This, usually, of iron with doors fitted at each side to hide the works, had a vigorous-striking bell. Early examples often had Gothic features—posts in the form of buttresses—but later the clock changed from iron to brass, and buttresses gave way to classical or pseudo-classical columns.

Still later, more elegant travelling-clocks were introduced from the Continent. These were square or round boxes with the dial on top, and were used as table-clocks too. They quickly became so popular that London makers couldn't meet the demand, and many were imported from France and Germany. Cases were often most exquisitely engraved, or chased and jewelled, for this art was more advanced on the Continent than here but most of the works were made in England. The English, unfortunately, weren't so good on the works either. They persisted in sticking

to the weight-driven clock when continental makers were making
the more complex and finer spring-clock. The more elegant
spring-clocks were made in gold, silver or silver gilt. There was
a fantastic clock at Whitehall Palace, probably imported, decorated with an "Ethiope" riding on a rhinoceros. The potentate was
attended by four slaves who, when the clock struck, all made
obeisance to their master.

Elizabeth owned a number of highly ornate clocks. One was
a golden bear, standing on top of a "tun" of gold embellished with
diamonds and rubies. Within the "tun" the clock was set. This,
notes Lady Howard with an astonishment which suggests a
rarity—not of ornament but of clock—was given to the Queen
by Margaret, Countess of Warwick "clock and all". Another, a
diamond-and-ruby-studded clock set in an apple of gold enamelled
green, was presented to the Queen four years later by Leicester.

In 1572, as a New Year's Day gift he gave her an unusual
present—an armlet of gold set with rubies, diamonds and pendant
pearls and having "in the closing thereof" a clock. This must
have been one of the first wrist-watches, and it was presented in
a splendid gold-embroidered case of purple velvet with a green
velvet lining.*

* By 1600 smallish watches were being made in London. There are
two very fine examples in the Ashmolean Museum, Oxford.

Of Silver and Curious Ornaments

Leicester always gave the Queen novel and exciting New Year's gifts and she, in return, was lavish with this favourite who, it is claimed, was the only man the Queen ever loved. In addition to lands, titles, and monopolies she gave him annually and for years, no less than 100 ounces of plate.

Plate was the usual New Year's gift made by a sovereign to courtiers, but Elizabeth's courtiers vied with each other not only in the costliness of gifts they presented to the Queen but in their curiosity and rarity of workmanship. Such gifts may have been inspired in part by hopes of benefits to come. But they were also expressions of love, loyalty and admiration. For it must be remembered that the Queen was generally adored by great and small. There was no make-believe, no pretence about it. It is an undeniable, historical fact. One which lights and warms the period. Even at this distance in time, one sees and senses still the faint, golden radiance of that adoration.

That the Queen should show preference for those with imagination as well as wealth; that she should approve of adventure and piracy, of trade and commerce, of splendour and magnificence is perhaps one of the chief reasons why the age was both prosperous and creative. Imagination was not considered to be faintly neurotic, nor was enterprise condemned as rather vulgar and American. These long-vanished gifts still glitter in the imagination; still delight and astonish the mind when we read about them in records of the time. Many sound as if they had come straight from Aladdin's cave—fairy-tale gifts, precious, exotic, jewel-studded, strange and fantastic. But, delight and astonishment apart, we can trace through them how a nation was transformed from the nearly bankrupt to the splendidly solvent, how the new gentry became rich, how small merchants became great, how tradesmen and citizens flourished.

In the early years of the reign gifts were mainly of money which Elizabeth needed badly. They were, in a sense, forced gifts as a tariff seems to have been laid down according to the rank of the giver, and even the clergy was not exempt. For

H

example, in 1561, we find that money presents from "Busshops" totalled £339 13s. 4d. in gold. The Archbishop of Canterbury presented his £40 in half-sovereigns in a red silk purse. Other bishops gave £30, £20 or £10 according, one presumes, to the importance of the see. For some reason the Bishops of Norwich and Rochester each gave £13 6s. 8d. In return, all bishops received gifts of plate from the Queen. In this year the Archbishop of Canterbury received one gilt cup with cover weighing forty ounces, "out of her Majesty's store". The Bishop of Norwich got the same, only his weighed but 20 ounces. The Bishop of Rochester did rather better for his £13 6s. 8d. as he received a gilt salt weighing 21¾ ounces. Earls in this year gave rather less than the Archbishop and received in ounces of plate rather more. Lords, barons, viscounts, gentlemen of the bedchamber, every member of the household and their wives, if any, gave and received presents. Lawrence Shref the grocer who gave the Queen a sugar-loaf, a box of ginger, a box of nutmegs, and a pound of "cynamon" was presented with a gilt salt, with cover, weighing seven ounces.*

By 1578, the year in which Leicester presented the golden and green clock apple (suggesting, no doubt, that he played Paris to Elizabeth's Aphrodite), money was still being given but gifts have changed in style, design and quantity. They take the form of jewellery, *objets d'art*, clothing, and ornaments for clothing in the Renaissance style. This continued for years until the end of the reign when, with many of the old favourites gone, gifts of money again became more frequent. When James I succeeded he made no bones about the fact that he infinitely preferred hard cash to any other kind of gift.

In a time so full of excitement, pageants, triumphs, and newly

* In the year of her accession, 1558, Elizabeth ordered payment of £11,000 to be made to Robert Brandon and Affabel Partridge, her chief goldsmiths, for 3,098 ounces of silver plate at 7s. 6d. per ounce. The plate was given away as New Year's gifts—some of it can still be seen in Moscow and Leningrad. But see Gerald Taylor's book *Silver*.

acquired money, personal adornment meant a great deal. Men
no less than women were judged by the richness and novelty of
their dress, the splendour of their jewels. But fashions in dress
changed so rapidly during the reign that many good people were
shocked—including William Harrison.

He objects to the enormity and changeability of fashions.
"Except it were a dog in a doublet", he says scathingly, "you shall
not see any so disguised as are my countrymen in England." He
is appalled by the prevalence of foreign fashions which "cause all
nations to deride us . . . for we do seem to imitate all nations
round about us like the chameleon". A return to good, old-
fashioned, dark and sensible attire was what the little parson
wanted to see. All these new colours such as goose-turd or

popinjay green, Drake's colour, Isabella colour, horseflesh colour, and a prevalence of orange, to say nothing of the fine silks, satins and velvets worn now by even ordinary people, were scandalous! a sign of decadence. . . . Worse, corrupting foreign influences had brought them into good, sturdy England.

Here, he was quite right, if not about the decadence at least about the importation of foreign styles. Although the English hated and despised foreigners they, then as now, adored foreign fashions.* Spanish styles were particularly popular despite the fact that Spain was THE enemy. The Queen, herself, had costumes of various countries and when Sir James Melvil saw her she not only boasted of it but to prove it wore the costume of a different country each day. In the end, when she had run through the whole gamut of fancy dress, she asked which he preferred. He told her "the Italian". At which "she was delighted because she delights to show her golden hair by caul and bonnet as in Italy".

On the subject of women's fashions, Harrison is even more sarcastic than he is about men's dress. He complains that women dress like "light housewives" and he just doesn't know how to describe their doublets. Nevertheless, he does describe them "with pendant codpieces on the breast full of jags and cuts" to say nothing of sleeves in sundry colours. And he adds, in rather more forceful language than we have learned to expect

---

* Harrison is supported here by Emmanuel van Meteren, an Antwerp merchant who lived in England during the whole of the reign. He was a cousin of Ortelius, the geographer, and travelled with him through England and Ireland. He has this to say of the dress of the period: "The English dress in elegant, light and costly garments but they are very inconsistent and desirous of novelties changing their fashions every year, both men and women." Van Meteren was also rather horrified by Englishwomen. He says: "They are well dressed, fond of taking it easy and commonly leave the care of household matters and drudgery to their servants. They sit before their doors, decked out in fine clothes in order to see and to be seen by the passer-by."

from a clergyman, "Their galligascons . . . bear out their bums"
. . . and make their bodies look deformed. "I have met with
some of these trulls in London," he continues, "so disguised that
it hath passed my skill to discover whether they were men or
women" and "women are become men and men transformed
into monsters."

This censure he applies more to the younger women, the
wives of citizens and burgesses, than to those of higher rank.
Visiting foreigners complained that the wives of tradesmen now
dressed so grandly that they could not be distinguished from fine
ladies. These foreigners were witnessing a phenomenon which
they failed to recognize as it was new in the world . . . the rise
of the middle classes. Today, of course, visiting foreigners can
witness the reverse.

Despite all this censure, fashions undoubtedly spread out from
the court and from men and women of rank. Certainly Elizabeth
was anything but simple in her dress on all public occasions.
Privately, we are told, she dressed relatively plainly, yet when

she died her wardrobe consisted of "3,000 gowns and 80 wigs of divers colours".[6] It was a far cry from the almost destitute baby who, after her mother's execution was so neglected by her father that she was without gown, kirtle, petticoats, smocks, sleeves, mufflers, kerchiefs, rails (night-gowns), biggins (night-caps) and handkerchiefs.

Perhaps Elizabeth did inherit her love of finery from Henry VIII whom she adored, but it may also have been her near step-mother, Anne of Cleves, who brought the trait out in her. Anne and Henry had remained on very affectionate terms after the "divorce". She was as a "sister" to him and he, no doubt grateful to be rid of an ugly princess who had not made a fuss about being got rid of, gave her a large annuity. Anne settled down comfortably in England and astonished the court by appearing in a magnificent new dress every day. Elizabeth and her young half-brother Edward, were devoted to Anne who was extremely fond of and very kind to all Henry's children. At Mary's Coronation Elizabeth sat next to gorgeously dressed Anne in the Coronation procession in a chariot drawn by six horses. If it be true that the young ape and emulate those whom they love and admire, it may be that Elizabeth, to a certain extent, was expressing love and admiration for Henry and Anne of Cleves by the splendour of her dress.

Added to a passion for finery, was her superb ability to gauge what people liked to see in a sovereign—particularly a semi-divine one. So on all public appearances, and they were numerous, she dressed the part of a Queen. She loaded herself with jewels, she wore magnificent clothes studded with gold, silver, pearls, rubies and semi-precious stones. She even wore high-soled shoes in public to make her appear taller. Even the old Greek gods were not above increasing their stature when they appeared to mortals and wished to look even more majestic and, therefore, more "condescending" than usual.

No woman at court dared outrival the Queen in dress though she may have tried to at home. Court ladies might emulate her

Of Silver and Curious Ornaments

on a less splendid scale, but woe betide them if they tried to outshine or surpass her by any new quirk of fashion. A box on the ears, a sleeve torn by the royal—and most beautiful—hands, a scathing comment, a sarcastic take-off would be the result.

So we find that New Year's gifts to the Queen, as time went on and she indulged her taste for finery, often took the form of clothes, ornaments, jewellery, or jewels for clothing. The link between jewellery and dress had become enormously strong during the Renaissance and on ceremonial occasions the great and near great, male and female, wore costumes sewn with jewels. Thus, a whole new class of artificers in metal came into being whose sole concern was with such small objects as jewels for personal adornment. Skill in the cutting and display of gems reached a hitherto unseen peak of proficiency while jewellery, as jewellery, showed no lack of robust individuality in design. In fact, design of a particular piece was often suggested by the shape of a curiously formed gem. Great, irregular baroque pearls would often end up as the body of a dragon with enamelled and jewelled wings, or as the hull of a microscopic galleon with gold rigging and sails beautifully gemmed. The engraving of gems also improved vastly at this time. A new type, the "portrait jewel", was evolved and became extremely fashionable. The Phoenix jewel in the British Museum is an exquisite example of this. It is a bust of Elizabeth cut in 1574 and surrounded by a wreath of red and white roses enamelled on gold.

Even buttons were minor works of art and so popular that the Queen received them as gifts on many occasions. Five dozen gold buttons shaped like crowns with a flower on top, each set with a pearl and eighteen pairs of gold clasps every pair enamelled and set with five diamonds and six rubies are among those mentioned. She also had innumerable sets of "aglets"—loops or eyelets which could be transferred from gown to gown. These were in gold, silver, or variously enamelled, and some were set with pearls.

But the Queen often lost things. On May 14th 1579, at Westminster, there was "lost from Her Majesty's back . . . one small acorn and one oaken leaf of gold". On another occasion she lost two of her gold buttons which were shaped like a tortoise and set with pearls. She also lost a pearl from another tortoise. And at Richmond, in 1583, when she was wearing a gown of purple cloth-of-silver, she lost a great diamond out of a clasp. She also lost a fish of gold out of her hat, and by mischance, dropped a silver fan into the moat of Hawstead Hall, while on a visit there.

These last two were undoubtedly genuine losses, but the loss of buttons, aglets, jewels from her gowns—and these were lost in quantity—was probably due to the intense desire people felt to possess something which belonged to the Queen. Something which had actually touched her magic person . . . and which therefore was a talisman, a lucky charm, or an amulet—perhaps against the king's evil. Something to venerate and to be handed down in the family. It is very probable that such things were snipped from her gowns by those who sat next to her at banquets, triumphs and pageants which were given wherever she went.

Such losses were as carefully recorded as the gifts in the household books—although there can have been small hope of recovery. But now the recorder used a silver "standish" for this exacting and detailed job, for these were rapidly replacing the old brass or pewter ones.

Among the rich, a standish was provided for the scrivener—it was not considered in the least dignified for a great man to write his own letters. The standish contained compartments for pens, ink horns and for powdered gum sandrac—or sand. Paper was used but parchment was necessary for official and family documents and its oily surface was prepared by rubbing in gum sandrac. Errors were erased with a penknife, the rough places sprinkled with pounce (probably pumice) and smoothed down with a dog's tooth or an agate. And, in passing, it is interesting to note that blotting-paper was known and had been known for years. Horman, writing in 1519 says "Blottyng paper serveth to drye wette wrytynge lest there be made blottis or blurris".

The Queen—not too grand to write her own personal letters—kept her writing-paper in two little silver cabinets of exquisite workmanship. She also had a number of writing tablets, among them a pair of gold ones ornamented with a grasshopper. It is said that she could write one letter, dictate another, listen to a tale and make suitable replies to it—all at the same time. "Boy Jack", she writes to Harington in a note accompanying a copy of a speech she made to Parliament in 1576 explaining as she continually did why she refused to marry, "I have made a Clerk write fair my poor words for thine use as it cannot be such striplings have entrance into Parliament Assemblies as yet. Ponder them in thine hours of leisure and play with them until they enter thine understanding; so shalt thou hereafter, perchance, find some good fruits thereof when thy god-mother is out of remembrance; and I do this because thy father was ready to serve and love us in trouble and thrall. . . ."

"Boy Jack" may have pondered but he certainly received no preferment through his godmother although he tried hard enough. It may be she considered him too much of a lightweight (which he was) to be a minister or member of the household, and too nearly "nephew" to be a favourite. Certainly she behaved to him, at times, as a loving but very fierce aunt; and he stood in such awe of her, he confesses, that once, after Essex's ill-fated Irish venture when she was extremely angry and bade him leave court, he did not wait to be bidden a second time but, as he says, "if all the Irish rebels had been at my heels I should not have made better speed for I did now flee from one whom I both loved and feared". As a symbol of his love (and his hope of advancement) he once gave her a heart of gold garnished with sparks of rubies and three small pearls. Out of the heart grew a tiny branch of red and white roses made of small diamonds and rubies. He hid his gift behind her cushion. Perhaps he felt it was not grand enough to compete with the usual run of splendid gifts. In return she gave him forty ounces of plate but nothing else. No other favour was shown him except, perhaps, a smile and a pretty compliment upon his new doublet.*

Jewels and bijouterie apart, the number of *objets d'art* which now ornamented the brand new Prodigy Houses and mansions of the great must have been colossal. Lily pots of gold set with semi-precious stones. Comfit boxes of silver, gold, and alabaster—plain or jewel-studded—shaped like scallop shells and giant walnuts. Golden flowers where a carved agate fly was enmeshed in a spider's web of silver filaments sparkling with diamond dewdrops; or where butterflies with jewelled wings outspread rested on curved petal or veined leaf. Golden cats played with gold, silver and agate mice. Frogs, whose warty greenness was made by closely set emeralds, stared with protuberant ruby eyes at nightingales studded with pearls, diamonds and rubies—or watched

* Harington writes: "The queen loveth to see me in my new frieze jerkin; and saith 'tis well enough cut'. I will have another made liken it: I do remember she spit on Sir Matthew's [Arundel] fringed cloth; and said the fool's wit was gone to rags. Heaven spare me from such jibing."

Of Silver and Curious Ornaments

enamelled salamanders glow within a ring of candle fire. All sorts of birds and beasts—real, imagined, mythological—were high in favour as ornaments. So were human figures. The Queen had a woman of gold with a ruby "set in her belly".

No less precious were miniatures—"likenesses in little"—and miniature painting of the period has the most wonderful jewel-like quality. These were set in jewelled frames and kept in cases fretted with jewels. When Sir James Melvil visited Elizabeth in 1564 as a special envoy from Mary Stuart, he was taken by her into her bedchamber and while he held the candle she opened a little cabinet "wherein" he says "were diverse little pictures wrapped in paper and their names written with her own hand upon the papers. Upon the first which she took up was written 'My Lord's Picture'". On being pressed for a sight of it, the Queen unwrapped the miniature and disclosed 'My Lord' to be, Robert Dudley, the newly created Earl of Leicester. This must have seemed a trifle odd to Melvil as Elizabeth had just suggested to him—quite seriously, according to Sir James Neale*—that Leicester would make a suitable husband for Mary. Possibly she was just getting her own back on the Queen of Scots who had cattily remarked that she'd heard Elizabeth was about to marry her horse-master. The Queen also showed Melvil a miniature of Mary, which she kissed, and "a fair ruby as great as a tennis ball". Melvil then, rather mischievously, asked the Queen to send Mary either Leicester's picture or the ruby but Elizabeth promptly told him that if Mary would follow her counsel, "she would in process of time get all that she (Elizabeth) had", and fobbed Melvil off with a diamond.

Who the other "likenesses in little" were, which she kept so carefully paper-wrapped, we don't know. Probably some were of various suitors for her hand. Others, no doubt, were miniatures which had belonged to her father, to her half-brother and her half-sister. Few, at that time, could have been of favourites

* See J. E. Neale, *Elizabeth and Her Parliaments*.

for she had been Queen for only six years and "My Lord" was sole favourite. It wasn't, however, until later on that miniatures proliferated, due as much perhaps to the great increase of ivory as to the increase in wealth.

Rich merchants and other citizens of sufficient means, who may have measured art by the size of the painting rather than by its quality, did not go in for miniatures but they delighted in having their portraits painted although this, too, was rather expensive. Even the less wealthy began to be interested in pictures as decoration and so a lively trade in cheap pictures, imported from the Netherlands, grew up (English painters had barely got their hand in). These were sold in London shops, located mainly between Charing Cross and the Temple, and also at fairs all over the country.

Trinkets, too, were sold at fairs, and farmers who were well enough off to "garnish their cupboards with plate"[7] could hardly object—though doubtless they did—to their wives and daughters garnishing their persons with strings of beads and bracelets of bugles, or their houses with the latest novelties from London— including an outlandish painting on wood or a painted text to hang on the wall. Even though many books and pamphlets of the time always warned that, in a wife, extravagance if not a deadly sin certainly led to one, such warnings were, undoubtedly, largely ignored. In vain might William Vaughan write of a wife, "she must not be too sumptuous and surpfluous in her attire, as, decked with frizzled hair, embroidery, precious stones, gaudy raiment and gold put about her, for they are the forerunners of adultery".[8] Women had heard that sort of thing too often before and were to hear it again. But if a woman couldn't over-orna-ment her person, due to the lately introduced sumptuary laws, she could at least ornament her house with the Elizabethan equivalent of Victorian knick-knacks. And if the children of the rich had silver toys to play with, then the children of the less rich could have carved wooden ones made gay with paint or vegetable dyes even if the colour did come off on baby's face as she sucked the toy brought for her at the Goose Fair, or supped milk from a holly-wood cup to keep off witches and the whooping-cough.

Curiously enough, coconut cups, known since medieval times, were all the rage, particularly engraved ones mounted in silver. One of these which possibly belonged to the Queen, was on exhibition at the Antique Dealers Fair in 1952. It is silver-mounted and on one of its panels is engraved the crown and the

royal cipher "E.R.", below which is a Tudor rose. On another panel is a porcupine. The porcupine was the crest of Leicester; it was also borne by his nephew, Sir Philip Sidney and so we do not know if it was a gift to, or from, the Queen. There were ostrich-egg cups too—that is cups made of an ostrich egg and not cups from which such eggs were eaten. What possible use these can have been as ornaments it is difficult to say, but they no doubt provided a touch of the fantastical which is one of the more endearing characteristics of the age.

To this realm of fantasy at Windsor Castle belongs a stuffed bird of Paradise some twenty-seven inches long. The description of it reads like no bird known this side of Hell or of Paradise . . . blue bill, top of head yellow; back of head "prismatic colours";

a red feathered back; yellow wings about four feet long while from its back, two big-ended fibres, or "nerves", grew out "with which, as it has no feet, it is said to fasten itself to trees when it wants to rest".[9] The bird was obviously a mock-up made by the Chinese for the big-eyed Western trade. There was also at Windsor, a twelve and a half foot long unicorn's horn valued at £100,000. Even though the unicorn's horn was believed to be an absolute antidote to all poisons, I feel one must treat this valuation with some reserve. The whole booty taken by Drake in one of his better piratical raids on a Portuguese ship was worth about £114,000, which was considered a fabulous prize. Now, as the Queen was always pressed for money, surely she would have sold this horn or a part of it, particularly as she had another one at Windsor—or so the rhyming Prince of Anhalt, who visited England in 1598 tells us. He distinctly remembers seeing *two*, "one quite smooth, the other of spiral shape nearly four ells long".[10] Perhaps the Queen did sell one, or she may have broken it up and given it away. Certainly the redoubtable Duchess of Somerset left among her gold-stuffed coffers two pieces of a unicorn's horn in a red taffeta purse.

There must have been numberless other treasures of which we know nothing. Some beautiful, some strange. At one royal palace there was a small room called Paradise where the eye was dazzled by the glitter of gold, silver and jewels. There was also a musical instrument made all of glass except for the strings. The Queen also had a draughts board—a gift from Christian I, Elector of Saxony—made of precious stones which included thirty-two emeralds.

She played chess, draughts, tables, and primero and, like her father, was very musical. Jacob Rathgeb tells us that at Hampton Court he saw, in addition to masterly paintings and writing-tables inlaid with mother-of-pearl, "organs and musical instruments which Her Majesty is particularly fond of". There is a fine pair of virginals with Elizabeth's cypher—rather badly displayed—at the Victoria and Albert Museum. She also played

Of Silver and Curious Ornaments

the lute, and once left her jewel-studded, ebony lute behind as a
present for the infant son of Sir Lionel Tollemache when she
visited him at Helmington Hall and stood godmother to the baby.
She was fond of children, singing-birds, apes, and little dogs.

And, like the second Elizabeth, she was also fond of earrings.
She kept them along with other small pieces of jewellery in a
small chest ornamented with pearls, or so Paul Hentzner says.
When he saw the Queen she was superbly dressed in a white satin
gown bordered with pearls "the size of beans"; her mantle was
of black silk shot with silver thread. Instead of a chain she wore
an oblong collar of gold and jewels, and her still beautiful hands
sparkled with rings. On her head was a red wig and on top of
this she wore a small crown, said to have been made of gold from
the Lüneberg table. In her ears she wore two pearls with rich
drops.

As there was a cult of the sovereign, we may be sure that
everyone who could imitated the Queen. She set the fashion, the
court followed and from there the fashion spread in ever-widen-
ing circles throughout the country. This was then, as now, good
for trade. Jewellers, goldsmiths and silversmiths, pewter workers,
clockmakers, weavers, dyers, lace-makers, tinkers, tailors and
candlestick-makers prospered with every new whim of fashion.
A certain Leonard Smith, a tailor in London (and tailors waxed
rich), had among other curios in his house the "hippocamp or
eagle stone—most curious and rare" and also a looking-glass
ornamented all over with pearls, gold, silver and velvet. Elizabeth, too, had many looking-glasses about her. One very clear
"ornamented with columns and little images of alabaster" in
which she at first must have watched herself age—and hated it.
We catch the reflection from the French Ambassador, de Maisse.
The Queen had been suffering from a raging toothache and
received the Ambassador in her night-gown—a costume for which
she apologized.

"She was", he tells us, "strangely attired in a dress of silver
cloth—or gauze—the collar was very high and the lining of the

131

inner part all adorned with little pendants of rubies and pearls. On her head she wore a garland of the same material and beneath it a great, reddish-coloured wig with a great number of spangles of gold and silver and hanging down on her forehead some pearls." Then, he says, "as to her face, it is and appears to be very aged. It is long and thin and her teeth are very yellow and unequal . . . and on the left side less than on the right. Many of them are missing so that one cannot understand her easily when she speaks quickly. Her figure is fair and tall and graceful in whatever she does; so far as may be she keeps her dignity, yet humbly and graciously withal."

This is how he first saw her. Later, when she knew him better and they were closely discussing his mission, she turned suddenly and said, "Master Ambassador . . . see what it is to have to do with old women such as I am."

She said it, as she did on many occasions to de Maisse and others, wanting desperately to hear the truth denied. De Maisse denied it. But the pitiless, very clear looking-glass ornamented with columns and little images would not have done so. And for that reason Elizabeth, during the last twenty years of her life, never looked in a mirror. The true image of herself could not be seen in any looking-glass, plain or ornamented. Goddesses could not age and lose their teeth. How old was Diana when she loved the boy Endymion? How old was Venus when the bright blood of Adonis jewelled the dark forest with anemones? Age-less . . . ageless . . . as she was. Even if Robert Dudley had died in Armada year—unromantically, of fever at Cornbury Park in Oxfordshire—there were still Adonises and Endymions about to prove it. There was beautiful Essex, and handsome young Charles Blount—to whom she had given a golden chess-queen as a mark of favour when he did so well in a tilt. Charles had worn the golden queen on his sleeve which had so offended Essex that the two had come to swords.

There was no need to look in a lying glass. The image of Gloriana, Belphoebe, Cynthia, peerless Oriana, Mercilla, the

Of Silver and Curious Ornaments

Lady of the Sea, the Phoenix of the World lay, imperishable and uncorrupted by Time, in the words of her poets; in the looks of her courtiers; in the devotion and jealousy of her favourites— in the bright blood of young Essex wounded, like Adonis, in the thigh by the cup-hilted rapier of the boy, Charles Blount.

I

CHAPTER FIVE

Of Food and Drink

THE streets of Sandwich were freshly garlanded overhead, and newly gravelled underfoot. At the gate of the town a great English lion and a great Tudor dragon "all gilt and set upon eleven posts"[1] stood guard. It was August 31st 1573, and Elizabeth was coming to stay for four days. She duly arrived, *en suite*, and was met by town officials including the minister of St. Clement's parish, and the schoolmaster who made an oration which the Queen, tactfully, liked so well that she gave it "singular commendation". She said it was "both very well handled and very elloquent". Then she was given a cup of gold and a New Testament in Greek (it was a source of pride to her subjects that the Queen read Greek easily). But probably the highlight of the four days' festivities—and certainly the function which affected the ladies of Sandwich the most—was the banquet given to the Queen in the school-house.

The Queen who was staying with Mr. and Mrs. Manwood, had to pass through their garden to reach the school where, before she entered, Mr. Isebrand made a speech and presented her with a silver gilt cup, "nere a cubit highe". When she was finally allowed in, the school had been transformed into a bower and there stood a table twenty-eight feet long with no less than one hundred and sixty dishes provided to tempt the appetite.

Elizabeth enjoyed this banquet so much that she had certain dishes "reserved and carried round to her own lodging". This signal mark of honour was greeted with the greatest satisfaction and delight by everyone.

Of Food and Drink

Here, Elizabeth must be given full marks for tact, graciousness, sympathy and understanding. At home she was moderate in her diet, but abroad she was accustomed to banquets of such involved magnificence and pageantry that a mere one hundred and sixty dishes might have seemed a poor effort. It would certainly have seemed so had she been a snob, or had any rich courtier fobbed her off with it. But the good people of Sandwich were not rich courtiers, they were her loving subjects and she gave them love for love. By reserving dishes especially to be sent round to Mr. and Mrs. Manwood's she told them more plainly than any words how much she appreciated their banquet.

Two years later, Leicester entertained the Queen at Kenilworth for eighteen days. It was a very different entertainment from that provided at Sandwich and cost Leicester around £1000 per day. Elizabeth was greeted by a pageant of welcome displayed on a temporary bridge, built over the base court to the main building. On the bridge were seven pillars where mythological deities offered symbolic gifts as she passed. Sylvanus presented cages of live birds; bitterns, curlews, hernshaws and godwits. Pomona's pillar held great silver bowls piled with apples, pears, cherries, walnuts and filberts. Other pillars held ears of wheat, oats, and barley; gigantic bunches of red and white grapes; great livery pots of claret and white wine, while on the pillar belonging to the sea-god, sea-fish in quantity lay upon fresh grass. As it was the hottest July in living memory this must have been an offence to the nostrils. The last pillar was devoted to the arts, and the arts were defined as arms, music and physic! All was explained at great length, by a blue-clad poet.

The whole of the visit was marked by one splendid entertainment after another. On one evening a water pageant was held. The Lady of the Lake sat on an island attended by a swimming mermaid twenty-four feet long, while Arion rode in on a huge dolphin to make the usual oration to the Queen. But Arion had drunk too freely, forgot his part, pulled off his mask and cried, "I am none of Arion, not I, but honest Harry Goldingham." The

Queen, we are told, was more delighted and amused by this than by anything else, though doubtless honest Harry got it in the neck from the pageant-master afterwards.

It was during this visit that Leicester provided the greatest banquet of the reign. Food came in in a thousand dishes of crystal and of silver and was served by two hundred gentlemen. All this is difficult to reconcile with Harrison's belief that the English were now less greedy than formerly.

"Heretofore", he says, "there hath been much more time spent in eating and drinking than commonly is in these days, whereas of old we had breakfast in the forenoon, beverages or nuncheons after dinner and thereto rear suppers when it was time to go to rest . . . now these odd repasts, thanks be to God, are very well left and each one in manner (except here and there some young and hungry stomach that cannot fast till dinner-time) contenteth himself with dinner and supper only."

Here Harrison, perhaps influenced by the thought that gluttony is one of the Seven Deadly Sins, offers up pious thanks for the new Elizabethan fashion of two meals a day. What he seems to forget is that gluttony is not necessarily measured by number of meals but by the quantity of food eaten at each meal. And the quantity eaten by the Elizabethans was prodigious. But Harrison spoke, in this case, for the upper classes only. Farmers and the members of their household ate three meals a day and began by break-fasting just after dawn. Thomas Tusser is quite clear on this point. In his poem "The Good Housewives Day" he says,

> Call Servants to breakfast, by day star appear,
> a snatch to wake fellows, but tarry not here.
> Let Huswife be carver, let pottage be eat,
> a dishful each one with a morsel of meat.

Nevertheless, the nobility and gentry did not break fast until they dined at eleven or twelve (an hour later than in Henry's time) and they supped at five, or between five and six. Merchants dined at twelve and supped at six. As for the poorer people "they dine and sup when they may, so to talk of the order of their repast it were a needless matter".[2]

Rich Elizabethans were prodigal of hospitality and many, gathering about them what seems to us constant if not chronic guests, still dined in the Great Hall after the old custom. Here, the host sat at the head table sometimes on a raised dais while guests, in order of degree, were seated near him. At a lower table less important persons sat. These included members of the household, strangers come on various minor matters, tutors, if any, and upper-servants. In the home of a moderately well-to-do country squire the servants might number as many as forty while in large houses, such as Haddon Hall, there were eighty retainers. On farms, servants and hired hands joined the family at high noon for dinner.

If masters, family and invited guests dined separately in a "dining parlour"—and these were coming in with a rush—the servants continued to eat in the Hall, probably under the eye of a steward. But as the reign proceeded and the Great Hall developed

into an entrance hall it could no longer be used for this purpose. So servants were given a private room elsewhere. This room was, and still is, called the Servants' Hall.

Food was prepared in vast quantities, and what was left over after host and guests had had their fill went to the servants. What was left after this went to the poor who at every meal-time clustered "round the rich man's gates". The poor may or may not have been numerous but it is unlikely—owing to the provisions made for their care (provisions which we now know as rates)— that they were literally starving although there was terrible misery in 1560, 1577, 1587, and 1596 which were years of dearth. Yet England was better fed than the Continent. Even in Mary Tudor's time a visiting Spaniard had recorded: "These English have themselves houses made of sticks and dirt but they fare commonly so well as the king." A remark which led Harrison to the smug and very English comment "coarse fare in rude cabins is better than their own thin diet in princely habitations".

In the many new princely habitations being built in England, kitchens were very carefully designed. A usual plan was a vaulted ceiling with four central arches which held the hearths. There was a brick oven for baking and probably a large working-table in the centre of the room. Kitchen equipment included—besides the usual spits and other implements for roasting and grilling—pots, posnetts, chafing-dishes, graters, mortars and pestles, boilers, knives, cleavers axes, dripping-pans, pot-racks, pot-hooks, gridirons, frying-pans, sieves, kneading-troughs, fire-shovels, barrels, tubs and so on. In addition to the kitchen there was a pantry and a buttery—both had been a necessary part of kitchen planning for centuries—but an innovation was the "pastry" furnished with one or two ovens.

Grander houses had wet and dry larders, spicery, mealhouse, sieving or bolting house and various other separate rooms which had specific purposes in relation to the preparation of food. Coals were kept in the "Squillerie" along with brass pots and pans, pewter vessels, and various kitchen herbs. An odd combination, but it is from Squillerie that we get our word scullery (butler comes from buttery where wine and other provisions were stored). In fact by the end of the century, service quarters were very highly organized and extremely well-planned—an art which was lost during the succeeding centuries to be rediscovered by the Americans.

From these vast kitchen regions, food was brought in covered dishes and placed on court cupboard or on various sideboards. From here it was offered to the diners. By the time it reached the lower table it must have been nearly stone cold. Wine or ale was served in goblets and cups but as gold and silver—to say nothing of pewter—had become so common and were so durable, wealthier people—setting an example of conspicuous waste—imported Venetian glass which was expensive and easily broken. This bit of snobbery was followed in poorer homes by the use of clay pots in various colours and shapes. Pompey in "Measure for Measure" speaks of stewed prunes in a threepenny fruit-dish "not china dishes", he says, "but very good dishes".

But even if the breakability of glass increased its snob value and was a symbol of the "greatness" of the owner, there were still those who hoped to discover the philosophers' stone which was to accomplish—among other miracles—that of making glass malleable!

Whatever the drinking-vessel, gold, silver, pewter, horn, leather, glass or earthenware, it stood on court cupboard or sideboard and from there was filled and handed to the diner. When he had finished drinking it was wiped clean, returned to its place and refilled, as and when required. This, it is claimed, was a custom which made for sobriety—a virtue not commonly associated with this roaring age (foreigners, rather spitefully, said it was due to sheer meanness). But various authorities assure us that drunkenness was not common and was even frowned upon! Salt meats—though this is difficult to believe—were not favoured because they gave a man too great a thirst and "they take it generally as no small disgrace if they happen to be cupshotten, so that it is a grief unto them".[3] Always excepting noblemen and aristocrats who did not wholly follow this practice and who, presumably with a wine cup beside them at table, drank throughout a meal as we do.

It appears from contemporary accounts, that these vigorous, vital and often vulgar ancestors of ours ate extremely well. Indeed, on the Continent England was regarded, among other unpleasant things, as being a nation of gross eaters. "Very sumptuous and love good fare" is the comment of the Dutch physician, Levinus Lemnius, who visited us in 1560. But earlier on we shocked the Frenchman, Etienne Perlin, by our table manners. No doubt he was a foppish and affected fellow, as he disapproved of everything English, but he was certainly horrified by the old English custom of belching roundly at meals "even in the presence of the greatest lords", he says, as if this added a sort of lèse-majesté to the belch.

But no one in England, even then, cared a hang what such niminy piminy foreigners thought and, as Harrison explains perhaps just a trifle apologetically, "The situation of our region being near unto the north doth cause the heats of our stomachs to be of somewhat greater force, therefore our bodies do crave a little more ample nourishment than the inhabitants of the hotter regions." Whatever the meaning of "stomach heat" it is certain that the nobility and rich merchants—and there were many of these—excelled in the number and changes of meat provided for themselves and their frequent visitors. Beef, mutton, lamb, veal, kid, pork, coney, capon, pig, venison, fish, domestic and wild fowls were plentiful and, on great occasions, all were offered together "so that every man might feed on what he likes best". They were great meat-eaters, unlike the Italians who ate much more bread, salads and "roots of small price". Feasts and even the more ordinary dinners, though varying in the number and splendour of dishes, began or "made entry" (no nonsense about *entrée*, although they were nearer the French in blood than we are) with the more delicate foods and lighter wines, and ended with the grosser foods and heavier wines plus a sweet, fruit and cheese.

How much more sensible and praiseworthy than the rude Scots who we learn, again from Harrison, "Of late years have given themselves unto a very ample and large diet . . . they far exceed us in overmuch and distemperate gormandize and so ingross their bodies that divers of them oft become unapt to any other purpose than to spend their time in large tabling and belly cheer." Harrison who, as far as we know had never travelled farther north than Coventry, unfortunately quite overlooked the fact that Scotland is even farther north than England and therefore the Scots stomach had every excuse for being even hotter and more forceful than the English. But Harrison, being English, was probably just as prejudiced against the foreign Scot as he was against the Italians and those who visited Italy. "What will encompass the ruin of the country", he prophesies with gloomy pleasure, "is the usual sending of noblemen's and mean (medium) gentlemen's sons into Italy, from which they bring home nothing but mean atheism, infidelity, vicious conversation and ambitious and proud behaviour . . . they return far worse than they set out." The moral diet of the Italians was obviously as contemptible as their material diet.

How very different it all was from England! Where even the farmers fed well, and more important, behaved well, particularly at "bridals and purification of women and such odd meetings". Less odd were Plough Monday, Shrove Tuesday, sheep-shearing and Harvest Home, the big country feast-days, when they ate and may even have behaved well too. Each guest brought a dish or two to the feast. The host was called upon to provide only bread, drink, sauce, house-room and a fire.

Otherwise these good people "live frugally as do artificers when not feasting and making merry, without malice and plain, without inward French and Italian craft".[4] Regrettably, it must be reported, this was not always the case. Leaving aside inward French and Italian craftiness, we hear that on rare occasions and among those of the "inferior sort" talk sometimes descended to the scurrilous and ribald. Vicious conversation it was, and among the untravelled too.

This sort of thing, however, caused no surprise to one, Thomas Coryat, who, unlike his contemporary, Harrison, must have approved of travel, for he was himself a great traveller. In fact he died in India after drinking too much sack, a drink to which he was quite unaccustomed. In any event he held an extremely low opinion of stay-at-homes finding them apt to be rude, slothful, rough, outrageous, foolish, barbarous, effeminate, wanton, given to sleep, banqueting, dice, idleness and "the ·enticements of all concupisciencies".*

Nevertheless, despite the rather astonishing claim that this was a sober nation (and drunkenness is not listed even by Coryat among the vices of the stay-at-homes), and despite the English dislike of foreigners, between 20,000 and 30,000 tuns of wine were imported annually. Yet the greatest "brunt of drinking" was born by strong beer and stale ale "of as many sorts and ages as it pleases the brewers to make".[5] Names of drinks are curious, rude and fascinating, huffcap, mad dog, angel's food are the more

---

* Travelling, however, was not easy. There were currency restrictions. Furthermore, those who wished to travel abroad were cross-examined by William Cecil on their knowledge of England. If, in his opinion, it was inadequate the traveller was told to stay at home and learn more about his own country before setting out for foreign parts. This "screening" obviously allowed Cecil to make reasonably sure that the disaffected could not get to Europe to stir up trouble for the Queen and England.

polite ones. There was also "artificial stuff" such as wormwood and hippocras or ypocras. A quick recipe for ypocras consisted of cinnamon, white ginger, cloves, nutmeg, grains of Paradise and pepper steeped for six days in spirits of wine. A few drops of this added to a bowl of wine turned it into ypocras while an excellent "Gossip's Cup" could be made by mixing a half-pint of ypocras with a pottle of ale. Metheglin, a spiced mead, was drunk in Wales, and a kind of inferior mead, or "swish water", was popular in Essex and other places. This was made of honey-combs soaked in water to which pepper and other spices were added . . . it was very efficacious in relieving the cough. Cider and perry were common in Sussex, Kent, Worcestershire, and other counties even though perry was condemned by Camden as "a counterfeit wine both cold and flatulent".

But it was not left to the brewers alone to make beer and probably every household in rural areas made its own, in quantity. Harrison's wife made his, and the little man whose stipend amounted to but forty pounds a year, recorded that he got ten-score gallons for a pound. That included the cost of malt, wood, servants' wages and food, wear and tear on equipment, and it works out at a bit better than a penny a gallon. Good beer was the colour of muscadel or malvesey, ale was "more thick and fulsome". Ale was often flavoured with mace, nutmeg or sage and sometimes a roasted orange stuck with cloves was hung in a vat of ale to give it a spicy flavour. Muscadel and malvesey were favourite wines of the time, so were vernage (an Italian white wine) catepument, raspes (a raspberry wine) romnie, bastard lire (bastard in this instance means sweetened) osy, capri, and clary; the latter a wine mixed with clarified honey, pepper and ginger. White and red claret were imported in quantity as well as thirty different kinds of Spanish, Grecian, and Canarian wines.

In this day and age when a bottle of Jugoslavian "Riesling type" costs eight shillings it is a melancholy thing to see that on Friday September 24th, in the year before Elizabeth came to the throne,

Bess of Hardwick paid 4d. for three pints of wine. In the early 1560's a hogshead of claret cost 50s.; a barrel of small beer 4s. 4d. and a barrel of double beer 7s.[7]

That noble visitor, the Duke of Württemberg, simply could not abide French wines and much preferred English beer. His secretary notes "the wine which comes from France (for there is no wine-growing in England) did not agree with His Highness nor could he bear it; but the beer, which is the colour of an old Alsace wine, was so delicious that he relished it exceedingly".

Spirits, though known as aqua vitae or aqua ardens, do not seem to have been drunk in any quantity—save in Ireland where usquebah was already the national tipple. Their chief use seems to have been medicinal. John Gerard, the great English herbalist, cites many of these uses but he also issues grave warnings on the abuse of aqua vitae. It was "hurtful to all that are of a hot nature and complexion" and most of all to choleric men. It was also "offensive" to the liver and "unprofitable" to the kidneys. Doubtless there were those who didn't mind offending their livers to the point of cirrhosis, or of rendering their kidneys positively bankrupt, but it is extremely unlikely that spirits were drunk in any quantity. Most certainly they were not drunk by the "lower orders" who, unlike their wretched counterparts in the eighteenth and nineteenth centuries, stuck to good, nourishing, English beer. Tea and coffee were still unknown and remained so until well into the seventeenth century.

Although bread was not eaten in the same quantity as in Italy, it was nevertheless one of the three components of the staple

Of Food and Drink

diet of the time. The other two were beef and beer. The "gentility" ate white bread made of wheat flour of which there were several grades. The first quality was made up into a flat, white, round loaf called a "manchet" which weighed eight ounces when it went into the oven and six when it came out. Queen Elizabeth's own manchet was made from wheat grown at Heston in Middlesex as it was held to be "the purest in many shires".[8]

In country districts much rye and barley bread was eaten, and in times of dearth bread was made from horse-corn, peas, beans, oats, tares, lentils and even acorns. A current saying runs, "a famine at hand is first seen in the horse-manger when the poor do fall to horse corn".

Next to bread in importance, came meat. England was noted not only for the quality of her meat but for its cooking. Probably the quality of the meat was excellent when it was fit to eat at all but the number of recipes which give instructions on how to make tainted meats edible leads one to suspect that the first Elizabethan stomach was singularly proof against food-poisoning. Of course, spices helped to overcome, at least in flavour, the minor results of no refrigeration. So did soaking the haunch in vinegar. And Sir Hugh Platt offers a sure cure for "greene venison", that is, venison which had gone beyond the aid of vinegar or spices. First remove the bones, wrap in an old coarse-textured cloth, dig a hole in the earth three foot deep and bury the venison for from twelve to twenty hours according to the degree of greenness. When dug up it will be found to be sweet enough to eat.

Sauces, too, helped overcome the flavour of bad meat and as the Elizabethans were aware of the dangers of the action of vinegar and other acids upon copper, sauces were made in sauce-pans of silver and served in "sawsers"—small shallow rimless dishes of silver, glass or china. Mustard, a favourite condiment, was served in a saucer, it was made either with vinegar or unfermented grape-juice.

However, the English were famous for the way they cooked meat,

145

green or not. Fynes Moryson, a much-travelled gentleman, who wrote about his travels shortly after the death of the Queen states, "English cooks in comparison with other nations are most commended for roasted meat." The indefatigable Harrison gives us a clue as to why this may have been so. He explains that meat was not baked with lard but with sweet beef or mutton suet and basted all over with sweet or salt butter. And here we come across a most curious fact, the poor ate butter as we do; the rich used it principally for cooking! As there was no method of refrigeration and scrupulous cleanliness was unknown, butter became an oily, rancid mess very quickly—particularly in summer— and must have been very like Tibetan ghee. In its rancid state it was often recommended as a laxative. May butter was reputed to have medicinal qualities if exposed to the sun for fourteen days before being taken. It was probably rancid by then, but it also must have absorbed Vitamin D from the sun. It is interesting to note that this "irradiated" butter was recommended as a tonic for aches and pains of the joints brought about by a cold damp winter.*

Milk could not be kept for any length of time, although its value as a food seems to have been known. It, together with

* The information about butter is given more fully in Drummond and Wilbraham's excellent book *The Englishman's Food*. Nevertheless, butter is listed on the daily menus for the Queen's table.

whey and buttermilk, was more of a country than a town food. Cheese, too, was eaten—green cheese and hard cheese. Green cheese meant a soft, new, curdy cheese of the cottage-cheese type. Strangely enough, all dairy products including eggs were known as "white meats".

Of "made up" dishes Platt gives a dire recipe for "Polonian sawsege"* while venison pasty was a dainty found in no other country. George and Meg Page invited Shallow and Slender to dine off hot venison pasty.[9] Brawn, too, was typically English and unknown elsewhere. It was eaten from November to February—due to the shortage of fresh meat—and chiefly as a special Christmas dish. It was made from the forepart of a tame boar a year or two old, fed up for the purpose on oats and peas. It was seethed, soused, had quantities of beer poured over it and was very highly spiced. Just what it tasted like is a little difficult to imagine as the following stories, told with obvious glee by the Protestant parson of Radwinter, illustrate. It appears that an English nobleman sent a great hog's-head of brawn to a Roman Catholic gentleman in France, "who supposing it to be fish reserved it until Lent and ate it most frugally every day". This unfortunate Catholic gentleman liked the brawn so well that he sent to England for more "as fish for next Lent". On this Harrison comments with ill-concealed delight and scepticism, "had he known it was flesh he would not have touched it for a thousand crowns—I dare say—without the Pope's consent". †

* Platt's recipe: "To make a Polonian sawsedge. Take the fillers of a hog; chop them very small with a handful of Red Sage: season it hot with ginger and pepper, and then put it into a great sheep's gut; then let it lie three nights in brine: then boil it and hang it up in a chimney where fire is usually kept; and these sawsedges will last a whole yeere. They are good for sallades or to garnish boiled meats, or to make one rellish a cup of wine."

† Yet at the Coronation Banquet of Katherine of Valois, wife of Henry V, Alderman Fabyan records "their feast was all of fish, for, being February 24th Lent was entered upon and nothing of meat was there

The Elizabethans at Home

Even more deplorable is the story of an Englishman living in Spain who served brawn to some Jewish guests. They, too, under the illusion that it was some uncommon kind of fish, enjoyed the dish heartily. When they had finished, their host—whose high spirits seem to have been matched only by his crass insensitivity—produced the boar's head and, no doubt nearly speechless with laughter, explained that this was the animal from which the strange fish had been made. The wretched Jews stayed not a moment longer. All rushed off to their homes where, stomach pumps not having been invented, they resorted to other violent measures to escape contamination. That brawn should have tasted "as fish" seems all the more remarkable since fish formed a considerable part of the Elizabethan diet. We are told —although this must be taken with reservation—that not even the meanest house in England was without some pond or hole in the ground where fish such as tench, eels, bream, roach, and dace were stored.[10] Sir Hugh Platt whose main interests seem to have been in soil improvement, household hints, and food preservation, recommends wrapping lobsters and crayfish in rags soaked in brine and then burying them in damp sand in "a convenient place". Oysters could be pickled, so he says, and kept for a very long time.

The eating of fish was indeed compulsory. Laws were passed early in the reign which stated that none of the Queen's subjects were allowed to eat meat during Lent or on Fridays. This had nothing to do with religious observances, though conveniently and wisely the church fast days were made use of. The law's expressly stated object was to maintain seafaring and to revive decayed coastal towns. This was essential for the preservation and expansion of the navy.

---

saving brawn with mustard". Brawn may have been a permitted Lenten dish in pre-Reformation England, or a special dispensation may have been granted. Harrison must have been aware of this but he was never averse to getting one back on foreigners and Roman Catholics even if it meant ignoring a fact or two.

Of Food and Drink

Although the fish laws were political rather than religious they also had a secondary object in preventing too great a consumption of beef and mutton during the winter. (Cattle could not be over-wintered successfully save in small numbers during mild winters in the south.) That they were enforced is shown by the fact that in 1563 a London tavern-keeper, a woman, was pilloried for having flesh in her tavern during Lent. The more usual penalty was a fine of three pounds with the alternative of three months in prison. By 1585 the navy must have been considered strong enough or the law too difficult to implement for in this year it was abandoned.

The Queen seems to have observed the laws strictly, herself, as a glance through her household accounts shows. For example, Wednesday, November 22nd 1576, must have been a fast day (it was Old Martinmas Eve) and her dinner consisting of two courses, was entirely of fish. The first course included pike, salmon, haddock, gurnard and tench; the second provided sturgeon, conger-eels, carp, lampreys, chines of salmon and perches. She ate no flesh at supper either. On Friday of the same week either she fasted, was ill, or was off on a visit, for no menu for the Queen's table appears although her servants were certainly fed—but not wholly on fish.

The Ancaster family laid in white herring at 23s. 4d. a barrel and Bess of Hardwick seems to have had a positive passion for shrimps (and how did they get shrimps to Derbyshire for her?), Time and again one comes across the entry in her household accounts "Item, shrimps, 2d." written in her own, bold, legible hand, or in the smaller, more beautiful and much more difficult script of a household official.

Fish was known in great variety and was also salted and sent inland. It was eaten in such quantity that even the Banks of Newfoundland were scoured for fish to supply the demand. In fact if it hadn't been for Europe's need for fish, Canada might not have been discovered until considerably later. We even exported smoked and pressed pilchards from Cornwall to Spain!

K

The Elizabethans at Home

In the matter of fowls, both wild and domestic, the Elizabethans were no less well provided. The crane, the "bitter", the wild and tame swan, the brant, the lark and two kinds of plover—not to mention the quail "who only with man is subject to the falling sickness".[11] Quail were imported live, in quantities, from the Lowlands. Then there were teal, widgeon, mallard, shelldrake and shoveller; the peewit, scamen, knot, olicet, dun bird, partridge and pheasant. It may be that not all of these were commonly eaten—one hopes that the peewit was spared—but Sir Hugh Platt gives a recipe for cooking sparrows and Bess paid 9d. for "a dozen and one sparrows". Larks cost her from 8d. to 10d. a dozen and they, like shrimps, are a recurring item in her accounts. Doves were eaten in quantity, the countryside was alive with dovecotes and pigeon-holes. Pigeons were even then "a hurtful fowl by reason of their multitude".[12] There were also cocks, hens, geese, ducks, "peacocks of the Ind" and turkeys. Cocks, turkeys and peacocks of the Ind were "gelded" and the flavour much improved especially that of the peacock of the Ind.

Harrison, ever willing to praise God with only slightly less enthusiasm than he reserves for England, the English and Englishness, says, "We do not, thanks be to God and the liberty of our princes, dine or sup with a quarter of a hen, or make repast with a cock's comb as they do in some countries; but if occasion serve the whole carcasses of many capons, hens, pigeons and suchlike do oft go to wrack (waste) besides beef, mutton, veal and lamb, all of which at every feast are taken as necessary dishes among the Communality of England." How the engrossed and gormandizing Scot managed to surpass this is not easy to imagine.

On ordinary days when there were no guests, the well-to-do family made do with a piece of beef, a loin of veal, two chickens, oranges and a sauce for dinner, and supped on a shoulder of mutton, two rabbits, pigs' "pettie toes", cold beef and cheese. A diet so rich in animal protein may account for the wonderful vitality and energy of the Elizabethans as it accounts for the vitality and energy of the Americans today.

Of Food and Drink

But food prices started a fairly steep climb during the reign and by 1572 London poulterers by "a combination" had put up their prices "to such distress of the citizens" that the court of the Lord Mayor and Aldermen stepped in and fixed them, as from April 4th, as follows: best swan 6s. 8d.; cygnet 6s.; stork 4s.; pelican 2s.; goose 1s. 2d.; best green geese, until May Day 9d.; best chickens 4d.; larks per dozen 8d.; blackbirds per dozen 1s. (so four and twenty baked in a pie would cost 2s.);

butter per pound until All Hallows 3d.; best eggs until Ash Wednesday four for a penny, or a farthing apiece.

Back in the '60's thirty-five dozen eggs had cost 5s. 10d. The new fixed-price eggs worked out at 8s. 9d. per thirty-five dozen. By the end of the reign they were a penny farthing apiece, or £2 3s. 9d. for thirty-five dozen—nearly eight times as much as at the beginning.

Despite rising prices, artisans, particularly in the towns, lived well. Like farmers they ate three meals a day beginning with breakfast at six or seven o'clock, a meal which consisted of bread, salt herring, cold meat, pottage, cheese and ale. At midday they usually fed at a tavern, or bought food at a cook-shop. London and other centres were full of cook-shops where hot sheep's feet, mackerel, soup, oysters, ribs of beef, and rancid meat pies were provided together with bread, fruit in season, and ale. They supped at home on cold meat, cheese, and wine. Again, the diet was rich in proteins while even the inmates of the House of Correction, at Bury in Suffolk, fared better than we did during the last war. Here, at every dinner and supper on flesh days, these enforced guests received eight ounces of rye bread, one pint of porridge, one quarter of a pound of meat and one pint of beer. On fish days in place of meat they had, at each meal, one or two herring and a third of a pound of cheese. Those who agreed to do extra work got extra rations, those who refused to work at all got only bread and beer.

But the village labourer in the country was probably healthier than the town artisan because he could add to his usual diet of veal, beans, fish, mutton and pickled pork those "white meats" which were scarce in town. He also ate vegetables and herbs, and drank milk, buttermilk and whey in addition to beer.

The Queen, in the matter of meals was all artisan. Not for her the two meals a day affected by fashionable women who rose too late for breakfast. Her Grace's Majesty rose early. So early that when she gave audience to Sir James Melvil, Mary's Ambassador, she bade him arrive at Whitehall at eight A.M. where he found her walking in the garden. By then she had already spent some time at her devotions, attended to various civil affairs and had had breakfast. Her breakfast usually consisted of manchet, ale, beer, wine and a good pottage, like a farmer's, made of mutton or beef with "real bones".

The menu for her dinner on November 17th 1576, although that date marked the eighteenth anniversary of her succession, was not a special one. In fact her menus seem to vary very little over the years. She had, as a first course, a choice of beef, mutton, veal, swan or goose, capon, conies, fruit, custard and fritters with cheat, manchet, ale and wine. The second course provided lamb or kid, herons or pheasant, cocks or godwits, chickens, pigeons, larks, tart, butter and fritters. Supper was also a two-course meal with a first course of boiled mutton, roast mutton, capon, herons, "chicken bake", congers, beer, ale, cheat and manchet. The second course sounds as if it had been made up from what was left over from midday dinner for again lamb or kid appear, cocks or godwits, pigeon and larks, with only partridge and plovers added.

Despite these spreads, we are told by various authorities that the Queen ate very little and rarely drank wine, preferring beer and ale, and these in moderation. Yet there had to be a choice, besides her ladies had to eat, so the palace cooks provided what, to us, seems an enormous number of dishes. The Queen always dined alone or with a few friends but when the day's work was done she often supped with friends and attendants "whom she would cheer up with mirth, discourse and civility".[13] After or during supper she would often admit Tarleton, the great comedian and talker, or other entertainers to amuse her with "stories of the town, common jests (and some were very common), and accidents!"[14]

Hentzner has left us a bulge-eyed account of the ritual attendant upon the Queen's dining or supping. First, two gentlemen, one bearing a rod, the other wearing a cloak, entered the hall, knelt three times, spread a cloth upon the table and then left. Second, two more gentlemen appeared carrying the salt, a plate, and bread. They, too, knelt three times, placed these things upon the table and disappeared. Third, came an unmarried lady (a countess, he says), and a married one who bore a tasting-knife. They curtsied three times, went to the table, rubbed the plate with bread and salt "with as much devotion as if the Queen were present". These ladies did not leave the room. Finally, the Yeomen of the Guard, bareheaded and in scarlet livery with a golden rose on their backs, came in bringing a course of twenty-four dishes served in plate, mostly gold. As each was brought in it was received by a gentleman yeoman and placed on the table. The married lady who wielded the tasting-knife then gave each Yeoman a morsel from the dish he had brought in to try it for poison (there had been attempts—foreign, of course—to poison the Queen). All the time while this was going on twelve trumpeters and two kettledrums "made the hall ring". Then the dishes were taken in to the Queen by the women; she selected what she wanted to eat and the ladies got the rest.

Those who made fortunes, or conversely lost their lives, in hazardous adventures at sea were less well fed than stay-at-homes. Sir Hugh Platt gives his inventive mind to the problem of how to keep meat fresh at sea, and suggests that it be placed in a perforated cask and dragged astern. The cold, salt, sea-water would keep it sweet and fresh. . . . But such an invention would hardly have done for shark-infested, tropical waters. A ship which in 1576 set off to catch the "Whale Fish" in Russia was provisioned with bread, cedar oil, hog's-heads of beef, salt beans, peas, salt fish, wine and mustard seed. Hakluyt who provides this information does not tell us what is meant by cedar oil. One might guess that it was some sort of pine-nut oil—since pine and cedar seem to have been interchangeable terms. But one might well be wrong. The ship may also have carried with it a quantity of scurvy grass, most ships bent on a long voyage did, for this, as its name implies, was a specific against scurvy.

Of vegetables and ways of serving them we have little direct knowledge. What we do know has to be ferreted out for the most part from a mass of medical material and from herbals of the day.* The word "herb" was, in those days, the generic name for all green things from grasses to trees as defined in Genesis "herb bearing seed after his kind", and we are told by Harrison, who had a garden of his own, that the finest herbs although well-known and plentiful in the time of Edward I had fallen into such

* There seems to be disagreement among authorities on vegetables of the period. Gerard lists many which may not have been in common use. It seemed to me that, perhaps, the best way of deciding the question was to go to the Netherlands and examine the wealth of still-life paintings of the period. These provided much interesting information and, as we imported vegetables from the Lowlands in the sixteenth century while many Lowlanders fled to England to escape persecution, bringing their gardening knowledge with them, Dutch paintings are a fairly reliable guide.

sad neglect that from the time of Henry IV to the latter end of Henry VII and the beginning of Henry VIII's reign there was little or no use made of them. They were thought suitable only for hogs and savage beasts.

Harrison, however, cannot be taken too literally as an authority on vegetables in any period other than his own. For the monks had been great gardeners and before the dissolution of the monasteries their kitchen, herb and physic gardens were famous. Dissolution and the breaking-up of monastic lands may well have contributed to the spread of gardening knowledge generally.

Among the vegetables which we know were eaten at the time were "turneps both great and small" and, though provoking wind, they were eaten raw by the poorer folk in Wales and by the less poor boiled or roasted. The greens were boiled or eaten raw in salad. Parsnips and carrots were boiled—the latter generally with fat flesh—the former occasionally made into fritters mixed with flour, egg, new milk, salt, nutmeg and then fried like pancakes. As for cabbage and colewort, there seem to have been thirteen known varieties, although one appears to have

been cultivated for its blue dye. Beetroot was also known, but certainly not well-known until late in the reign. It is said to have been introduced in 1546, but probably remained a curiosity in private gardens for some time before coming into general use. Salsify, or Tragopogon, was recommended boiled and buttered. It grew plentifully in the fields about London, Islington and Putney. Artichokes were eaten raw with pepper and salt, or boiled. Asparagus or "Sperage" was boiled and eaten with salt, oil and vinegar. Peas and beans had, of course, been known and eaten in quantity from early times. The great garden bean, parent of our broad bean, and seven kinds of kidney bean were eaten usually "boiled with their cods" though Gerard brands them as "windy meat". Less provoking in this respect were Romane or garden peas, lentils, and even lupin seeds.

Tusser, in his list of herbs and roots to boil or butter, gives "Roncivall" or "Runcivall" peas as a delicacy. This is a corruption of Roncesvalle, where disaster overtook Charlemagne's army, though why the name should have been given to large, marrow-fat peas, no one seems to know for sure. Or why a Roncesvalles spoon—better known as a runcible spoon—should have been so named is again not clear. (The runcible spoon was of two kinds. One pronged like a fork had an outside tine with a sharp cutting-edge, like the American salad-fork, but it was curved like the bowl of a spoon. The other was usually made of horn with a bowl at either end, one the size of a teaspoon, the other the size of a tablespoon. It had a hinge in the middle which allowed one end to fold back over the other. No amount of research on my part has elicited the information as to which kind of runcible spoon was de rigueur for dining on Edward Lear's "mince and slices of quince".)

Chervil, young sow thistle, corn salad, leaves of clary, and spotted cowslip all seem to have been used along with many others as pot herbs. And sallets or salads were very popular and highly recommended by the medical men of the day. Innumerable salad herbs are mentioned, in addition to lettuce of which there were a number of varieties. Purslane, tarragon, cress, succory, endive, root of rampion (boiled), borage—and particularly flowers of borage "to make the mind glad"—[15]all found their way into salads, as did radishes. Onions were so popular that they were imported from Flanders as they still are. Leeks had been known for centuries, but chives were thought to make one thin and to engender "hot and gross vapours". In fact, the mild and delicate chive had few defenders, it was also thought to be "hurtful to the eyes and brain" and to cause troublesome dreams.

There were also pompions (pumpkins), boiled and buttered, sliced and fried or baked with apples. There were several kinds of melon and a variety of cucumbers including a long, thin, repulsive-looking one known as "adder's cucumber". The adder look was achieved by putting the fruit when very young inside a hollow tube or reed and allowing it to grow through the tube and out the other end. Gerard, with Lysenko-like science, assures his readers that if the seed from one of these artificially attenuated and elongated cucumbers be saved and planted, the resultant plant will produce adder cucumbers *without* the aid of a hollow tube or reed.

Besides such genetic marvels there were more ordinary things like skirret, horseradish, gourds, raspberries, strawberries, mulberries, peaches, apricots, cornels, currants, raisins of the sun, and imported oranges, lemons, and olives all to provide variety and possibly lightness to what must have been an extremely heavy diet.

The Elizabethans at Home

The Elizabethans were very fond of fruit and no country house was complete without its orchard. Walled gardens with trees trained against the walls to produce early fruit were recommended; this was a secret brought from Italy by Lord Darcy. The gooseberry, a rarity in Henry VIII's time was now widely grown. Strawberries were of the wild, woodland variety, white and red. Their runners were collected from woods in the autumn to furnish gardens great and small. Raspberries too came in during this period. They had been known before but ignored probably because, as William Turner had remarked back in 1548, "the taste of it is sour". But the sourness could be overcome by sugar and the Elizabethans had a lot of this. Thomas Tusser gives a list of twenty-seven kinds of fruit, including soft fruits, which should be set or transplanted in January and Tusser, unlike Gerard, is a very reliable guide.

There is a charming letter in the Cranfield papers written by Judith Beecher to Lionel Cranfield on August 1st, 1600. After thanking him for a keg of sturgeon and candy sugar, she hopes that he will soon bring Mrs. Cranfield to visit her for, she writes, "There is now such a store of plums and pears as would tempt her greatly." It seems odd that pears would be ripe on August first, yet they are also mentioned as part of the decoration of the pageant of welcome given by Leicester that excessively hot July.

Fruit was stored for winter too. Apples, pears, cherries and plums were dried and grapes could be kept for weeks by cutting them with a bit of vine-wood attached. The woody bit was stuck in a large apple and the grapes were nourished and kept fresh by the juice of the apple. Fruit was also imported from the Low Countries; and raisins, prunes, and figs were brought in from Portugal and the Levant.

And then there was the potato—both varieties. The sweet potato or yam, sometimes called "skyritts of Peru", was eaten roasted in ashes, sopped in wine, or dressed with oil and vinegar and even boiled with prunes. These roots which, it is claimed, were first brought home by John Hawkins in 1564, were often made into a confection "no less toothsome, wholesome and daintie than of the flesh of quince. And likewise the comfortable and delicate meates called in shops Morselli, Placentulae, and divers others such like."[16] Sweet potatoes were also used as a base where "cunning confectioners and sugar bakers may worke and frame many comfortable and delicate conserves and restorative sweetmeats". And Hakluyt says that the sweet potato "is more delicious than any sweet apple, sugared".

Despite the comforting and restorative qualities of sweet potatoes plus the fact that they nourished and strengthened the body, we are warned that their side effects, so to speak, are wind and bodily lust—both of which seem to have troubled the Elizabethans greatly. Nevertheless, Gerard says that he succeeded in growing this sweet and dangerous potato in his own magnificent garden at Holborn. This may possibly be true but, alas, Gerard, enchanting as he is to read, is not to be relied upon too greatly. He is a shocking plagiarist (so is Hentzner) and pages of his *Great Herbal* are lifted wholesale from continental sources.

The other potato, to which Gerard gives much less attention, is the one which has since become a staple in our diet. It was called first, the Potato of America and possibly the Noremberga potato since that was the name of the place it came from prior to the place-name being changed to Virginia in honour—and by kind permission—of the Virgin Queen. It was equal, we are told rather off-handedly, in goodness and wholesomeness to the common potato; that is, the sweet potato, which was so much more widely known and valued. It too, was roasted in embers or boiled and eaten with oil, vinegar and pepper or "dressed in any other way by the hand of some cunning in cookery",[17] but this was a rarity.

That the potato was regarded as an exciting and unusual thing is indicated by Falstaff's remark "Let the sky rain potatoes". While the devil Luxury, according to Thersites in *Troilus and Cressida* had "potato-fingers". Whether this refers to the sweet potato or the Virginia potato we do not really know. Probably the former as the Virginia potato did not become popular until two hundred years later. No doubt the sweet potato was preferred because the Elizabethans, like the Americans today, were inordinately fond of sweet things.

Sweets, particularly those made for great occasions, were wonderful, elaborate confections which carried out the prevailing taste for riotous and fantastic ornamentation. There were jellies of all colours, varieties and flavours made to represent

flowers, fruit, herbs, trees, beasts, fish and fowl. Almond paste and marchpane mixed with isinglass and sugar were shaped into rabbits, ducks, geese, dredged with cinammon and made to look as if they were the real thing roasted. Often sweets were made in the shape of arms or escutcheons, brightly coloured and extravagantly gilded, while everything which could be candied was candied. Falstaff who is always urging the elements to do something really extraordinary cries, "Let it snow eringoes".

Eringoes were the candied roots of sea-holly. Roses, marigolds, gillyflowers, violets, rosemary, borage were preserved whole in sugar syrup, or their petals were crystallized. Suckets of lettuce stalks, orange pips and green walnuts were made and eaten in quantity. "Kissing comfits" were candies perfumed to sweeten the breath. Candied nutmeg and ginger, candied lemon and oranges were commonplace. Candy, as the Americans use it, is a good Elizabethan word, though the Elizabethans got it from the Arabic or Persian.

Again, if we take a random selection of New Year's gifts made to the Queen over various years we find all sorts of sweets cropping up. Revell, the Purveyor of the Works, gave her a marvellously wrought marchpane in the shape of St. Paul's complete with steeple. John Henyngway "Poticary" presented a pot of some orange condiment and "pine comfits, musked". The grocer, Lawrence Shref, gave a sugar-loaf, a box of ginger and other spices; while George Webster, a master cook, presented another marchpane made to look like a chess-board. The Queen was very fond of chess and marchpane. Mrs. Morgan presented a box of cherries and apricots, doubtless they were candied. Another cook produced yet another marchpane, with a very fine St. George in the middle and, not to be outdone, the serjeant of the pastry in the same year presented "one fair pie of quinces, oranged". It is odd to find the Queen's physicians, Doctors Huick, Julio and Bayley, all presenting her with exactly the same thing—green ginger, preserved. Did they agree beforehand, or were they deadly rivals who, by some unfortunate coincidence, had hit upon the same gift? We shall never know the answer. Yet the ginger did differ slightly. Dr. Julio's was plain. Dr. Huick's had orange flowers in it and Dr. Bayley had had his made up with lemon.

Of course, she received comfit boxes in quanity every year and they were undoubtedly filled with comfits or suckets. Suckets were made by dipping almost anything from orange-pips to green walnuts in boiling syrup, letting them cool, then re-dipping.

The process was repeated until the sucket was thickly coated with hard sugar. Oranges, lemons, nutmeg and ginger were candied too. And whole oranges were preserved in sugar and then filled with marmalade.

Codinac was a favourite kind of quince marmalade, and marmalade seems to have been kept in boxes—which sounds rather messy. There were various cakes and pastries—soft saffron-cakes were eaten with beer. For puff pastry "cold butter" was used. A contemporary recipe for puff or short pastry which could be made "without butter or sewet" called for the yolks of three eggs, a pint of cream, sugar and a sufficient quantity of pre-baked flour to make a thickish paste. Rosewater seems to have been used in nearly everything, including marmalade. Sugar-bread, gingerbread, flan (made with new cheese), seed cake, to say nothing of a plain pudding which seems to have been a cross between a boiled and baked custard—with the addition of flour—were everyday affairs. Mince-pies were eaten, at any rate mincemeat of a very heavy order was made and liberally spiced. Spices appeared in practically every dish. Pepper, in particular, was used in vast quantities and at one time sold for from 2s. to 2s. 6d. a pound.

Sir Francis Drake in his globe-encircling voyage which lasted thirty-four months (1577–80) concluded a treaty with the Sultan of the Moluccas or Spice Islands giving the English the exclusive right to buy the produce of the islands and took aboard as a first instalment six tons of cloves. Unfortunately he got stuck on a reef in the East Indian Archipelago and had to toss overboard half the cargo of cloves in order to lighten ship sufficiently to get off the reef. With cloves the price they were the loss of three tons must have been a financial disaster of no small proportion.

But the Elizabethans seem almost to be made of sugar and spice! Barbary sugar was known and used, while ordinary sugar was imported in loaves of 100 lb. and broken up for selling. At the beginning of the century sugar cost from 4d. to 10d. a pound. But by 1600 the price had risen to 1s. or 1s. 6d. (Food prices

Of Food and Drink

generally rose by about 120 per cent in the 100 years between 1541 and 1641—wages did not.) A special fine white sugar was made for sweetening wine—and most people sweetened their wine. Falstaff's favourite drink was sack sweetened with sugar and, indeed, his friend Poins calls him Sir John Sack and Sugar.

Honey—English honey was naturally the best because of nature's prodigality with wild thyme—was used not only for sweetening but by physicians in various remedies. It was white as sugar and far less "choleric" than imported honey. Physicians would never dream of using imported honey in their nostrums. The honey brought from Spain or Pontus was specially eschewed because it was believed to have a "naturally implanted venemous quality".

Xenophobia could hardly go further! Spanish bees could not be trusted not to put hemlock nectar into the waxy combs destined for England.

CHAPTER SIX

Of Ailments and Their Cure

THE Privy Council was worried. It was the Queen who worried them. She very often did on matters of State but this time it was different. Elizabeth had a terrible toothache. It had come on after the festivities at Kenilworth and her doctors seemed powerless to relieve the pain. In fact they fell into acrimonious dispute over the matter. They quarrelled and argued while the ache went on raging—and probably the Queen did, too. Finally, the Council took matters in hand and, with certain grave misgivings, sent for "an outlandish physician of the name of John Anthony Fenatus" a celebrated pain curer. It was felt by many that it was "very risky to entrust the Queen's tooth to a foreigner who might be a Jew or a Papist".[1] But everyone, including Elizabeth, was by now desperate. Something, no matter how risky, had to be done.

Fenatus prescribed various remedies in Latin and at great length but advised that "if the tooth were hollow . . . it were better to have it drawn". The Queen flatly refused. She hated surgery and was terrified by the very thought. One glance at the surgical instruments of the day, a cross between carpenters' and blacksmiths' tools, is sufficient to explain the terror. So Fenatus recommended the tooth be filled with fenugreek* held in place

---

* Fenugreek, i.e. *Trigonella*, a hardy annual of the order Leguminosae, first introduced into England from S.E. Europe in 1562. Its seeds were used by farriers in treating horses! The Romans called it Foenum Graecum, Greek Hay.

with wax. This, he claimed, would in time so loosen the tooth that it could be removed by the fingers, but, he added doggedly, "drawing it away is best".

Poor Elizabeth simply couldn't face it, and the Council couldn't persuade her to. Then the Bishop of London, Thomas Aylmer, solved the problem. He assured her that the pain of having the tooth drawn was far less than she feared. He was, he said, an old man with only a few teeth left but he'd gladly allow the surgeon to draw one out in her presence to prove that it didn't hurt too much. This the surgeon did, and Elizabeth was so much encouraged by his example that "she did likewise".[2] To the great relief of everyone.

Toothache was a minor, if extremely common ailment, and this particular story has a happy ending. But, in view of the medical knowedge of the day, what is really astonishing is how sufficient of our ancestors survived long enough to perpetuate the species. War, pestilence, and famine—always the chief executioners of the human race—still were, even as late as the sixteenth century, most ably assisted by the medical men of the day, and by an almost total lack of even elementary hygiene. Corpses left rotting on the gallows, London Bridge tastefully embossed with heads of the executed; floors which would disgrace the modern deep-litter system of keeping hens; slops and filth of all kinds thrown into the streets; inadequate bathing facilities (the bath houses were little more than brothels); polluted water and rancid food, all must have provided richly nourishing material for germs, viruses, fleas, lice, rats and mice.

Fortunately for the Elizabethans—and for our subsequent history—the Queen was the healthiest of all the Tudors. She did not suffer from gout and asthma as her grandfather Henry VII had done—(gout was held to be responsible for the famous Tudor temper). She escaped the congenital syphilis which was said to be her father's legacy to the wretched and unhappy Mary Tudor. She did not contract the wasting sickness or consumption which had carried off Arthur, her father's elder brother, and which, complicated by something which may have been Raynaud's disease, ended the life of her half-brother, the sixteen-year-old Edward, in such agony that the child's last anguished words were, "Oh Lord God, free me from this calamitous life."

Nevertheless, the Queen suffered from several severe illnesses during her life but, happily, survived them no less than the ministrations of her physicians. At fifteen she had scarlet fever which may have left her with a septic throat; certainly she was subject to sore throat. At thirty she survived smallpox, although probably her hair didn't. Her natural hair had been "redder than yellow and curled apparently from nature" according to Sir James Melvil who saw her in 1564, but from sometime after that to the day of her death she wore an auburn wig.

Another trial was migraine—a Tudor affliction. And at one period of her life—around the age of forty—she suffered a varicose ulcer of the leg. This she used, from time to time, as a diplomatic illness . . . it handily kept her from doing things she didn't want to do. Yet if, for any reason she wished to prove that she was perfectly healthy and well, she would dance all night—and she danced beautifully—although the ulcer must have given her great pain.

In 1572 she was dreadfully ill with food poisoning—which is hardly surprising, and all but died of the cure—which is even less surprising when we learn that it was excessive bleeding, purging, and fasting. The year before this, on returning to Richmond after a Royal Progress through Essex, she had suffered a violent bilious attack. It came on suddenly and was as suddenly relieved by vomiting: or so William Cecil wrote to the French Ambassador. The Queen's health was never a matter of indifference to her Council, nor to her people who felt that the security of the realm depended upon the single thread of the Queen's life. They were right. It did.

Yet, even though the College of Physicians had been founded

years before, in 1518, medicine of the period remained almost
wholly medieval and was based fundamentally on the Greek
system of Aristotle and Hippocrates—as modernized by Galen
in the second century A.D. As such, it was a mixture of philo-
sophy, observation, and experience to which were added astrology and magic. Apart from Galen's innovations, pathology was
still deeply rooted in the ancient theory of the four fundamental
principals or elements of the natural world; Air, Fire, Water
and Earth. Each had its own quality or character—cold, heat,
moisture, and dryness. As man was a part of the natural order,
it was believed he partook of these qualities and that the blending
of any two produced his "complexion" or, as we should say,
temperament. Further, each complexion or temperament had
its own associated humour.

Thus, heat and moisture mixed produced the sanguine man
whose humour was blood. Coldness and moisture were responsible for the phlegmatic man whose humour was phlegm. The
hot and the dry, blended, produced the choleric type whose
humour, not unexpectedly, was green or yellow bile; while the
melancholy temperament of Robert Burton was due to the
blending of cold and dry—Air and Earth. The associated humour
was black bile.

If the proportions of the blend were right then, apparently,
you were all right. But if for some reason or another there was
an imbalance, a thought too much of this, a trifle too little of that,
then you were headed for trouble (natural causes of disease were
unknown). The imbalance had to be corrected by bleeding,
purging, drugs, herbs, diet, amulets—and consulting the stars.

Food, like everything else, was of the same four elements and
its nutritive and digestive qualities were determined by this.
But worse, food had "degrees". For example, what we think of
as the simple and uncomplicated cabbage was hot in the first
degree and dry in the second. Whether this made it a choleric
cabbage—which sounds highly unlikely—or meant that a
choleric man should avoid it as having a tendency to produce

too much of the explosive yellow or green bile, we do not really know. It seems very doubtful, however, if the average Elizabethan paid very much attention to "degrees" in food save in times of illness. Certainly the Elizabethans who ate so enormously—despite Pliny's warning, which they well knew, that "many dishes bring many diseases"—could not have had their minds on the degrees of heat, cold, dryness or "slime" possessed by every mouthful of food they took.

The Elizabethans seem to us to be nothing if not sanguine, which is defined as being hopeful, lusty, amorous, and confident. As sanguine man was believed to have perfect digestion this may account for the Elizabethan ability to eat so much. The sanguine type, as defined in those days, was one with red hair, large veins and arteries, full pulse, perfect digestion, red and white skin,

a tendency to be fleshy, a heavy sleeper, given to sweating, short-tempered, and subject to both violent and pleasant dreams. This seems to fit, at least superficially, Henry VIII—and to a lesser extent his daughter Elizabeth.

Yet even sanguine man could be made melancholy by foods which caused an excess of black bile. Foods which brought on this unhappy condition were spleen, pears, apples (though a roasted apple did wonderfully comfort the stomach), peaches, milk, cheese, salt-meat, red deer, hare, beef, goat, peacock, pigeons and fenny fowl, fish bred in standing waters, peas, beans, dark bread, black wines, cider, perry, and spices. If such foods could induce sadness in hopeful, lusty, confident sanguine man they must have driven the "naturally" melancholy man to the extremes of acute depression.

But sanguine man—hot and moist as he was and able to eat everything—was not totally free from the necessity of watching his diet. The purer his complexion or temperament "the sooner corrupted and the blood infected".[3] He was advised to avoid immoderate excesses in fruit, herbs, and roots such as "garlick", onions and leeks, and to refrain from old flesh, brains, and the udders of kine. Moderate sleep and diet, were advised, or else he became too fat and gross.

Phlegmatic man who, like prunes, was cold and moist, and choleric man, hot and dry as red pepper, also had to observe no less involved dietary and other rules suitable to their particular colours or temperament. Thus diet and medicine were often enough indistinguishable. A good cook was believed to be half physician, for, as Boorde tells us, "the chief physic, the council of physicians excepted, comes from the kitchen. Therefore, the physician and cook for sick men must consult together . . . for if the doctor without the cook prepare any meat, unless he be an expert, he will make a worse dish and the patient will be unable to eat."

Curiously enough, children were believed to be born phlegmatic and were therefore fed upon foods which were moist and only moderately hot. Luckily, such foods were milk—believed to be related to blood—cream, whey, curds, and white meat which, as we know, meant dairy produce. As the child grew it became more sanguine or choleric (few, it seems, became melancholy) and so, from about the thirteenth year, children were allowed the "grosser meats" and wine if mixed with water. Water, itself, was thought to be "cold, slow, and slack of digestion". It may not have been that but it must often have been polluted.

For the infant there was no alternative to breast feeding,

The Elizabethans at Home

though a primitive sort of a bottle made from a cow's horn was known. Babies produced by the well-to-do were farmed out to wet-nurses and were not weaned until they had cut four or more teeth. Queen Elizabeth's weaning, at thirteen months, was an affair of Parliament. But from what Juliet's nurse says in *Romeo and Juliet* her star-crossed charge must have been around three on that hot day—the day of the earthquake—when the nurse first laid wormwood to her dug. What with the earthquake and the weaning wormwood both happening on the same day, poor little Juliet must have felt not only rejected but completely and forcibly cast out. It is surprising that child psychologists haven't fallen upon this and revealed it as the key to the whole of *Romeo and Juliet.*

Yet it was not the milk of the wet-nurse which was considered of prime importance, it was her moral qualities! The hapless infant, it was thought, could imbibe vices along with the milk. This doctrine must have been of great convenience to a rich and naughty mama who could be as naughty as she liked without the least fear that her naughtiness would be passed on to her child. We have no record of the infant mortality rate of the time but a glance at some Elizabethan tombs indicates that it must have been high. Another thing which indicates that babies died young—if they survived the shock of birth—is that they were baptized almost immediately upon arrival and were thus assured of instantaneous admittance into heaven. It was quite common for mothers to die of puerperal fever—an infection which was thought to result from the coldness of the Christening chamber.

As children were supposed to have naturally phlegmatic stomachs, so old people's stomachs were thought to revert to the childhood phlegmatic. They were therefore advised to return to a child's diet. The advice was probably good even if, as we may think, the reasons were wrong. But even we cannot quarrel with the precept to drink wine with pork or to subsist on fruit when afflicted with fever (although for fever an even better

170

remedy, if you were rich, was powdered pearls dissolved in lemon juice). The statement "diet is the mother of disease let the father be who he will"[4] has a curiously modern ring.

So diets, some of them as eccentric as modern diets, played an important part in medicine and were keyed to the complexions and humours of man. Even the hours of sleep varied with the complexion. Sanguine and choleric types needed only seven hours, while the phlegmatic required a good nine. As for the melancholy, they were allowed as long as they liked. Waking frequently was known to be both a symptom and cause of melancholy inducing "dryness of the brain, frenzy, dotage and making the body dry, lean, hard and ugly to behold".[5]

In general, it was held that a healthy man—no matter what his complexion—shouldn't sleep during the day or if, after stunning himself with a meal, he felt that he must—then he should sleep standing against a cupboard or sitting bolt upright on a chair or settle, form or stool.

For those who took to their beds in sickness there were some useful sick-room rules. The first, bespeaking a pessimism born of long experience, enjoined the patient to make a will and receive the last rites. Good nurses or keepers "diligent, not sluttish or lazy"[6] were desirable. The room should smell sweet —evil odours bred diseases. The patient should not be pestered with conversation—especially that of women—and should follow the counsel of the physicians called in to minister to both soul and body. It is probable that the counsel of the former was of more benefit than that of the latter since the final instruction is, when death approaches "only godly matters should be spoken of".[7]

When death approached Lord Burghley one of his attendants was a woman—the Queen. She, who had so often driven him almost to despair, now came every day to feed the old minister with her own hand. For her "Faithful Spirit", as she always called him, she had a deep and abiding love and his death left a great gap in her life. She could never after hear his name spoken

The Elizabethans at Home

without tears coming to her eyes. In the year of Burghley's death, 1598, the first treatise on tropical medicine was printed in England. Its title was *The cure of the diseased in remote regions; preventing mortality incident in foreign attempts of the English nation.** Such a treatise would have been an impossibility in 1558 when the young Elizabeth, a shrewd judge of character, picked canny William Cecil as her chief minister.

Yet medicine and even more surgery, were evolving during the reign. Strangely enough, this evolution was due to the two great impulses of the Renaissance—Art and Adventure. Art with Leonardo da Vinci had discovered anatomy, and Andreas Vesalius of Padua whose great work on anatomy had appeared as early as 1543 might well be called the scientific successor to Leonardo. But it was a French army doctor, Ambroise Paré (1510–90) who first perceived the importance of this new knowledge of anatomy and related it to surgery. Paré, "the greatest surgeon of the Renaissance, and one of the greatest surgeons of all time",[8] put an end to the dreadful tortures of red-hot cautery after amputation by means of a simple ligature which he invented. He designed artificial limbs and used them on soldiers. He discovered that gunshot wounds were not, in themselves, poisonous as was commonly believed and therefore did not need to be treated with boiling oil, which was the usual practice, but needed to be soothed with salve. He also advocated a method of turning the child in the mother's womb before delivery in certain abnormal cases. In England, Thomas Gale, a noted surgeon, wrote a book on the treatment of gunshot wounds, so did William Clowse, while John Woodall, also a surgeon, wrote on amputation. † War, then as now, gave great impetus to medicine and surgery.

* By G. W.; perhaps George Whitstone.

† Although William Harvey (b. 1578) began practising in 1602, his great work on the circulation of the blood, which completely revolutionized medicine, was not published until twenty-five years after Elizabeth's death.

Of Ailments and their Cure

As for adventure—its expanding spirit had led to the discovery of new countries and to the extension and expansion of trade. This, in turn, had provided England and Europe with new drugs. The Spaniards who brought back with them the treasures of the Incas brought also, it is said, a particularly virulent form of syphilis contracted from the Peruvian natives. But they also brought ipecacuanha and quinine, although the curative power of the latter was not known until the seventeenth century. Sir John Hawkins, who kidnapped negroes in Guiana and forced them upon the Spanish settlers in the West Indies, brought back tobacco which was first used as a fumigant and, more importantly in an age without anaesthetics, as a narcotic. Mandrake, too, was used as a narcotic ("cold and dry even to the 4th degree"). Steeped in wine it was given by surgeons to those whom they proposed to "cut, saw, burn or take off a limb". It was highly dangerous and unless administered with great care it caused "dead sleep and maketh the body insensible".[9]

Yet the dissemination of even this new knowledge of medicine, and surgery was, by present-day standards, slow and was confined in the beginning to Italy and France. The English, in general, intensely nationalistic and individualistic as they were, were as suspicious of continental nostrums as they were of continental politics.

Foreign remedies might, just possibly, be all right but one, Timothy Bright,* thought English ones better and, with nationalistic fervour, brought out a book called *A Treatise wherein is declared the sufficiencie of English Medicines for cure of all diseases, cured with Medicine.* It was Bright, too, who, before Burton, brought out a *Treatise of Melancholie.*

Disease, however, is the great internationalist and knows no frontiers. The Queen although she escaped poisoning at the hands of foreigners—and she told a French Ambassador there had been

* Timothy Bright: (1551?–1615) was also the inventor of modern shorthand. His *Characterie* (1588) was a work on the lost art of shorthand which he re-invented.

173

The Elizabethans at Home

seventeen attempts to poison her—did not, as we know, escape smallpox. Nor did her subjects.

To prevent the dreadful scarring which was the lifelong badge worn by those who managed to survive the disease, red cloth was fastened over the windows of the room in which the small-pox patient lay—a custom which had been followed since the time of Edward I.* In the palace of the Queen the cloth, no doubt, was of the finest quality and dye, but in the cottage a red petticoat sufficed. It is only recently we have discovered that this must have been effective. The work of Dr. Niels Finsen of Copenhagen has shown that it is the actinic rays of the sun which are responsible for scarring. If these are filtered out, little or no scarring results. The strange thing is, red glass, mica or paper —or even, presumably, a red petticoat—will filter out these rays!

Smallpox apart, it was fortunate for physicians—if not for their patients—that the variety of new herbs and plants had been increased during this period for at this time a new theory, the "Doctrine of Signatures", was enjoying a considerable vogue. This theory was invented by Bombastus, a Swiss-German who understandably enough preferred to be called Paracelsus. He died before Elizabeth came to the throne but his Doctrine of Signatures had many avid followers during the reign. Briefly, Bombastus taught that every plant was "signed". That is, it is associated by colour, shape, odour, or habitat with a specific disease and is, therefore, the specific *for* that disease. For example, chest complaints could be cured with Lungwort (Pulmonaria) since the leaves were thought to resemble the lungs which, in a minor sort of way, they do. But the word "wort" itself when attached to a plant or herb had, since Anglo-Saxon times, indicated in England that the plant had medicinal properties.

* Gaddesden, personal physician to Marguerite of France—second wife of Edward I—records his "red treatment" of Edward of Caernarvon first Prince of Wales.

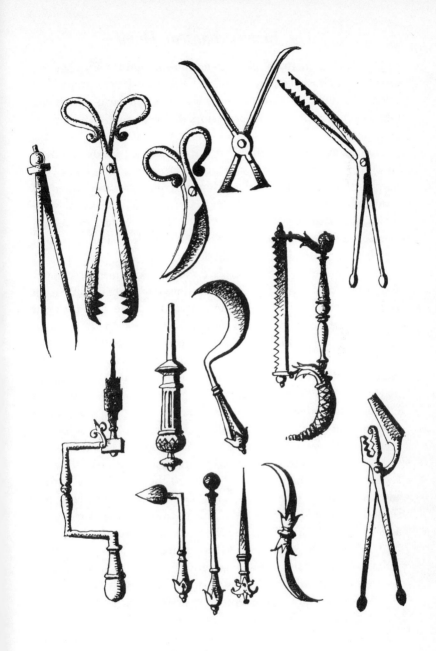

The list of signatures seems to us endless, and the Elizabethans obviously saw signs in plants—and planets—where we would see none. But Bombastus's theory was very popular here and was taken up by medical men, professors of magic, and many intelligent people.

Bombastus died of drink or was murdered by jealous rivals— an event which happened when the Queen was only eight, but his theories vigorously outlived him and very probably killed off thousands, as they were put into practice by physicians, apothecaries, herbalists and astrologers who, since the stars influenced disease, and the planets were associated with various remedial metals, were also counted as physicians.

Dr. John Dee was Elizabeth's favourite alchemist, astrologer and magician. He had picked a propitious day for her Coronation and shortly after was sent for in a great hurry because a waxen image of Elizabeth, pierced to the heart with pins, had been found in Lincoln's Inn fields. He was able to reassure members of the Privy Council, who were in a great state of agitation, that no ill-effects would reach the Queen because of this bit of sympathetic magic. He was then sent off, post-haste, to Richmond to reassure Elizabeth too—if she needed reassurance. He also went off to Germany, in 1577, to consult other learned men about the Queen's teeth, which were deplorable even in an age of bad teeth. At one time, gentle Dr. Dee formed a partnership with one, Edward Kelley, who claimed to have discovered the philosopher's stone and also to be able to raise spirits. Dr. Dee and Mr. Kelley had several spirit guides. One, Madimi, began her guiding as a child and was a good linguist. But she grew up rather too suddenly into a handsome woman who had entirely forgotten languages and who, rather surprisingly, practised nudism. As she was by no means disembodied this led to sad trouble with the wives of the two seers, and to the eventual break-up of the partnership.

Edward Kelley was a rogue. Dr. Dee wasn't. He was, apart from his credulity, a highly intelligent man with an inquiring mind. Among other things, he proposed sound schemes for a

Of Ailments and their Cure

Royal Naval Reserve and for improving the fishing industry (neither was used). He instructed the Queen in astronomy no less than in occult knowledge, and was consulted by many famous people—among them Burghley, Leicester, Walsingham, and Bacon. He was also one of the first, if not *the* first, to use those two words which are regarded almost as unpermissible today, "British Empire".

Elizabeth seems to have been fond of Dr. Dee and visited him several times at Mortlake to see his scientific instruments and his library, but she seems to have done very little for him in the way of preferment. It was perhaps this which led him to take up with Kelley. Dr. Dee was no business man and, as Kelley claimed to have discovered the philosopher's stone which would have made them rich, it may have been this which led him into a foolish partnership.

Alchemists everywhere were busy claiming to have discovered the philosopher's stone; an elixir which not only turned base metals into nobler ones but which was also the elixir of life. A certain Cornelius Alvetanus dedicated his treatise, "De Conficiendo Divino Elixire sive Lapide Philosophorum", to the Queen who read it in Latin and was so taken with it that she gave Cornelius comfortable quarters in Somerset House and bade him get on with it. Curiously, the Queen seems to have been less interested in living for ever than in the immediate needs of her treasury for she gave Cornelius a contract to produce 50,000 marks of pure gold "at a moderate price". Cornelius failed. In 1567 he was committed to the Tower "for abusing the Queen's Majesty"[10] by falsely promising her the elixir.

The whole of the fraudulent business of alchemy with its strange and to us almost unintelligible "scientific jargon" is held up to ridicule by Ben Jonson in his play *The Alchemist* with the greedy and credulous Sir Epicure Mammon as the goat. In fairness, it must be said that many alchemists were genuine seekers and, oddly enough, it was Bombastus—Paracelsus—who gave a new direction to alchemy when he stated that its true object should be, not the making of gold, but the preparation of medicine.

Since most Elizabethans believed firmly in signs, portents and the influence of stars (early on in the reign Burghley consulted an astrologer about the Queen's marriage and was told that Elizabeth would marry a foreigner—which must have given him a shock—and would have one son, who would be a great prince, and one daughter), it is hardly surprising to find that many believed, equally firmly, in ghosts, elves, fairies, and evil spirits. These manifestations of the supra-mundane world could, of course, do good if they had a mind to but they seldom seem to have been so minded. There were also witches and sorcerers—a sorcerer was a rather superior witch or wizard—to worry about.

Bishop Jewel, an enlightened man, was so upset by the wicked goings on of witches and the way they were ruining people's health, that in 1572 he delivered a strong sermon against them. The Queen was present and the bishop didn't mince words. "These eyes", he thundered, "have seen most evident and manifest marks of their wickedness. Your Grace's subjects pine away even unto death, their colour fadeth, their flesh rotteth. Their speech is benumbed, their senses are bereft."

The good bishop obviously felt very strongly on the subject yet it seems extraordinary tactless of him to have preached about witches in front of the woman whose mother was believed to have been one; Anne with her witch's mole and her vestigial finger . . . a "devil's teat". But the average Englishman—the rural inhabitants and the poor—pinned his faith in herbs and simples, in amulets and charms.

Many cures of the day were wholly charms. Spring water drunk at night from the skull of "one who has been slain" cured the falling sickness. To cure a scorpion's bite—surely not common in England but a handy first-aid hint for travellers in the tropics—the bitten must whisper in an ass's ear "I am bit by a scorpion". A woman could be released from travail if someone threw a stone over the house where she lay—a stone which had killed three living creatures, a man, a wild boar, and a she-bear. Such stones cannot have been easy to come by, and charlatans probably made a fortune by selling bogus ones. But one of the most curious charms was that against the "quotidian ague".* For this the sufferer was advised to cut an apple in three sections; on the first section he must write "The Father is Uncreated"; on the second, "The Father is Incomprehensible"; on the third "The Father is Eternal". Ordinary ague could be cured rather more simply by "a spider in a nut shell lapped in silk". Burton's mother used this remedy—or amulet—on the poor of Lindley in Leicestershire where she lived, and was laughed at for doing so by her clever son, Robert, who asks, "Quid aranea cum febre?" Later, however, when he discovered mention of this same cure for ague in the Materia Medica compiled by Dioscorides, a first-century Greek physician attached to Nero's army, he changed his opinion and gave the spider-in-a-nutshell cure his approval. What he had considered to be an old wives' tale had received the prior sanction of a science which was, by then, at least fourteen centuries out of date! We dare not laugh too merrily over this, as the old wives' tale that raspberry leaf tea helps women in labour seems now to be in danger of being proved true by modern research. Furthermore, even modern physicians know and are baffled by the fact that obstinate warts can be "charmed" away.†

Among the countless herbs in use for a variety of afflictions were those believed to have an affinity to certain parts of the body. Thus, afflictions of the head responded to concoctions

* Quotidian ague was an intermittent fever occurring every day.

† Even Robert Burton seems to be in two minds about science and the old wives' tale for he quotes Fuchsius on the subject and approves his statement that "Many an old wife or country woman doth often more good with a few known and common garden herbs than our bombast physicians with all their prodigious, sumptuous, far-fetched, rare conjectural medicine."

containing aniseed, betony, calamint, eyebright, lavender, bay, roses, rue, sage, marjoram, and foal's foot. It will not have escaped notice that most of these are sweet-smelling. Those who suffered from headache were particularly advised to avoid bad smells, the "contagiousness" of marshes, and to smell only "sweet savours". They were also advised to keep the head cool, not to sleep too much or drink too much wine. They must eschew rheum-making foods, and on no account were they to cry, sing high, or shout out "hallo!"

For the lungs—and the Elizabethans like us were particularly subject to bronchitis—comfrey was advised (and comfrey is still used in bronchial mixtures today) together with calamint, liquorice, enula, campana, hyssop. Horehound and water germander were thought particularly efficacious. (I am in no position to sneer at this, for in my childhood in Canada I was always given a delicious horehound candy whenever I had a cough.) The consumptive was advised to avoid sour and tart things, to use restoratives and cordials; avoid fried or burnt meat, anger and pensiveness, and to eat stewed pig, cock in jelly, boiled rice, raw eggs and to drink goat's milk. Again we may pause and wonder, why goat's milk? The Elizabethans could not have known that it is, by nature, T.T. although they may have known it has a higher butter-fat content.

The heart could be strengthened and assisted by borage, bugloss, saffron, balm, basil, rosemary and roses, but foxglove (digitalin) seems to have been unknown as useful to the heart until the seventeenth century. The stomach responded to wormwood, mint, betony, balm, centaury, sorrel, and purslane. And here we might note that those suffering with the "Illiacke", that condition which may have been regional ileitis or appendicitis, were warned to beware of cold, to keep the bowels laxative, to abstain from new bread, new ale, beer, cider and cinnamon, all foods containing honey, and to avoid like the plague, all things which "engender wind", notably peas, beans, and pottage.

Of Ailments and their Cure

The liver—and the liver was the seat of all humours—could be brought round by earth pine, germander, agrimony, fennel, endive and, naturally, liverwort. The spleen was comforted with maidenhair, fern-fingers, dodder of parsley, thyme, hops, betony and the inner bark of the ash tree. There was mugwort, pennyroyal, and savin for the womb; camomile, St. John's wort, origan, rue, cowslip, and the lesser centaury for the joints. Gouty people were also to avoid tight boots, salmon and oysters.

But gouty people with enough money went to Buxton in July to cure the ailment. Buxton was a very fashionable Elizabethan spa and here, in 1577, we find Sir Thomas Smith, Sir William Fitz William, Mr. Manners, Lady Harington and Lord Burghley all drinking or bathing in the waters of the warm spring—as the Romans had done long before. The Earl of Shrewsbury was there, too, with a gouty hand, an affliction which was as nothing compared to the pain and distress his wife, Bess of Hardwick, caused him. She was perfectly horrid to the Earl who had been made custodian of Mary Stuart. Perhaps it was jealousy, but it was certainly Bess, herself, who put it about that the Earl was enamoured of his prisoner. After years of quarrelling and temper she left him in 1584. In the meantime she afflicted him more sorely than his gout.

The stone was also a great misery of the time and for this saxifrage root steeped in the blood of a hare, baked, powdered and taken morning and night was recommended. For "fatness and fogeyness" much purging and little pepper was prescribed. Kybes, or chilblains, which were "of an extreme cold and phlegmatic humor" could be eased by avoiding snow, keeping the feet warm, and washing the affected parts—which should never be pricked—with urine or neat's-foot oil. For lousiness, bred by a corruption of hot humours, sweat, rankness of body, unclean shirts, or by going about with dirty people—and lousiness was very, very common—an ointment made of oil of bay and mortified mercury had remedial properties. Mercury was dog's mercury and could be mortified only by the spittle of a fasting man.*

Most families, town or country, had their own family recipes for curing various ailments, as well as their own herb gardens. Or, if the danger seemed great, they consulted a physician, a local wise woman skilled in healing, an apothecary or even the grocer. A herbal was as necessary as a cook book, and every literate man or woman considered it vital to know the curative power of herbs and to keep up with modern discoveries in medicine and magic. Drugs and medicines were sold by apothecaries and grocers who would very often make a collection of various prescriptions given by physicians and sell them for profit—or do the "doctoring" themselves. They probably didn't do any more harm than the physicians.

Yet there were two schools of thought among physicians, apothecaries and, probably, even grocers. One held that simples were best; the other believed in compounds. Compounds were "compositions and inexplicable mixtures" and they were particularly beloved by Bombastus and his followers. Compounds could, and did, contain quite extraordinary things such as dried toads and excrement and minerals such as gold, silver, mercury, and antimony.

A foreigner, Dr. Alexis of Piedmont, caused quite a stir in medical circles by a potent recipe for an ointment called "oil of a red-haired dog". The wretched animal was boiled whole in oil until it fell apart. Then, and then only, scorpions, worms, certain plants, hog's and asses's marrow together with various other

* Mercury, or quicksilver, and other metals were introduced into the Pharmacopoeia by Paracelsus who also invented alcoholic tinctures which suggests that he may have died as a result of taking his own medicine. The leading exponent of Paracelsus' teaching in England was the alchemist Robert Fludd (1574–1637). Many of Paracelsus' followers and exponents in this country and Germany were Rosicrucians who carried on his work for a century after his death which occurred in 1541.

repulsive ingredients were added in a strict and specified order. The resulting fearful mess, the doctor claimed, had cured a Portuguese gentleman—who for some unspecified reason lived on Mount Jordan—of the gout. But even more miraculous, it had restored life to the withered arm of a brother of the Order of St. Onuphiro. The arm, Dr. Alexis says, was "tutto secco, che parea veramente un tranco di ramo d'arboro", or, "all dried up like the stump of a tree branch". After sixty-three days' application of the ointment, the mummified left arm became as fleshy and full of life as the right arm. In England this created a sensation but we have no evidence that it was tried here. It is doubtful if even an Elizabethan would have boiled a dog in oil.

In addition to herbs, simples, compounds, minerals, amulets, magic, consulting the stars, wise women, physicians, apothecaries, and grocers, certain stones were believed to have certain virtues. A garnet, worn about the neck or taken in a drink, kept sorrow at bay. Jacinth and topaz allayed anger and grief and also diminished madness. The beryl helped the understanding, repressed vanity and evil thoughts while the chelidonius—a stone apparently found in the belly of a swallow—if wrapped in a fair cloth and tied to the right arm cured lunatics and madmen of their lunacy and madness. It went even further than this and made them "Amiable and merry". Emerald and sapphire were also good for pacifying the mind while carbuncle and coral were splendid in driving away devils, overcoming sorrow, repressing nightmares and the fears of children and keeping them safe from fits, sorcery, charms, and poison. Coral could also be used for diagnostic purposes. That enchanting Elizabethan, Sir Hugh Platt who, among other accomplishments, invented the first alphabet blocks for children says, "coral has some special sympathy with nature, for the best coral will turn pale and wan if the party that wears it be sick, and it comes to its former colour again as they recover". Although we may not believe in coral as a medium for what might be called non-specific diagnosis yet, undoubtedly, we must believe that coral has some virtue in

The Elizabethans at Home

warding off something, since present-day Elizabethan infants are usually presented with a necklet or bauble of coral as a christening present by grand- or god-parents.

Apart from the major torments of the time, plague, small-pox, syphilis, there was a host of minor ailments some of which defy definition and have such perfectly horrifying names, that Thersites in *Troilus and Cressida* uses a string of such complaints as pure invective. After explaining, in excessively plain English, exactly what "male varlet" means, he elaborates: "The rotten diseases of the south", he says, "the guts-griping, ruptures, catarrhs, loads of gravel i' the back, lethargies, cold palsies, raw eyes, dirt-rotten livers, wheezing lungs, bladders full of imposthume, sciaticas, lime kilns i' the palms, incurable bone ache and the unrivalled fee simple of the tetters . . ." it is not to be wondered at that the Elizabethans believed "the south wind doth corrupt".

There were, of course, the ordinary and quite recognizable afflictions too, scurvy, tetters (ringworm), shingles, sore throat, chicken-pox, scarlet fever, jaundice, tearing toothache, corns, dropsy, hemrods (there is a paralysing cure for this in the *Anatomy of Melancholy*). There was also quinsey, or squinancy, ague, worms, lice, giddiness and the hickets. But the Elizabethans were also subject to corrupt and rotten ulcers, the dumb palsy, the falling down of the mother (peculiar to women), stopping of the spleen, frenzy, coldness of the stomach, slackness of the sinews, ripe and unripe botches, the white morphew, and the pin and the web—an affliction of the eyes. Sore eyes figure prominently in the records of the time. Dimness, films, weakness, styes and a dozen other ailments were rife. They were, it seems, more common in spring and were probably due to a lack of vegetables and fruit during the winter months.

Yet there seems to have been no pellagra since so much whole-wheat bread was eaten—manchet could not have been so white as our white bread—and although a good deal of rye bread was also eaten there is little to suggest that the Elizabethans suffered

Of Ailments and their Cure

from gangrenous or convulsive ergotism (a condition still known on the Continent today). St. Anthony's fire—or Holy Fire as the disease was then called—seems to have been rare, even though Gerrard described it as if it were quite common. If toes and fingers did fall off it was more probably due to Reynaud's disease, frost-bite, or to tuberculous dactylitis.

They may have been vulgar, ostentatious, and greedy these Elizabethans, but they also must have been tough to be able to endure not only the diseases but the cures. Plague for them was what the bombing of civilian populations in crowded areas is to us. Those who could, evacuated to the country; those who couldn't burned fumigants in the streets and chalked "Lord have mercy upon us" on their doors.

They lived in fear of witchcraft, relied on charms, swallowed medicines with disgusting ingredients. They had bad teeth, bad breath, and rheumatics. They suffered amputations without anaesthetics. They died in unrelieved agony of things we wouldn't dream of dying of. They mistrusted physicians, not without reason, and trusted astrologers. But they seemed to have had faith in God and hope of the next world. Yet they did not attempt to map this next world. They were, perhaps, too vitally concerned in mapping the one they lived and died in—or perhaps they had too much sense to attempt to know the Unknowable. They may have feared death, though they seem not to have done so greatly, but certainly they did not fear life. They died younger than we do, yet some lived to a great age.

That other Elizabeth, the formidable Bess of Hardwick, died of what sounds like pneumonia—or it may have been sheer superstition—at the age of ninety. Bess had a mania for building and a gipsy soothsayer once told her that when she ceased to build she would die. A terrible spell of cold weather caused her workmen to stop work on the rebuilding of Bolsover. Building materials were held up, snowdrifts reached the tops of the walls, workmen dropped numb from ladders. Bess, hearing this, took her carriage and drove from Hardwick to Bolsover over the dreadful Derbyshire roads to urge, bully, and command them to continue. It was hopeless. They could not continue. They had no materials to continue with. Bess returned to Hardwick—and the short journey took ten hours. Once there, she drank a hot posset, told everyone she felt perfectly well but, nonetheless, took to her great carved bed with its fabulous hangings. There she lay, a great pain in her side, eyes bright with fever, mouth sunk beneath the aquiline nose, issuing orders that her workmen must continue—her life depended on it. And so she died.

On a table near her bed were several books—*Calvin upon Jobe*, covered in russet velvet, and *The Resolution of Solomon's Proverbs*. There was also an hour-glass.

CHAPTER SEVEN

Of Pleasures and Pastimes

IT was the dragon who caused the trouble. High above the castle walls he spewed out squibs, which went off with a wonderful bang, and fiery golden apples, which should have burnt out in flight but didn't. Four houses in Warwick and "in the suburbs" were set alight and there was considerable panic in the streets.

Henry Cowper's mill by the river below the castle was severely damaged, even though several noblemen and gentlemen—among whom were the Earl of Oxford and Mr. Fulke Greville—rushed down from the castle to lend the miller a hand. They had been watching the fireworks in honour of Elizabeth's visit to Warwick, and had seen a fireball land on the thatched mill roof. We don't know what the noble Earl and the gallant gentleman managed to save—if anything—but we do know that the guests up at the castle were so sorry for Henry Cowper that they took up a collection for him. The sum realized was £28 12s. 8d.

As the Elizabethans loved fireworks, the damage they so often caused was just one of the usual hazards connected with having a good time. And having a good time was a strenuous business, particularly when it came to outdoor sports. "Sometimes their necks are broken, sometimes their backs, sometimes their legs, sometimes their arms; sometimes one part thrust out of joint sometimes another; sometimes their noses gush out blood, sometimes their eyes start out . . . the best goeth not scot free but is either sore wounded, crazed and bruised so that he dieth of it."[1]

187

The Elizabethans at Home

This is not a description of various poor wretches stretched upon the rack, it is merely a contemporary account of the game of football as played with great delight and gusto by the Elizabethans. By all accounts there must have been almost as much blood let in sport as was let by physicians.

At cudgel play—a sport much favoured at country fairs and on village greens—it was a small matter for the loser to be concussed or to end with a fractured skull, as the prime object of the game was to draw your opponent's blood by a good hefty blow on the head with a stout club. A red streak pouring from the scalp down the face signified the loser—conscious or unconscious. The winner might, happily, escape with broken arm or dislocated shoulder.

Wrestling and broadsword encounters were equally liked and equally likely to imperil life and limb. Crushed ribs in wrestling must have been a commonplace, and country and village sports were rougher and bloodier than those practised by the more sophisticated, even Spenser's "Calidore" nearly broke his opponent's neck in a wrestling match and Calidore was a model of courtesy.

Courtesy originally meant the elegance of manners practised by courtier or courtesan. It was much thought of in Italy where books on good manners and courteous behaviour—following on Castiglione's *Il Cortigiano*—were very popular reading. Even a Borgia banquet was a thing of mannered elegance and calculated beauty. Rough, practical jokes were frowned upon as barbarous, although poisoning an invited guest or one's wife was not—if done with sufficient finesse. To the Italians of the era, the least courteous, the most barbaric, and the dirtiest race on earth were the Germans. While even Boccaccio, earlier on, had spoken of French savagery, Spanish coarseness and English craft. So, judged by Italian standards we were still just a pack of crafty barbarians enjoying barbarous and meaningless sports. Nevertheless, the Elizabethan courtier, gentleman and noble prided himself on his prowess at running, jumping, fencing, shooting and in the tylt yard.

Of Pleasures and Pastimes

At Whitehall there was a "tylt rail", bowling alleys, cock-pits and tennis-courts built by the Queen's father who had enjoyed them all in his extravagant fashion. The Queen, it appears, was more keen on watching tylts than tennis since the tylt was a colourful affair, full of panache and flattery, pageantry and rivalry, and it centred around her. Tennis figures less prominently in Elizabeth's time than in Henry's (women did not play). Henry had, when younger, been so keen on the game that once when

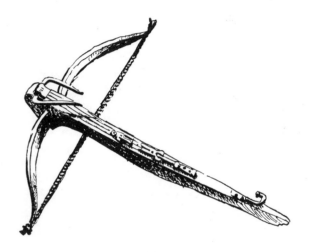

in France he played it day after day laying enormous wagers—as much as 2,000 crowns—on himself. He cannot have been as good on the tennis-court as in the tylt yard for he invariably lost. Katherine of Aragon, in the interests of economy, finally persuaded him to stop.

Archery, riding, hunting, hawking and less strenuous sports such as bowling, pall mall, skittles, quoits and fishing were courtier and country favourites. Fishing, pall mall (possibly an early version of croquet) and bowling were much favoured by the ladies and most of them went in for riding and hunting as

The Elizabethans at Home

well. The Queen was a superb horsewoman* and no mean shot with the cross-bow. She could bring down a buck with the best of them, and so enjoyed riding and hunting that at Nonsuch in 1600 when she was sixty-seven, she was out on horseback every second day. In a letter which Leicester wrote to Burghley, during the Queen's stay at Kenilworth, he says, "Even by and by Her Majesty is going to the forest to kill some bucks with her bow, as she hath done in the park this morning. God be thanked, she is very merry and well-disposed now." Previously she had been in a very bad temper because something had gone wrong with the supply of ale and beer—it was far too strong.

Stag, roe, and buck—all great houses had a deer park and there were many parks and forests belonging to the crown—hare, badger, otter, boar and even the goat were quarry, but "the pursuers or conquerors of the chase (speaking of hunting only) are but one kind of creatures, namely, hounds".[2]

The Elizabethan ear for music was carried even into the kennel. In a most wonderful description of hounds "dew-lapped like Thessalian bulls" Shakespeare says they are "matched in the mouth like bells",† and Gervase Markham tells us how to match them; "If you would have your kennels for sweetness of cry then you must compound it of some large dogs that have deep, solemn mouths . . . which must as it were bear the bass in consort, then a double number of roaring and loud-ringing mouths which must bear the counter tenor, then some hollow, plain, sweet mouths which must bear the mean or middle part and so with these three parts of music you shall make your cry perfect."

* Rathgeb remarks that in England "Horses are abundant, yet, although low and small they are very fleet; the riding horses are geldings and are generally excellent. The Queen has forbidden any horse to be exported out of the kingdom without license." (Also see 4th Eliza. Black Letter, Proclamation.) Yet in 1580, Elizabeth imported six Hungarian horses to draw her coach. They were light greys with manes and tails dyed orange.

† *A Midsummer Night's Dream.*

Of Pleasures and Pastimes

As the middle- and upper-class Elizabethan family could pick up a music-book and sight-read the parts straight off it is hardly surprising they so delighted in the choral effects of the hounds when they opened or hit a scent.

Hounds apart, the Elizabethans were as doited about dogs as we are. "There is no country that may (as I take it) compare with ours in number, excellency and diversity of dogs", says Harrison, who had probably never set foot outside England, and he enumerates them at length. Hounds and curs. Of the latter or "homely" kind, were shepherd's curs and the mastiff—also known as the tie or band dog because it was kept tied up lest it should do "hurt abroad". Harrison, at one time kept a mastiff and the great beast was so devoted to Harrison's children that whenever parson-papa picked up a stick to chastise his offspring the dog refused to allow the punishment and gently took the stick from Harrison's hand. But mastiffs, usually, were extremely savage and used for bear- and bull-baiting and even for lion-baiting—all of them very popular spectator sports of the day. There were two famous bear-gardens on the south bank of the Thames where mastiffs were kept and trained for the sport—a favourite Sunday diversion.

Yet the Elizabethans were not, generally speaking, as cruel to animals as they were to each other. John Harford, Mayor of Coventry, was walking one day, in the surrounding fields with his two greyhounds when he met William Haly, walking his spaniel. Either the Mayor's greyhounds attacked the spaniel or Haly feared they would because to save his dog he beat the Mayor's. The Mayor to save his greyhounds, beat Haly. Haly died of the beating and Harford was deprived of his office—by order of the Queen.

Lap-dogs were much favoured by ladies—especially the Maltese spaniel—the smaller the better. Harrison has no use for these "sybaritical puppies" or for the type of woman who affected them. He is very scathing about this fashion in dogs. "Meet play fellows", he calls them, "for mincing mistresses to bear in their bosoms, keep company in their chambers . . . and lick their lips as they lie like young Dianas in their wagons and coaches." Such women loved their dogs better than their children, he says sharply, and is very leery indeed—as well he might be—of the standard excuse that a dog borne in the bosom is a cure for a weak stomach.

Elizabeth may not have gone quite so far as the young Dianas gadding about in their wagons and coaches but she certainly had several lap-dogs. Zuccaro's sketch of her made in 1575 (now in the British Museum), shows an odd little dog sitting on a pillar to the right and behind the Queen. M. Gheerhaert's portrait* shows Elizabeth, full length, with the sword of state and a small, shaggy dog at her feet. The dog looks as if it had dropped from an equally small, shaggy fan the Queen holds in her left hand. In fairness, it must be admitted that neither dog looks like a bosom companion or a "sybaritical puppy". Christopher Hatton also had his portrait painted with his dog—an animal which looks for all the world like a dyspeptic, pigmy lion.† Sir John Harington was devoted to his dog, Bungay, so it seems very obvious that devotion to dogs was as much a part of the Englishness of the English, then as now. Just as country sports were and are, although they have changed in character.

Country sports and games of a less violent order than cudgel-

* Duke of Portland's Collection.

† Attributed to Cornelius Ketel (in the possession of the Trustees of Winchelsea Settled Estate).

Of Pleasures and Pastimes

play included such pastimes as Blindman's Buff—or Hoodman's Blind—Leap Frog, Prisoner's Base, and Barley Break. Barley Break was very similar to Prisoner's Base but "home" was, appositely or not, called "Hell". All Hid, was Hide-and-Seek played out of doors and as popular with adults as with children, probably for a very different reason. Dun, or Dun-in-the-Mire was a singularly unattractive game played with a log of wood. The log, or dun (dun meant cart-horse) was supposed to have fallen into the mire, or if there were a real mire handy which more often than not there was, the log was pitched into it. The game was to get it out. Each player tried and each attempted to obstruct the others. As often as possible the log was allowed to fall on someone's foot. Presumably, he who finished with a single toe unbroken won. Loggets was a kind of rustic bowls and Span Counter, a boys' game.

Indoor amusements were no less varied if less bloody. The new long tables in the new long galleries were used for Shovel-Board, or Shove-Penny, but the counter or penny was of silver. The most popular coin for the game was the Edward—the broad shilling of Edward VI—so the shovel board was known as the Edward board, particularly in country inns and taverns. Chess was very popular. Backgammon or Tables and a similar game called Tick-Tack, or Tric-Trac were quieter pastimes as were Draughts. Billiards though not generally known was also played.

Cards and dicing—always the province of the sharper at fairs and in taverns—were also popular in the home. Cheating cannot have been regarded as quite the same crime as it is now for Sir Hugh Platt mentions as one of his happier inventions, a ring cleverly set with a tiny mirror whereby the wearer could see his opponent's cards. He claims that such a ring will guard *against* cheating but it sounds as if it could equally well encourage the very thing it was designed to put down.

Card games such as One-and Thirty, Noddy, Primero, Gleek, Pope July, were extremely popular. In Primero, a game which the Queen much enjoyed, the cards had three times their original

The Elizabethans at Home

value; four were dealt each player and the principal groupings were flush, as in Poker; prime—or one card of each suit and point—reckoned as in Piquet. In Gleek, a three-handed game, twos and threes were removed, twelve cards dealt to the players and the remaining eight could be bought in. The object was to get three cards alike, so Gleek may have been an early great-grandparent of Rummy. When the Queen played and won, she insisted on being paid on the spot (a habit which some Victorian historians considered to be very un-Queen like).

The card game which originated in England during this period —and the game which is still the most popular of all in rural areas—was Whist. It was then called Triumph—Triumph gave us the word "trump." Trumps, before the development of Triumph, were called Tiddy, Tumbler, Tib, Tom and Towser, while a pack of cards was called a pair or a deck and the knave was known as the jack; both the last two terms are still in use in Canada and the United States.

Dice games must have been even more numerous than card games, and even more of a trap for the unwary and the innocent visiting inns and taverns, particularly in London. There was a very brisk trade in false dice, made in quantity by prisoners in the King's Bench and Marshalsea prisons and, possibly, in the Fleet and Clink as well. From the names of the different kinds of false dice it would seem that you bought your crooked bones according to your favourite game. There were barred cater-treys which never turned up fours or threes; barred cinque-deuces, barred six-aces and their opposites called "flat" cater-treys, flat cinque-deuces and flat six-aces. There were "bristle" dices where an invisible bristle fixed on one face influenced the throw. "Contraries" were loaded, as were Fullams or Fulhams (so named because Fulham was a notorious resort of crooks and sharpers). There were High and Low Men, loaded to cast high or low, long dice, with two sides smaller than the other faces; "Light Graviers", possibly light on one side and heavy on the other and dice made with a cavity which were known as "Gourds".

Whether the Elizabethans cheated like mad at cards and dice at home is difficult to say. They may have, as it was a sort of no-holds-barred kind of life they lived anyway and, if some contemporary accounts are to be believed, rogues and beggars made up about half the population. Certainly, those not gifted with a natural talent for petty crime could be trained in a school for rogues. Even children were taught to cut purses under the tuition of various sixteenth-century Fagins. Few respectable citizens were safe in a crowd or at a fair, unless they were constantly on guard.

This, however, didn't keep anyone away from a fair or show of any kind. The Elizabethans adored fairs. Popular festivals were regularly kept up all over the country; the last fling before Lent on Shrove Tuesday, the "Church Ale" on Whit-Monday, the Twelve Days of Christmas with its Lord of Misrule whom many regarded almost as the devil incarnate. There were also lesser fairs and festivals of a regional and local character. Hallowe'en —the old Celtic New Year—was more of a country festival and the farther west or north you went the more it was celebrated with seed-cake and ducking for apples. This festival crossed the Atlantic and is still kept there, rather riotously, on October 31st. May Day was primarily a country festival—though even in London the milkmaids wreathed their pails with flowers and danced in the streets. In the country, the Maypole, painted or garlanded with flowers, was put up in every village and danced around by men, women and children—not as a self-conscious survival or revival of an ancient tradition but as a natural part of a living festival. In some parts of the country people would set a tree in the front yard and deck it with flowers as we now ornament a Christmas tree. Children went from door to door singing May carols, and the now "old" custom of singing the "Hymnus Eucharisticus" on the top of Wolsey's Tower, Oxford, as the clock strikes five on May morning was a fairly new custom then. It was part of a Requiem Mass sung annually for the repose of the soul of Elizabeth's grandfather, Henry VII.

With superb illogicality but praiseworthy national fervour the English kept May Day not as a relic of a pagan religious festival but as the day consecrated to Robin Hood and Maid Marian. Thus, archery and Morris dancing were part of the festival. In addition, there was feasting and drinking, the usual country sports of the break-bone kind, and much music.

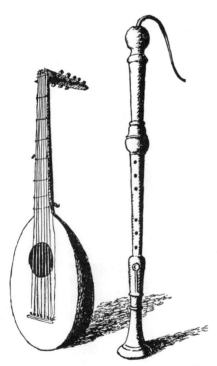

And here is where the Elizabethans startled the rest of the world. Our painting, our sculpture could not touch the work of the Renaissance masters of Europe but we were acknowledged the most musical nation on earth. The Queen was extremely musical, a talent she inherited from her father and

Of Pleasures and Pastimes

also, although this is often forgotten, from her mother, Anne Boleyn, who was most accomplished. We are told that Mary Tudor, though less musical than Elizabeth, at the age of three entertained "three French gentlemen of rank", [3] by playing upon the virginals. She had, poor baby, "a light touch with much grace and velocity" according to one of the gentlemen.

Music was, in the true and real sense of the word, a popular and a family art. The average Elizabethan could take his part in one of the new and exquisite madrigals being written with an ease which would astonish a madrigal singer today. Books of music and musical instruments were left lying about in great and less great houses so that guests could amuse themselves with music— as we now provide thrillers, bedside anthologies, T.V., wireless and crossword puzzles. (Lutes were even provided in barbers'

shops.) After dinner it was quite common for family, guests and servants to get together and sing. In country inns—and our inns were excellent, clean and providing good service and food—the landlord, guests, the local squire, the yeomen and their families would all get together and spend several hours singing with such skill and enjoyment that foreigners were astonished no less by the art than by this display of democratic tendencies.

At every town and village the Queen visited on a progress, music played a most important part in the

N

festivities. On one occasion, at Norwich, a musical surprise was planned to speed the Queen on her way as she left the city. An enormous hole was dug by the river and camouflaged with green canvas and branches. As Elizabeth passed by, river nymphs popped up and made little rhymed speeches while musicians, concealed in the pit, played so that the music seemed to be issuing from the earth. Unhappily, a terrible great cloud-burst rather spoiled the intended effect and half-drowned the subterranean musicians.

To the love of music was joined the love of dancing. Everyone danced. Elizabeth was so enamoured of dancing that it is said, wrongly, Christopher Hatton owed his preferment solely because of his ability to dance. This popular misconception does both Hatton and the Queen an injustice. He may have, in the first place, caught the Queen's eye by his beautiful dancing, but Elizabeth was no fool. She played favourites with her courtiers but she chose her chief ministers and law officers with such unfailing distinction that they grew old and died in her service. When Leicester, jealous of Hatton, offered to introduce Elizabeth to a dancing-master who, he assured her, danced much better than Hatton, Elizabeth answered, "Pish! I will not see *your* man—it is his trade."

"She takes great pleasure in dancing and music," de Maisse writes to his sovereign Henry IV, in 1598. "She told me she entertained at least sixty musicians; in her youth she danced very well and composed measures and music and had played them herself and danced them. She takes such pleasure in it that when her maids dance she follows the cadence with her hand and foot. She rebukes them if they do not dance to her liking and without a doubt she is mistress of the art having learnt in the Italian manner to dance high."

Mary Stuart, so Sir James Mevil told the Queen, danced "not so high nor disposedly" as Elizabeth. This sounds as if Elizabeth were a rather stately dancer, but "disposedly" also meant merrily.

There must have been hundreds of dances—pavanes, galliards,

allemands—the names of some are delightful. Lady Carey's Dompe or Dump—a slow dance; Flaunting Two—a country dance; Mopsy's Tune; the Bishop of Chester's Jig; the Spanish Lady; Farnaby's Woodycock; Nobody's Jig; Dusty My Dear. There was also a craze for Scots dances such as, All Christian Men Dance (surely John Knox couldn't have approved of this), Long Flat Foot of Garioch, The Lamb's Wind, Leaves Green, Shake-a-Trot, the Alman Hey, Rank at the Root, and the Dead Days were among those which came south of the border.

On a larger and more ornate scale were masques and pageants —and no Elizabethan would miss seeing one if he could help it. Masques and pageants given for the Queen are inexhaustible— and exhausting—but there were Puritan voices raised against mummery, as against nearly all other pleasures and pastimes. Bacon's Puritan mother writes to her son, Anthony, that she trusts "they will not mum, masque or sinfully revel at Gray's Inn" where Anthony and his better-known brother Francis lived. Among Francis's contemporaries mumming and masquing at Gray's Inn was Lawrence Washington.* On February 7th 1589 they were elected together into the Society as Ancients.

Four years before this election there had been a Gesta Gray-orum—a masque and ordinary revels—of which Lady Bacon certainly would not have approved. Jokes, practical and other-wise, played an important part in all revels and among the verbal jokes at this one were such hilarious efforts as, "If any woman be subject to the falling sickness she must not travel Westward Ho because she must avoid the Isle of Man . . ." Hardly had the audience had time to wipe away the tears of laughter when the joker continued "and for this evil let her for a charm always have her legs crossed when she is not walking".

Another joke which must have delighted the Xenophobic English was "No native physician be excellent for all excellent simples are foreign". And what of this? "A cannibal is the loving-est man to his enemy; for willingly no man eats what he loves

* A cousin of Lawrence Washington of Sulgrave Manor.

not." One fell from paroxysm to paroxysm of laughter. "A great lady should not wear her own hair, for that's as mean as coat of her own spinning." Or "Musicians are healthy because they live by good Air." Such jokes were so well thought of and so popular that they were collected and printed. Joke books had a great vogue all over the country.

The theatre too, was enormously popular, though it offended Puritans. Actors were often beautifully costumed, frequently because noblemen on their death left some of their clothes to their servants who made a profit by selling them to actors. Thus, a stage Lord might be clad in the expensive and ornate garments of a real, if defunct, Lord. Realism of a most horrid kind was

part of the joy of the Elizabethan theatre. In battles and murders blood and guts liberally strewed the stage—having been procured for the purpose from a local butcher. *Titus Andronicus*, which most of us today find more than repulsive, is a perfect indication of the taste for horrors.

Plays were acted in broad daylight without the aid of scenery, lights or orchestra, though trumpet calls, flourishes, tuckets and alarums are frequent in stage directions. The actor, unsupported by scenery and not cut off from audience by a curtain, had to gain his effects by a direct attack on the emotions and the imagination. Yet stage carpenters must have been ambitious and resourceful. Stage directions from the Rose theatre include,

Of Pleasures and Pastimes

"Exit Venus, if you conveniently can let a chair come down from the top of the stage and draw ⸜er up." And even more difficult, "Upon this prayer she departeth, and a flame of fire appeareth from beneath, and Radagon is swallowed." Or more simply, and no doubt very effectively, "Jonas the prophet cast out of the Whale's belly upon the stage." But actors had props too. An inventory of the properties belonging to the Admirals Company in 1598 lists a variety of curious props; a Hell mouth, a tomb of Dido, a bedstead, a pair of stairs for Phaeton, Old Mahomet's head, one golden fleece, one bay tree, one ghost's crown, one chain of dragons, Neptune's fork and garland, Tamberlain's bridle, Tantalus's tree, Mercury's wings, Cupid's bow, the Pope's mitre, Kent's wooden leg and—most sinister indeed—"a caldron for the Jew".

Countless Elizabethan plays must have perished but, as continuous runs were unknown, the number of new plays written and produced must have been enormous. During one fortnight in February the Admirals' men on twelve acting days acted in ten diff;rent plays. Thus the actor was a busy man with no time for elaborate rehearsing and, in an emergency, he could improvise at length. Italian actors were so brilliant at improvisation that provided they were given a story or plot they could make up the whole play as they went along.

Audiences, unsophisticated in their tastes, loved high-sounding words and long speeches. Heroes had to be heroes, villains villainous. Terror must be a real physical thing. Tragedy was not muted nor was comedy polite. Playwrights knew what audiences wanted and gave it to them in full measure. Plays were stuffed with long speeches, rhetoric, classical and mythological allusions.

So were books; Harrison is full of long diversions and harkings back to Latin authors. Reading, to judge by the number of books and pamphlets, broadsides and ballads printed must have been one of the major pastimes. A half-century of printing, together with far better and wider educational facilities for more people meant books to read and people to read them. The Elizabethans in fact developed a voracious appetite for reading-matter. And reading-matter was turned out in such quantity that Thomas Coryat remarked, gloomily, that there would soon be more books than readers.

Londoners bought books from stalls clustered round St. Paul's cathedral. Country people were served with ballads, broadsides, pamphlets, jest and riddle books by itinerant pedlars. The new, round world of the Elizabethans was what the Universe is to us. Their space travel is our known geography. Travel books were so popular that it seemed people could never have enough of them—which is how Harrison came to write his book. It was intended as a part of a much larger work undertaken by Reginald Wolfe, printer to the Queen who, planned to bring out "a universall Cosmographie of the whole world, and therewith also certaine particular histories of every known nation". For the historical part he engaged Ralph Holinshed and others. But, after twenty-five years of work, Wolfe died. His backers, afraid to continue so vast an enterprise, decided to do only Holinshed plus a description of Britain and England. Harrison had long been working on a Chronologie of his own, so he was asked to furnish the necessary descriptions—which he did, though he says in his introduction that he "scrambled up . . . this foul frizeled Treatise".

Part of the desire to read travel books arose from the fact that travel and exploration in the public imagination spelled riches.* Those who never travelled farther than the next village for Michaelmas fair took to voyaging and discovering treasure through books. Sir Walter Ralegh's short book with the long title— *The Discovery of the Large, Rich and Bewtiful Empire of Guiana, with a Relation of the Great, Golden City of Manoa (which the spanyards call El Dorado) and the Province of Emeria, Arromaia, Amapaia and other Countries with Rivers adioyning*

* The capital put up for Drake's voyage around the world was £5,000. The return was £600,000.

went into three editions in the year of publication (1596). Who could resist such words as Large, Rich and Bewtiful Empire, or Great Golden City or the strange poetry of Emeria, Arromaia, Amapaia?—certainly not the Elizabethans even if most of them disliked and mistrusted the author. Arrogant, they had heard he was, and he looked foreign, too, with his dark face and eyes, like a Spaniard.

An entirely different kind of sailor-author was Henry Robarts who produced pamphlet after pamphlet glorifying British seamanship and the exploits of privateers. Robarts, a staunch believer in patriotic propaganda even manages to attribute acts of high piracy to the providence of God. This was a very popular notion of the day. But the idea that material success, no matter how achieved, is signal proof of God's favour was neither invented by, nor did it die with, the Elizabethans.

A popular ballad of the time puts national fervour in a nutshell

> You gallants all o' the British blood
> Why don't you sail o' the ocean flood?
> I protest you're not all worth a filbert
> If once compared to Sir Humphrey Gilbert.

Yet what would the sailors have done without Richard Hakluyt? His was the greatest name of the time and his *Principal Navigations* is still one of the finest books in our language. Hakluyt, like Harrison, was a parson and, like Harrison and Robarts, was a propagandist for his country. He believed that the maritime power of England had a mission through trade and colonization, to "increase the Queen's dominions, enrich her coffers, and reduce many Pagans to the faith of Christ". Times change. Today we are reversing the process which the first Elizabethans set in motion. But it should be remembered they were as firm in their belief that it was right to initiate the process as we are that it is right to reverse it.

With our own interest in science and science-fiction, it is perhaps a little surprising to find the Elizabethans no less interested in what they termed science. With few physicians available every householder felt obliged to know something of medicine. With stars so influential it would be folly not to know something of astrology and astronomy. With alchemy always on the verge of discovering the philosopher's stone it would be stupid not to keep abreast of news in this field. The, to us, almost unintelligible and seemingly endless jargon of *The Alchemist* was understood by the middle- and upper-class Englishman far better than we understand our own mushrooming scientific language.

Digests, which we think of as typically modern, were also popular. John Maplet, in 1567 brought out a positively encyclopaedic digest designed for the busy and the unlearned man, under the charming title *A Greene Forest, or a Naturall Historie*. Maplet wanted to simplify university training and make it available to the ordinary man. His *Greene Forest* was a digest and home-study course rolled into one. Divided into three sections, Animal, Vegetable and Mineral, its information was necessarily brief but what facts there were, were set out in English translated and condensed from the Latin treatises used at the universities. Maplet popularized Aristotle, Pliny, Theophrastus, Dioscorides and Cardan and brought them within reach of those who had neither Latin nor Greek; just as Chapman, but for other reasons, "Englished" Homer. Most of the erudite works of the day were written in Latin, and it was a courtier accomplishment to translate various books from Latin into English. Elizabeth, in her later years, occupied herself in spare minutes by translating Boethius as a pastime.

Of the digest type—and equally popular—were books of miscellaneous information. Books of "secrets", such as that attributed to Albertus Magnus, ran into edition after edition. Magnus's book contained esoteric lore about herbs, stones, beasts, as well as useful information about the seven planets "governing the Nativitie of Children". Children born on the same day, same hour, same year were supposed to have a strong affinity for each other—Synastria it was called—and Synastria explained the closeness of Elizabeth and Robert Dudley—or so he said. For it was believed that the Queen and he shared their birthdays right to the very moment of birth. It may not be true, but if they believed it, it explains much.

A translation of Antonio de Torquemada's *The Spanish Man-deule of Miracles* had a great vogue, for the age was as credulous

in its own way as we are in ours. Among the wonders recounted and lapped up, was that of a woman wrecked on an African shore who mated with an ape and produced two sons. This sort of thing was accepted with the excitement and interest as we, until recently, accepted Piltdown Man.

Then there were hundreds of booklets of popular learning of the Teach or Do-it-Yourself variety. Thomas Hill was a most prolific turner-out of such work which let tradesmen, the un-Latined and un-Greeked, into the secrets of Nature. These revelations included useful information plus a certain amount of mumbo-jumbo on gardening, astrology, astronomy, physiognomy, palmistry, botany, medicine, chemistry, bee-keeping, dream-interpretation and prediction; to say nothing of a secret recipe for turning water into wine. But the new horizons of the physical world had certainly led to new horizons of the mind, and trades-men and apprentices could now speak with more knowledge than the clerk of the Middle Ages. There were no longer two classes there were three, and the new middle-class, always en-larging, took to books and reading with the same avidity it took to trade. Men were not equal. If they had been there would be no point in bettering oneself. The tradesman's son—and the tradesman may have started as a countryman—very often went to Oxford or Cambridge. And many a tradesman's son earned, or tried to earn, a living by his pen. Christopher Marlowe's father was a cobbler; Gabriel Harvey's, a rope-maker; Robert Herrick's a goldsmith, Anthony Munday's, a draper; George Peele's a salter; John Webster's, a merchant tailor; John Donne's an iron-monger. William Shakespeare's father began as a glover. . . . and ended as a prosperous burgess of Stratford. There seems no reason at all for deciding that by birth and education Shakespeare couldn't have written Shakespeare. He could read and there was much to read. And like the brilliant Italians, once given a plot, he could improvise. Elizabethan authors on the whole were lucky; they had a public so eager to read and to learn that almost anything in print sold well—from the newly Englished masterpieces of the ancient world right down to the most ephemeral ballad.

And of ephemeral reading-matter there was no lack. Broad-sides and ballads were innumerable and were, in a sense, the equivalent of our newspapers. Nearly everything could be, and was, translated into ballad form. To a nation which loved songs—even bad ones—as much as the English did, the ballad was obviously designed to be extremely popular. It did not matter how scurrilous the content nor how appalling the verse; complaints against taxes and monopolies, the purported last thoughts of executed criminals, the hatred of Pius V, the adventures of Drake and Hawkins, the competition engendered by the importation of foreign artisans, the knavery of tradesmen, the evils of wine, women and tobacco all were subjects for ballad maker and monger. The common man of the day lived in an age half-way between the Troubador and the Tabloid.

As for fiction,there was plenty of that. Sir Philip Sidney's *The Arcadia* was very popular in court circles as was Lyly's *Euphues: the Anatomy of Wit*. There was Robert Greene's *Menaphon: Camilla's Alarm to Sleeping Euphues*; and his pastoral romances such as *Pandosto: The Triumph of Time* (Shakespeare liked this so well that he borrowed the plot for *The Winter's Tale*). Greene, who called Shakespeare an "upstart crow" was a prolific writer and the big best-seller of the day. Thomas Lodge, who abandoned law for literature and literature for medicine, was popular too. His pastoral romance, *A Margarite from America*, contains a scene wherein the heroine Margarite, a good girl, and Fawnia, a naughty one, meet a lion in a forest. The lion devours Fawnia but lays his head in Margarite's lap and licks her milk-white hand. The lion, being royal, punishes vice and rewards virtue. No Elizabethan would question the lion's behaviour as the medieval belief that moral goodness was recognized and rewarded by the king of the beasts was, if not fully believed, still accepted as a very proper thing. Lodge's other pastoral romance *Rosalynde: Euphues Golden Legend*, written during a voyage to the Canaries, was also extremely popular. (Shakespeare liked this so well he used it as his plot for *As You Like It*.)

On a rather less-exalted level than Sidney, Greene, and Lodge were translations from the Spanish, French, and Italian.The taste for Spanish romances, endless and inane, told with little skill and less artistry, destroys any illusions that we may have that the literary taste of the first Elizabethans was universally good. Middle-class readers were less concerned with taste than with

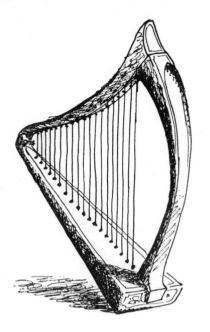

morals (though moral excellence was certainly not always found in the original Spanish romances). Here, again, one sees a touch of the Victorian in them—or again it might be called a further example of the Englishness of the English. Yet there were realistic and low-life novels too. Some were based on the erotic novelle of the Italians like *The Palace of Pleasure*. Others were less novels than pamphlets, and exposed the tricks practised by rogues on "rabbits". Greene wrote four booklets on this theme, "for the benefit of Gentlemen, Apprentices, Country Farmers and Yeomen". They became known as "Cony-Catching" pamphlets and detail very vividly the well-laid snares and traps set to catch bumpkins and other innocents unaccustomed to the wicked ways of London.

Yet with all this new reading-matter, the Elizabethans still dearly loved Pliny for he was full of marvels and wonders. "Dragons there are in Ethiopia", he says, "ten fathoms long" and few Elizabethans doubted or had any desire to doubt that this was so, although it is possible that some may have disbelieved that there were wild dogs with human hands and feet. And the exemplary conduct of the lion, though not a native beast, must certainly have reassured children. The king of the beasts was full of "nobleness and clemency and will sooner assail men than women and *never* young children unless it be for great famine".*

* Nor would the king of the beasts destroy his human colleague in office. Even Falstaff knew that. "The lion will not touch the true prince", he says (*Henry IV*, Part I. ii. 4).

Of Pleasures and Pastimes

The Elizabethan moppet sitting frog-eyed on his three-legged stool while an elder brother or sister read Pliny's *Natural History* aloud must have viewed the lion with an affection and composure unknown to the modern child whose monsters are men from Mars bent on destroying the earth. The sixteenth-century child must have delighted in the dolphin too, "the most swift fish of the sea" who above all other fishes loved "young children and the sound of instruments". The dolphin also loved the human voice and nothing rejoiced him more than to be addressed as "Simon".

Edward Topsell, one time chaplain of St. Botolph's, Aldgate, out-plinied Pliny in the matter of dragons with his book *The History of Serpents*. From this, child and adult learned that the Ethiopian dragon was thirty yards long—a good ten yards longer than the measurements given by Pliny. One variety, the Epidaurian, had a golden-yellow skin; another, a fierce mountain breed, was noted for its eyelids which rattled like brass. The Macedonian kind was the "most tameable" and fortunate Macedonian children kept these dragons as pets "riding upon them and pinching them as they would dogs without any harm and sleeping with them in their beds".

It seems quite contrary to modern opinion to learn that many dragons are not carnivorous and certainly did not roast princesses with a fiery breath and then devour them. Dragons grow fat on eggs. An adult dragon swallows them whole then rolls about until the shells are crushed inside him. A baby dragon can't manage this, so he holds the egg with his tail, pierces it with a handy scale, and then sucks. Nothing was worse for a dragon's digestion than apples. (Is this why a dragon was set to guard the tree which bore the golden apples of the Hesperides?); if forced, by some unhappy circumstance, to eat one he wisely eats wild lettuce to counteract the poison. Some dragons appear to be such charming and devoted saurians—one loved a neatherd for his beautiful golden hair and brought him a present every day—that it is a little sad the medieval church fathers felt in necessary to choose the dragon as the personification of sin and Satan.

The Elizabethans obviously must have divided dragons into two categories—good and bad. Henry Cowper the miller probably had a poor opinion of the dragon who damaged his mill. But those who had made the creature, meant him to represent the splendid golden dragon which long ago King Arthur's father had taken for his standard. It was this, the red-gold dragon of Wales, which the Tudor family bore as their badge and which, with the lion, now supported the English shield.

The dragon was one of Elizabeth Tudyr's beasts.

CHAPTER EIGHT

Of Gardens and Gardening

A ROYAL Garden Party in the time of the first Elizabeth wasn't something the Queen gave; it was given for the Queen. On her summer progresses if the weather were fine—and even if it weren't—part of the entertainment offered by her hosts invariably took place in the fine new gardens of the fine new houses which were completely transformed for the occasion.

Thus, the Earl of Hertford, having been warned that the Queen intended to pay him a surprise visit on September 20th, 1591, prepared his park and gardens at Elvetham accordingly. He must have been warned of the surprise some time in advance for he had a miniature crescent-shaped lake scooped out (by hand) and, on a hillside overlooking the lake, he built a summer-house—although technically summer would have expired by the 21st. The summer-house was a splendid affair; the interior hung with arras, the ceiling decorated with ivy leaves, and the floor strewn with rushes and sweet herbs. The exterior resembled an outsize rustic bower as the whole of the framework was concealed by boughs, branches and clusters of ripe hazel nuts.

Elizabeth arrived at three o'clock to find her path to the house flatteringly obstructed by large blocks deliberately strewn about by green-eyed Envy. These were swiftly and joyously removed. Then six garlanded girls carpeted the rest of the way with flowers.

On the Tuesday, which was wet, a great garden fête had been arranged:

> Eliza is the fairest Queen
> That ever trod upon this green.
> Eliza's eyes are like the stars
> Inducing peace, subduing wars.

sang a chorus of sprites and elves (the elves were there as a play on the name Elvetham). And they went on singing line after line after tedious line. It seems to have been a watery and musical affair all round culminating in the summer-pavilion beside the newly dug lake.

Here Elizabeth sat, watched, and listened to "three virgins in a pinnace" who played a "Scottish Jig" on cornets, and to Neaera and three voices who, "to please Eliza's ear with harmony", sang "to one lute".[1] These gaieties were followed by other "sea people" who frolicked about in a most sportive manner with "a large squirt". Here, too, was an island fort in the lake—defended in mock battle by armed men—to say nothing of a "Snail Mount". This resembled a monster with horns and was full of "wild fire". Food and drink were lavishly provided, Nereus presented the Queen with a jewel in a red purse and—"it rained extremely".

It sounds a perfectly ghastly garden party, what with the squirt, the wild fire and the rain. But the Elizabethans loved gardens and being in a garden; from the Queen down to the smallest cottager. And wherever the Queen went over the dreadful roads, through tiny villages, past outlying and lonely cottages or farms, her "good people" rushed to strew the way with flowers or to present her with nosegays picked from their own front or back yards. Here our North American cousins in their use of the word "yard" are nearer the Elizabethans than we are when we speak of a garden. For "geard" is Anglo-Saxon and "yerd" is Middle-English and both are nearer the first Elizabeth than our corruption of the French "jardin".

Nevertheless, the true, the astonishing, the very English passion for making things grow began during the reign and a little before. It was in the sixteenth century that gardens and gardening became a popular as distinct from an exclusive art. The breaking-up of the monastic estates, the passing of land into many hands, the great prosperity, the increase in the building of houses—prodigy and otherwise—made gardens and gardening more important to many people than ever before. Furthermore, the persecution of the Protestants abroad meant that many of them sought sanctuary in England and they brought with them new crafts and skills. The Huguenots from the Lowlands fleeing religious persecution, were, in particular, noted as gardeners.

Gardens were often designed with a house. If a newly rich Elizabethan bought a "platt and upright" from an "architect", such as John Thorpe, Thorpe designed the garden, too. It was no mere adjunct or afterthought but was believed to require as much, if not more, skill as designing a house. "Men come to build stately," Bacon says in his exquisite essay *Of Gardens*, "sooner than to garden finely". This certainly sounds as if he thought gardening the more difficult art; an art which he practised himself as he laid out the walks and gardens of Gray's Inn.

Yet it would be a great mistake to think Elizabethan gardens in the least like ours. Apart from the fact that we have many more and different kinds of flowers, the whole conception of the garden was different. We belong to the landscape and artful wilderness school following on Kent and Capability Brown, while Elizabethan ornamental-shrub gardens were distinctly Eastern in character and design. The ancient four-fold plot, as described in Genesis ("and a river went out of Eden to water the garden and from thence it was parted and became into four heads") still survived.

Eastern gardens, due to the constant need for irrigation, were invariably laid out on this plan; a plan which may still be seen in the design of certain Persian carpets. Briefly, it was a cross of water dividing the garden into four squares or rectangular plots. These plots, if the area were large, were further reticulated by

o

smaller canals or ditches. The "chess-board" gardens of Western Europe from the Crusades to Stuart times follow this pattern, although, certainly, there can have been very little need for this kind of close irrigation in England. But it was the Crusaders who had brought the idea back with them, along with leprosy, captives, strange beasts and articles of commerce, and the Elizabethans still stuck to this basic design, though they added many "novelties".

The Elizabethan garden was, therefore, a square divided into four plots, not by water but by walks and paths. Bacon advises his contemporaries that "the garden is best to be square encompassed on all four sides by a stately arched hedge". This was the ideal. Gardens were often walled, though the battlemented walls of medieval gardens were no longer necessary or even customary. Inside the wall, and at some distance from it, there was usually a hedge of various shrubs or small trees such as whitethorn, privet, sweetbriar and the occasional rose "enlaced together" often with windows or arches cut through so that from this hedged walk one could walk round the perimeter of the garden and see into it. Bacon's idea of a fair hedge was one planted upon a flower-embroidered bank. Above the arches little turrets were to be set large enough to hold a cage of birds "and over the space between the arches some other little figure with broad plates of round coloured glass gilt for the sun to play upon". Alternatively, lattice-work or poles were set along the walk and plants trained up them to arch overhead. It is very probable that, among other climbers the vine was used for this purpose.

There were other and more modest ways of fencing a garden too; pailings of "drie thorne" or "white thorne" "artely laid" were recommended by that prolific writer Thomas Hill who sometimes wrote his gardening books under the enchanting name

of Didymus Mountain. He also suggests a novel method of planting a hedge. The gardener was to collect seeds of white-thorn, briars, gooseberries, and barberries in the autumn; steep them in meal, then set them to overwinter in "a long worn roape . . . being in a manner starke rotten". In the spring two furrows about three feet apart were ploughed around the space to be hedged. The rope was easily and conveniently laid in the furrows. Hill assures his readers that within a month "more or less" the seedlings will appear, and within a few years the garden will be compassed by a strong double hedge.

Prodigy houses and manors were fittingly set in great parks and woodland with, beyond, the farms and fields belonging to the owner, but the land immediately around the house was treated formally. Usually there was a forecourt, often walled, with ornamental gateway and lodge on the entrance side—and, if the house were a very grand one like Theobalds, there were other courtyards leading from this. On the kitchen side of the house were the kitchen gardens and the all-important wood yard. The third side was generally given over to orchards while the fourth side was the square or ornamental garden, often connected by walks to the orchard. Thus the house, itself, occupied the central position in an area divided into four plots. And the four-plot plan was again carried out on a smaller and more ornate scale in the square or ornamental garden.

The simplest plan for ornamental gardens was cruciform; four paths leading to a little square or circle in the centre where there was a statue, fountain, mound, or sundial. The approach from a house of any size was usually from a raised terrace which fronted the house. From here the garden as a whole could be surveyed. A broadwalk, or "straightforward" as it was called, usually ran from the terrace across the garden to the far wall and, if the garden were very large, there would be more than one straight-forward. Straightforwards were intersected by other walks running parallel to the terrace. Thus the chess-board design was made.

It may be that this, although of Eastern origin, was an unusually satisfying pattern for the English. Dr. Nikolaus Pevsner has recently pointed out that rectilineal forms—horizontals intersected by perpendiculars—have long been a favourite design or pattern in English Art and Architecture. And it was certainly a favourite, if not the only design, for an Elizabethan ornamental garden.

The spaces between the walks were laid out in knots, mazes or flower-beds, usually in geometric or heraldic designs. Beds were either raised or level with the paths. If raised they were now not so high as in medieval times though they were still faced with brick or stone, or latticed or railed. Flowers were not massed in single blocks of colour but were mixed and contrasted with charming informality. Curiously enough, pots of flowers were often set out on beds already planted with flowers. But sometimes beds contained no flowers at all. They were covered with different coloured sands—a practice of which Bacon thoroughly disapproved. He thought such beds looked little better than tarts, presumably of the open-faced, edible variety. Or one bed might be a Troy town or maze. Such mazes were nearly always low and lavender-cotton was a favourite plant used to make their pigmy walls. Or, again, a bed might be turfed, and by turf the Elizabethans did not mean a shaven lawn. Turf was longish grass starred with small, common wild-flowers, daisies, cowslips, and the golden dent-de-lion.

Turf was also used to make garden seats. These were sometimes built against a wall, sometimes around a tree. The arms were brick, stone, or wood and the seat, though faced with stone, was of earth raised a foot or eighteen inches from the ground and turfed over with ordinary turf, or with sweet-smelling camomile, violets, or pennyroyal. Such seats must have been delightful in warm, dry weather, but impossible otherwise unless covered, which they occasionally were.

But the knot garden, which could occupy a bed or a number of beds was most typical of Tudor times. It came in with the first Tudor, Henry VII, and went out with the last, Elizabeth I. Knots or clusters of shrubs and flowers made up the design as they did, and still do, in certain types of embroidery. The outline was made of close-planted shrubs and the interstices filled with flowers or more usually with different shrubs. Lavender, thrift, dwarf-box (a recent introduction), hyssop, germander, savoury and other sweet-scented shrubs were favourites. They were kept low-clipped and the clippings used for strewing. Some contemporary authorities maintain that herbs and box were never used for bordering paths or outlining knot designs but that "dead material" was preferred. Lead "plain or cut out like unto the battlements of a church", oak boards, tiles, or the shank bones of sheep were highly thought of as decorative edgings. Even better and more fashionable than shank bones were "round white or blewish pebble stones". It seems a little strange that simple and obvious stone-edging shouldn't have been thought of before, but apparently it wasn't. John Parkinson, who was born in 1567 and brought out his great book on gardening as late as 1629, says quite flatly, "It is the newest invention."

The knot gardens at Holyrood were shaped like a fleur-de-lis which must have pleased Mary Queen of Scots. But such gardens could take any form that fancy dictated, and Elizabethans were very fancy. Stars, crescents, concentric circles and even the favourite strap-work all provided motifs for knots. Noblemen and gentlemen frequently had their arms laid out in knots while country housewives spread their linen out to dry on the shrubly knots in their own small, square gardens. The floral clock at Edinburgh is doubtless a descendant of the Elizabethan knot garden and it is the kind of fantasy which would have delighted the Elizabethans if, indeed, they themselves didn't produce something similar. But evidence points to the fact that Elizabethan knot gardens were mainly made up of shrubs, because flowers were few and were mostly spring flowers, at least in the early Elizabethan period. This explains the real meaning of the old nursery song, "Here we come gathering nuts in May"—words which have puzzled so many generations of logical children. The word "nuts" is really a corruption of "knots". Knots of May were clusters of spring flowers gathered from the fields by old custom on May Day. The Queen went gathering knots of May at Lewisham the year before she died. So Elizabethan knot gardens were knotted with perennial shrubs ranging in colour from silver lavender to green box and black yew which, when laid out in designs and patterns, gave the Elizabethan garden both its winter interest and its summer delight.

Garden walks—and there were many of them—were regarded as being of the utmost importance. Broad open ones were turfed, sanded or planted with burnet, wild thyme, watermint, camomile and other sweet-scented herbs which, when trodden on, gave

off a delicious sweetness. Shady alleys with willow, lime, syca-
more, and whitethorn arched overhead; pergolas where the vine
was trained or even the vivid scarlet-runner; arbours, or "roosting
places", were also prominent features of any good-sized garden.
Arbours were often made in trees and were, not uncommonly,
two or three storeys high. There was a famous arbour of this
sort at Cobham where a great lime tree had been so trained that
the branches grew from the trunk in three flat tiers upon which
planks were laid. One imagines that it must have looked rather
like a giant Victorian cake-stand. The first tier, we are informed,
could hold fifty men and there were stairs leading to it from the
ground, as well as stairs leading from it to the upper tiers. But such
arbours were a feature of greater gardens and there were many of
these since a Prodigy House demanded a prodigy garden.

On Elizabeth's very first progress into what Lord Burghley,
on a later occasion, called "the wilds of Kent", she visited Harrison's patron, Sir William Brooke, seventh Lord Cobham, at

Cobham Hall—newly enlarged and rebuilt. The entertainment in the garden made a great impression on a youngster, Francis Thynne. Later in life he set it down on paper.

"In which first year of her Majesty's reign falling in the year 1559", he says, "this Lord did most honourably entertain the Queen with her train at his house of Cobham Hall with sumptuous fare and many delights of rare invention."*

Among the numerous delights and rare inventions which caught young Thynne's eye, was the banqueting house built especially for the visit, "with a goodly gallery thereunto, composed all of green, with several devices of knotted flowers, outposted on each side, with a faire row of hawthorn trees". He relates with obvious pleasure that "Dr. Haddon made some verses in Latin" which were placed "in the fore-front of the banqueting house". These, he says, "do not only show the joyful welcome of Her Majesty to that Honourable Lord but also to the whole country of Kent".

Thynne may have copied the verses down on the spot, or possibly Dr. Haddon was pressed to pass copies around among his friends. In any event Thynne does not spare us his own translation of the Doctor's Latin poem.

> The kingly progeny and stock of Brutes most famous race
> Elizabeth, most welcome is to people of this place.
> Which way thou cast thine eye, thou mirth and joy doth see
> For joyful of thy princely face both men and women be.

* Francis Thynne was probably not much more than thirteen at the time so he may not have remembered in any great detail, when he came to write about the event, what the garden was like on that high occasion. Later in life he helped with the revision and continuation of Holinshed's Chronicle for which Harrison wrote his *Description of England*. Thynne may have inherited his literary and editing talents from his father, William Thynne, clerk of the kitchens and of the green cloth to Henry VIII, who was a great student of Chaucer's works and Chaucer's first editor.

Of Gardens and Gardening

The beardless boys, the hoared age, the maids of tender years
And trope confus'd flocks to thy sight in which their love
appears.[2]

There is more, but it is perhaps kinder to leave it at that. The
Queen, a brilliant Latin scholar, may have done rather better
with the line "and trope confus'd flocks to thy sight" than did
young master Thynne. Yet it is perhaps prudent to remember
that the Brutes mentioned in line one were not savage beasts but
the descendants of Brutus, or Brute, first king of the Britons and
great-grandson of Aeneas. Having, by an unfortunate mischance,
killed his father, Brute took refuge in Greece, then in Britain and
called the capital of his kingdom Troy-novant—now known as
London.

Lord Burghley delighted in making gardens, fountains, and
walks at Theobalds and directed that £10 a week should be laid
out in keeping the poor at work in his garden. As the average
weekly wage at the time was probably around five shillings there
must have been at least forty people employed in the gardens in
addition to the regular gardeners. The walks at Theobalds were
particularly fine: "one might walk two miles in the walk before
he came to their ends" as a later English account tells us;[3] while
that contemporary foreigner, Hentzner, says the gardens were
also "encompassed by water large enough for one to have the
pleasure of going in a boat and rowing between the shrubs", and
adds, "here are a great variety of trees and labyrinths made with
a great deal of labour, and a *jet d'eau* with its basin of white
marble, and columns and pyramids of wood and materials up and
down the garden". Columns and pyramids of wood and materials
sound like topiary work and topiary work reached almost fantastic proportions, although not so fantastic as in the eighteenth
century. It was common even in small gardens despite Bacon's
disapproval. He preferred "a pretty pyramid" or "fair columns",
the rest he considered as toys or trifles for children.

The "rest" peopled the garden with figures of armed men,

sometimes engaged in silent combat, monochromatic peacocks with their tails unfurled, green cats, greyhounds, deer, hares and rabbits cut from privet, yew, and even rosemary, and this population was further augmented by carved wooden figures painted and gilded. At Hampton Court where Henry VIII had greatly enlarged the gardens, there were no less than 159 of these figures—strange creatures such as dragons and griffins; wild animals like leopards, tigers, antelopes; and more ordinary ones such as bulls, greyhounds, and horses. Queen Elizabeth had thirty-four heraldic beasts in her privy garden at Whitehall. These, carved, painted, and with horns brightly gilded, stood on wooden pedestals

holding aloft vanes (pennants) bearing the Queen's arms. Sir James Melvil records that when he came to London to see Elizabeth, she granted him audience at eight o'clock in the morning in her garden at Westminster where he found her "walking in an alley". This, unfortunately, is all he tells us about the garden, but we do know from other sources that Elizabeth, like her countrymen, loved gardens passionately, and despite strange beasts and bizarre topiary, the English violet was her favourite flower.

It may be that these inanimate beasts which became such a feature of Tudor gardens were in imitation of the menageries which had for centuries been a feature of Royal Gardens. Henry I, who made a great park at Woodstock, had a menagerie there where he kept lions, leopards "strange spotted beasts", porcupines, camels, and other such animals sent to him, goodness knows how, from "divers outlandish lands".

Elizabeth's grandfather, Henry VII, had a pet monkey who one day tore to bits the diary the King kept—thus immortalizing himself to the great detriment of future historians. Hentzner, when visiting the Tower of London in 1592, saw there a small house "where were kept three lionesses, one lion of great size called Edward the Sixth because he was born during that reign", a tiger, a lynx, a wolf—excessively old—a porcupine and an eagle. All were kept "at the Queen's expense". Obviously wooden animals were less expensive in upkeep and far less dangerous to have around. The "Queen's beasts" recently set up in Kew Gardens hark back to the first Elizabeth.

The Elizabethans also delighted in mounts—a garden feature which persisted well into Stuart times. The mount was a man-made hill crowned by a summer-house or planted with fruit-trees. How or why a mount became a garden ornament is difficult to discover. Originally mounts had a sacred significance, they were representations of high and holy places. Even the ancient Britons made mounts for some religious purpose or another—which possibly explains Silbury Hill. London, itself, it is said, derives its name from such a mount, "llan" meaning sacred—as it still does in Welsh—and "din" meaning an eminence or high place. Tradition has it that St. Paul, the patron saint of London, preached from this llan-din, now disguised under the name of Parliament Hill, but whatever the reason for, or origin of, mounts, the Elizabethans insisted on having them in their gardens. Even Bacon approved of the mount. In fact, he describes the mount as a central feature of a prince-like garden (and by a prince-like garden he meant one of some thirty acres). "I wish", he tells us firmly, "in the middle a fair mount with three ascents and alleys enough for four to walk abreast, which I would have a perfect circle, without any bulwarks or embossments; and the whole mount to be thirty feet high surmounted by a fine banqueting house with some chimneys neatly cast." One detects here the suggestion that not all Elizabethan mounts were simple, circular structures and that Bacon must have seen many which were bulwarked, ornamented, embossed, embellished and possibly even mazed out of all recognition.

At Hampton Court, Henry VIII in his usual extravagant fashion had had an enormous mount constructed, topped by a splendid summer-house. Indeed, no smart garden of the time was complete without a summer-house or pavilion of some sort and in London gardens there was a positive craze for them. Again, this idea very probably stemmed from the East where pavilions were an essential and necessary part of any park or garden, and were as delicate, as beautiful, and as wonderfully coloured as the butterfly from which the word pavilion derives. Before Xerxes set off on his disastrous campaign against the Greeks, he entertained the princes and nobles of Media and Persia at a seven-day feast in the garden of his palace at Susa. The feast was held in a garden pavilion and the description of it must have been almost as familiar to the Elizabethans as it is to us, since it occurs in the Book of Esther (Ch. 1, v. 6).

The great garden pavilions of Tudor and Elizabethan times were frequently erected for banquets, and we know the one at

Of Gardens and Gardening

Theobalds must have been used for this purpose if for no other reason than that it contained the enormous table of black basalt. It was a very spectacular, semicircular summer-house, and in the lower part, in addition to the black-basalt table, twelve

Roman Emperors displayed themselves in white marble. The upper part was "set around with cisterns of lead"[4] which were filled with water in the summer and were "very convenient for bathing".

The Elizabethans at Home

At Gorhambury, Sir Nicholas Bacon, Lord Keeper of the Great Seal and father of Francis and Anthony, had a banqueting- or summer-house of so-called modest proportions built in his gardens. It cannot have been so very small as the liberal arts were depicted on its inner walls, while above, as a sort of dado or frieze, were pictured the learned men of various eras who excelled in each. Verses describing their accomplishments accompanied the pictures. Pythagoras, Stifelius, and Budaens represented Arithmetic—Robert Recorde, the eminent mathematician and court physician to Edward VI and Mary Tudor, was not there although he had written the earliest important English treatise on Algebra and had also invented the "sign of equality"(=). Aristotle, Porphyry, and Seton illuminated Logic. Music, curiously enough, was honoured by Arion, Terpander and Orpheus—this in an age surpassingly rich in national composers and musicians. Rhetoric issued from Cicero, Quintillian and Demosthenes. Geometry fell to Archimedes, Euclid, Strabo, and Apollonius; and Astrology, by which Astronomy was meant, was graced by Regiomontanus, Haly, Copernicus and Ptolemy—Dr. Dee was not among them. When the Queen visited Gorhambury she was extremely interested in this "modest" pavilion and most particularly in the Astrology section. Sir Nicholas—of the strange, fascinating, and totally un-Elizabethan face—explained Astronomy to the Queen to her great satisfaction. At Beddington House, in Surrey, the gardens were noted for their choice fruits and for having the first orangery in England. Here, too, was a famous garden pavilion, its top decorated with a painting of the Armada of 1588, and containing a red-and-white marble table.

These were the fabulous summer-houses of the rich; the less well-to-do went in for slender columns supporting a roof and even plainer summer-houses or "bowers" were made of wooden poles roofed and sometimes roughly sided with lattice-work over which was trained honeysuckle, jasmine, lady's bower and the ubiquitous and flamboyant scarlet-runner. Today the garden summer-house or pavilion in which food is served is the hired marquee.

Of Gardens and Gardening

No garden was complete without a fountain or water of some sort. Ornamental pools were favoured by many, though not by Bacon who considered that they attracted flies and frogs. Rathgeb was most impressed not only by the gardens at Hampton Court, "some planted with nothing but rosemary, others laid out with various other plants which are trained, intertwined and trimmed in so wonderful a manner and in such extraordinary shapes that the like could not easily be found", but by a fountain which stood in the middle of the first court. This he describes as being "a splendid, high and massy fountain with an ingenious water work whereby you can, if you like, make the water play upon the ladies and others who are standing by and give them a thorough wetting".

He tells us that His Highness took a delight in this garden but does not relate whether the Duke, with typical Teutonic high spirits, gave any ladies present a thorough wetting. Such fountains were by no means rare; there was one at Whitehall and

another at Nonsuch. The one at Nonsuch seems to have been a pyramid of marble full of concealed pipes "which spit upon all who come within their reach". [5] The one at Whitehall was a *jet d'eau* concealed in a sundial. Any unwary visitors bending to tell the time of day were often showered with water since at a distance there was a little wheel, turned by a gardener, which spouted water out of the dial most unexpectedly. This must have been great fun . . . particularly in cold weather.

But the practical-joke fountain was not the only kind. There were beautiful and splendid fountains which were quite harmless. At Kenilworth, a great octagonal basin caught the jetting water and held carp as well. On the sides of the basin Proteus and his sea-bulls, Thetis in her dolphin-drawn chariot, Neptune and Triton together with whales, sturgeon, conch shells and other sea motifs were richly carved. In the centre of the basin two athletes stood back to back carrying a ball on which Leicester's heraldic device—the Bear and Ragged Staff—was mounted. In the privy gardens at Nonsuch there were two ornate fountains, one with birds spouting water from their beaks; and in "The Grove of Diana"—a part of the park—Actaeon, transformed into a stag, suffered a shower at the hands of the goddess and her nymphs. Statuary for fountains was not always of marble; it was often of lead, gilded. Gardens were also ornamented with jars, vases and statues. Of the latter Bacon disapproved. To him they added "nothing to the pleasures of a garden". Such ornaments must have been a Tudor or Elizabethan idea since there is no mention of them in medieval times. It is very probable that the use of statues, vases, and many fountains came to England either via Italian craftsmen or by the English who, then as now, travelled in Italy. It was in the sixteenth century that Cardinal d'Este built his superb villa with its magnificent gardens at Tivoli near the site of Hadrian's Villa. He ornamented his villa and its gardens with the statues, vases, and columns which were unearthed when the foundations of the Villa d'Este were laid and its wonderful terraces built, and so set the fashion for classical ornaments in the Renaissance garden.

But Cardinal d'Este (Ippolito the Younger) was not the only high dignitary of the church to possess a beautiful garden though his is still the most perfect example of a Renaissance garden extant. Dr. Cox, Bishop of Ely had one, too, at Ely Place on Holborn Hill. When Christopher Hatton, Vice-Chamberlain, decided he wanted a new town house complete with garden, he cast covetous eyes on Ely Place but the Bishop refused to negotiate. Elizabeth, who disliked Dr. Cox as fervently as she liked the

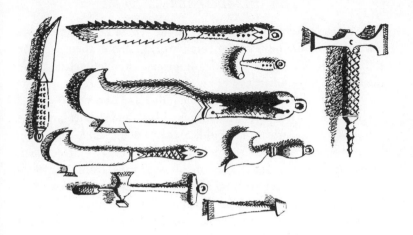

looks and dancing of her Vice-Chancellor, was extremely angry with her Bishop. So angry that for a long time it was believed she wrote him the famous letter which for brevity, bluntness, and blackmail is hardly surpassed.

"Proud Prelate" (the letter reads) "You know what you were before I made you what you are now. If you do not immediately comply with my request I will unfrock you, by God! Elizabeth."

The letter is now held to be a forgery but it most certainly expresses what Elizabeth felt about Dr. Cox—an intolerant, narrow-minded, grasping man who refused to minister in the Queen's Chapel because it contained a crucifix and candles on the altar. And Dr. Cox must have received a blast of some sort from the Queen for he gave in and Christopher Hatton was given the gate-house of the Bishop's palace plus several acres of Holborn Hill—now known as Hatton Garden. The Bishop managed to reserve to himself and his successors in the See the right of walking in the garden (which must have annoyed both Hatton and the Queen) and permission to gather twenty bushels of roses annually, which gives us some idea of the extent of the rose garden.

One of the most exciting things about gardens and gardening to the Elizabethans must have been the new flowers, herbs, trees

P

and shrubs introduced during the reign. These new plants came from all over the newly discovered world, among them was the tulip which came from Constantinople via the Netherlands, and the Crown Imperial from Persia, also via the same route. There was Persian lilac and Persian ranunculus and the now familiar love-in-a-mist, dittany, everlasting, lilac, and laburnum; the yellow crocus, African marigold, Sweet Sultan, sunflowers from Peru (Gerard says that those in his garden grew fourteen feet high) Michaelmas daisies, candytuft—perhaps from Crete or Candy—tobacco and nasturtiums from America and also from there the tulip tree and the red maple, to mention but a few.*

Parkinson's classification of flowers for the garden again affords insight into the Englishness of the English. He divides flowers into two categories. "English Flowers" and "Outlandish Flowers". Among the outlandish he mentions the Crown Imperial, the small Fritillary—or "Turkie or Guiniehen Flower"—and the hardy cyclamen. Strictly English, were primroses, marigolds, daisies, violets, columbine, roses, and gilliflowers. But the word gilliflower seems to have been a pet name for various kinds of flowers. Stock gilliflowers were stocks; wall gilliflowers, wallflowers; Queen's gilliflower, Hesperis or Sweet Rocket. Clove gilliflowers were carnations and pinks.

Pinks—and the name of the colour comes from the flower—were dearly loved by the Elizabethans and (*pace* Parkinson) they were probably introduced some 500 years before, either accidentally or deliberately, by our Norman conquerors. The best loved of the pink family was the carnation which seems to have acquired its name in mid-sixteenth century either because it was so often used in making coronels and chaplets, or because it was

* My own count of the number of new trees, shrubs, vegetables and flowers introduced into England between 1548 and 1597 is 121. I do not suggest that this is accurate but it does serve to show what great impetus was given to gardeners and gardens by the opening up of the world. As all plants were thought to have medicinal value most gardeners of the time were also apothecaries.

Of Gardens and Gardening

dented and toothed "like a litall crownet". Certainly everyone grew pinks and carnations—they were wonderfully rewarding in small gardens, sweetening the air without bother or trouble— and in grand gardens they could be experimented with and developed into showy blooms.

A certain Master Tuggy, whose garden was in Westminster, was the great carnation fancier of the late sixteenth century. He was the Allwood of his era. He bred and improved them and gave his new strain names, such as "The Princess" which Parkinson, no mean gardener himself, says was "the most beautiful that I ever did see". As for Master Tuggy's "Rose gilliflower", it was, says Parkinson, "a different sort from all others in that it hath rounded leaves (petals) without any iagges (jags) at all on the edges; of a fine stamell colour* or rather much like unto the red rose campion both for form, colour, roundnesse but larger for size".

Whether Master Tuggy put his carnation seed into a hollowed-out bean, stopped the hole with soft wax and set it in "proper ground" we do not know. But this was held to be the secret of producing double carnations of great size. So it seems that the English have loved pinks and carnations for nearly a thousand years and we, the neo-Elizabethans, seem just as devoted to them as were the first Elizabethans.

Gerard must have grown nearly every new plant in his great garden at Holborn and even Harrison, whose stipend was only £40 a year, tells us "such hath been my good luck in purchase of a variety of simples that notwithstanding my small ability there be very nearly 300 of one sort and another contained therein no one of them being common or usually to be had. If therefore, my little plot void of all cost in keeping be so well furnished, what shall we think of Hampton Court, Nonsuch, Tibault's, Cobham Garden and sundry others."

Harrison, on gardens, is a sheer delight. He so obviously loved them, marvelled at them and at the wonderful workmen who

* Stamell or stamel was a coarse woollen cloth or linsey—woolsey usually dyed red.

were "not only excellent in grafting the natural fruits but also in their artificial mixtures whereby one tree bringeth forth sundry fruits, and one and the same fruit of divers colours and tastes, dallying as it were with nature and her course, as if her whole trade was perfectly known to them". It is a little difficult to fathom, in the absence of more specific details, what "the same fruit of divers colours and tastes" could be—unless, perhaps, it was the plum which ranges from damson to greengage. He also informs us that some gardeners knew how to "bereave" certain fruits of their kernels and others of their core; how to endow them with the flavour of musk, sweet spice, and amber. He was also amazed at the way in which plants and trees were treated for sickness and disease "with no less diligence than physicians do commonly show upon our own bodies which to me doth seem right strange". Even apothecaries' shops, he exclaims, seemed to be "needful to our gardens" and even the "very dishwater" was not without its use to some plants.

Despite the muffling centuries, one is still saddened by the thought that the rector of Radwinter could not afford to "hazard" £10 on the slip of a marvellous rose which was to be seen in Antwerp. A rose which he tells us had "180 petals on one button"—a far greater novelty than that rose of sixty petals mentioned by Pliny.

For the rose was then, as now, the favourite flower no less than the symbol of

England. Briar, musk, damask, cabbage, York, Lancaster—all were grown and loved in great gardens as well as in small. And small gardens were more numerous by far than great ones. In their simplicity and sweetness the farmhouse and cottage gardens were much as such gardens are today. For the favourite flowers of the unsophisticated first Elizabethans are still country favourites, pinks in profusion, pansies, sweet-william, hollyhocks, wall-flowers, bachelor's button, columbine, primroses, violets, lily of the valley, marigold, daffodils, paeonies, poppies, Star of Bethlehem, snapdragon and, undoubtedly, the yellow aconite which grows in England, so it is said, only in those places where Roman blood was spilled.

Thomas Tusser, that practical farmer, gives lists of herbs necessary to grow in the garden for "Physick" as well as a long list of strewing herbs. The latter include such flowers as cow-slips, roses and violets in addition to the more usual strewers. But he recommends the growing of sweet-william not for "meat or medicine" but for pure pleasure. "Man only", says William Bullein, "doth smell and take delight in the odors of flowers and sweet things."⁶

It is perhaps strange to realize that the Elizabethans were modern enough to use garden frames. These were built of wood and ran on wheels so that they could be pushed along the broad, level walks to catch the sun or escape the wind. It is odd to realize that they used window-boxes, too, made of wood and lined with pitch—even if at that time the pelargonium was not known.

But it is neither strange nor odd to hear the word "Paradise" used so often in connection with Elizabethan gardens, for the word is from Persia via Greece and means Park . . . and that was the middle-eastern idea of bliss. The translators of the Septuagint borrowed the word and used it to designate the Garden of Eden. The early Christian fathers used it to mean Heaven. But in medieval times it was a popular belief that Paradise, an Earthly Paradise, did exist—a land of beauty and peace where death and decay were unknown. It lay far away beyond China, or in the ocean off India, or three days' journey from the kingdom of Prester John, and it could be found for the searching. But the globe-encircling, romantic, adventurous Elizabethans never found it. We have no evidence that they really believed in its existence. Yet the basic plan of an Elizabethan garden was that of Eden. Perhaps, after all, they did attempt to create what they could not discover—or no longer believed in.

CHAPTER NINE

Of Cosmetics and Perfumes

THE Dark Lady of the Sonnets, whoever she may have been, was decidedly not the Elizabethan ideal of feminine beauty. Gentlemen, as usual, preferred blondes; pink and white and golden. Or, as Spenser put it in a phrase which might have come straight from a Victorian novel, "roses in a bed of lilies". Women were less choosy. They simply preferred men and were prepared to endure almost any torture to achieve that pink, white and golden look which men liked.

It cannot be said that the Queen set the fashion for a particular type of beauty, although she was fortunate in being born with the right coloured hair. Renaissance women all over the Continent were busy attempting to look fair and fragile even if they were tough, resilient, brilliant and shrewd at business. Italian women, (harlots, principally in Venice) could be seen in flocks sitting on flat-roofed houses, faces covered, hair spread out over wide-brimmed crownless hats so that the sun—so ruinous to the complexion—would assist the work of whatever bleach they had applied. Ladies sun-bleached their hair more privately in secluded gardens and on the roofs of palaces.

Englishwomen were, on the whole, more fortunate than their Latin sisters; many had fair hair and a pale skin, and even the dark-haired often had a fair complexion. This, however, was not enough. There were other and more detailed specifications for the ideal English beauty. We are indebted to John Marston, the poet-dramatist, for a fairly exhaustive description of how a woman should look. The face should be "round and ruddy"; the forehead, smooth, high and white; the eyebrows small, delicate, and marked with a pencil; the lips coral or like cherries; the eyes, "lamplike but downcast". The cheeks should show "the rose and lily in combat" and be dimpled like the chin; the neck, snow-white and round like an ivory pillar "holding the head high"; the ears, round and compact; the hair, a rich, golden yellow.

So much for head, neck and face—the body had its ideal specifications, too. The space between the shoulders must be wide; the breasts high, fair, and round; the hands, small and white with long fingers and red nails; the waist, slender; hips, large; legs, straight; feet, small with a high instep.

If not born with all these requirements the Elizabethan woman set out to make good any deficiencies by that art to which Jezebel, unfortunately, had given such a bad name. She painted her face, dyed or bleached her hair, plucked and darkened her eyebrows, dropped belladonna into her eyes with a feather, reddened her lips, and skilfully pencilled in blue veins on a falsely whitened bosom which, if she were unmarried like the Queen, she displayed in such a manner that little or nothing was left to the imagination. She went in for lotions and beautifiers of all kinds —hair washes, freckle and spot removers. She wore a mask to keep her face from browning in the sun or running off in the rain; added to her own hair; washed and dried her teeth; laced her busks tightly to achieve a "monkey waist"; padded her hips and, as usual, scandalized parsons and puritans.

There are always exceptions, of course, even among parsons. William Harrison was shocked, John Donne wasn't (as a young man he spoke up strongly in defence of women painting[1]) but, for the most part, those who disapproved took the same line— it was wicked, not to say sacrilegious, to attempt to improve upon the face which the Lord had given one. To go in for beauty aids and cosmetics would be of no help at all to a woman on Judgment Day. "Will these painted women be able to look up

Of Cosmetics and Perfumes

to God with a face He does not own?" Thomas Tuke asks in *A Treatise against the Tincturing and Painting of Men and Women*. But the arguments against painting were not on religious and moral grounds only. Men of science warned against the use of the poisons and unrefined minerals which went into the home-made cosmetics and beauty preparations of the day. Judging by most of the recipes which have survived, it is not surprising that science—or even common sense—inveighed against cosmetics. The really astonishing thing is that women didn't die of lead-poisoning more often than they did.

The requisite lily whiteness of face, neck, and breast was achieved by the use of ceruse. It sounds an innocent and even cheerful word but it was white lead mixed with vinegar and painted on the skin. Borax and sulphur were also used as a whitener but ceruse gave the best immediate effect. The long-term results were: a dried and mummified skin, snow-white hair, gastro-intestinal disturbances, and palsy. The combative rose, coral, and cherry for cheek and lips was provided by fucus, a red dye perhaps made of madder or red ochre. Fucus had been used by Roman women but theirs, as the name implies, was made of a harmless sort of sea-weed whereas the best fucus in England—one which produced a very pretty and lasting vermilion—was made from red crystalline mercuric sulphide. Unfortunately, it ate into the flesh and so could be used only for as long as flesh remained. Far safer, if less ruinously permanent, was a rouge and lip salve made by mixing cochineal, white of hard-boiled egg, milk of green figs, alum, and gum arabic. It may have been this particular brand which caused Paulina in *The Winter's Tale* to warn Leontes against kissing Hermione,

> . . . forbear
> The ruddiness upon her lip is wet;
> You'll mar it if you kiss it; stain your own
> With oily painting.

Hermione was, at that point, supposed to be a painted marble statue, a deception which must have been very easy to get away with when statues were nearly always painted and women tried to make their skin look white as marble. An unpainted statue to an Elizabethan probably would have looked as dreary as an unpainted woman. So the woman who wanted to go on looking like marble and not like a bit of old leather cautiously used a "white fucus" which was less dangerous, though less effective, than ceruse. It was made from the burned jawbones of a hog or sow, ground, sieved and "laid on" with oil of white poppy. Most cosmetics were laid on thickly with white of egg rather like tempera painting and this gave a slight glaze or polished marble effect.* Kohl was used for the eyes—women had been using Kohl ever since Egyptian times—but belladonna to produce great, velvety pupils was relatively new and was a custom probably imported from Venice.

Exactly what Elizabeth's true colouring was, apart from her hair and her eyes—dark as ripe olives, is not easy to say. Most portraits of her, particularly in her later years, are "cult" portraits more intent on showing by the magnificence of her dress, the majesty of her bearing, the splendour of her jewels that she was a great Prince. The face is almost mask-like and often so pink and white that it might be anyone. Even contemporary prose and verse portraits differ. Some say her complexion was sallow; some say olive; some, fair. . . . Richard Puttenham—the man who may have written *The Art of English Poesy* and who invented the wonderful phrase "fleering frump" to describe a mocking, scornful person—very wisely does not commit himself on this point. In his poem *A Fragment of a Partheniad written of our Sovereign Lady*, he describes Elizabeth thus:

> Of silver was her forehead high,
> Her brows two boes of ebony,

* It should be remembered that many women suffered a disfiguring pitting of the skin as a result of smallpox and tried to disguise it with very heavy make-up.

Of Cosmetics and Perfumes

Her tresses trust were to behold
Frizzled and fine as fringe of gold.

Two lips wrought out of ruby rock
Like leaves to shut and to unlock.
As portal door in prince's chamber;
A golden tongue in mouth of amber.

Her eyes, God wot, what stuff they are!
I durst be sworn each is a star;
As clear and bright as wont to guide
The pilot in his winter tide.

Her bosom sleek as Paris plaster,
Held up two balls of alabaster;
Each byas was a little cherry
Or else, I think a strawberry.

This tells us nothing at all. It could be a description of any
woman of fashion of the day. It presents the conventional ideal—
although the clichés were not so worn then as now. But the
Queen, although she might be a goddess and was addressed as
such (though not by Richard Puttenham), like any other woman
used cosmetics to achieve the ideal. And, as she aged, she used
them more and more. Her skin became whiter, her cheeks and
lips redder, her eyes more lamp-lit. It may be that because she
was near-sighted she could not see quite clearly what she was
doing to her face. Or it may be, as she refused to look in a
mirror during her declining years, her tiring women were
responsible for the mask of paint she wore. Yet even if it is
customary for novelists and some historians to describe the Queen
as over-painted and raddled, as if this were a defect of character,
it was, in fact, a custom of the time—save among Puritan women.
Elizabeth was a Protestant but she was not a Puritan.

Cosmetics were, of course, only the finishing touches, what
came before their application was of even greater moment.

Lotions and applications of all sorts for face, hands, neck, and bosom were in constant use. Master Alexis of Piedmont whose miraculous "Oile of a red haired dogge" had so benefited the Portuguese gentleman's gout and the withered arm of a brother had a very special recipe for a "Water to make women beautiful for ever". This eternal beauty was obtained by taking a young raven from a nest, feeding it on hard-boiled eggs for forty days, killing it and then distilling with myrtle leaves, talc, and almond oil. Master Alexis was a foreigner and one could never be quite sure that foreigners weren't out to poison one. More English— and more popular—was "Tristram's Water". This remarkable lotion did everything and could be used internally and externally. It removed spots from the face and body, cured toothache, overcame halitosis and, if rubbed on the head every morning, kept one youthful—possibly not for ever but for long enough. Tristram's Water was a mixture of spices, wine, rhubarb, oil of bay and took a month to prepare. If it did no good it, at least, had the unusual merit of doing no positive harm.

There were other blemishes which had to be dealt with rather more energetically and specifically. From the number of recipes given as a cure for freckles it might be thought that the Elizabethans were afflicted with these small sun-spots to a vast extent, but "freckle" was a generic name for all kinds of spots. An unnamed traveller had cured himself of "freckles" by washing his face at moon's wane with elder leaves distilled in May. Another freckle eradicator was a dose of birch-tree sap taken in March or April. This, it was said, "makes the skin very clear". Probably it did, as it must have contained a useful quantity of Vitamin C, sadly lacking in a heavy winter diet. Birch-tree sap also had the property of being able to dissolve pearls, according to Sir Hugh Platt; a secret, he says, which is "known to many". But he doesn't say what the purpose of the secret is.* Very obstinate freckles or pimples could be cured by mixing ground brimstone with oil

* Probably a cure for fever.

Of Cosmetics and Perfumes

of turpentine which, when applied to the spot, "makes the flesh to rise spungeous". When the flesh had thus spungeously arisen it was anointed with "butter risen from milk in the morning".

Although milk did not enjoy the reputation it had in Roman times as a beauty bath, it was still used for that purpose (so was wine) and it was firmly believed that a child washed every night in either breast or cow's milk would "wax fair and resist sunburn"—and sunburn or tanning was something every Elizabethan took all possible precautions to avoid. In addition to wearing hats and masks, she used quantities of lemon water in which a handful of "sublimate finely powdered" was dissolved to bleach away any trace of darkness. If she suffered from the "white Morphew", a scaly condition common to both men and women, and very prevalent, there were dozens of panaceas to be tried. Master Rich of Lee, cured himself and an unnamed "gallant lady" of this distressing complaint with a home-made remedy which he highly recommends to all sufferers. Into a pint of distilled vinegar Master Rich put two new laid eggs, shells and all, added three yellow dock roots, two spoonfuls of flowers of brimstone and let it brew itself for three days. He then steeped a clean cloth in the mixture and three times a day wiped his own and the "gallant lady's" face with it. In a few days, so Master Rich says, they were relieved of their affliction.

A red face was also not considered beautiful, even on men; and many must have followed the example of a certain Mr. Foster of Essex, "an Attorney of the Common pleas" whose face "was for many years of an exceeding high and furious colour".[2] Mr. Foster quite cured himself of his beetroot complexion by wearing double-linen socks into which he put well dried and pounded Bay salt. These he wore for fourteen days and nights; drying them each morning and evening by the fire. It may have been more difficult for a lady whose face was of a high and furious colour to follow Mr. Foster's example for men were able to conceal such socks under hose and shoes. Ladies, unless they went slip-shod, probably couldn't get double-linen-socked feet into the

The Elizabethans at Home

shoes they wore . . . so they doubtless took to more ceruse to cover the redness. Certainly, no one seems to have thought that a lighter diet; fewer hot spices, and less wine might have toned down a fiery complexion.

But then there was Soliman. Soliman, when all else failed, really did get rid of all blemishes, freckles, spots, warts, and blobs by the simple expedient of removing the outer layer of skin. It was used, presumably, on the same principle as the "sandpapering" technique of modern plastic surgery. The only snag was that Soliman happened to be sublimate of mercury, and was described even then as being "dead fire malignant and biting". It removed spots and blemishes but it also quietly consumed the flesh underneath and left dreadful scar tissue . . . to be removed by more Soliman. It also had some very unhappy side effects, it brought on "the shakes", blackened the teeth, and made the gums recede.

Teeth, as we know, did not last, partly because of the quite extraordinary kinds of dentifrices used. Some were made of honey and salt burned to ashes; others of powdered rabbit's head, pomegranate peel, and red peach blossom. A favourite was plain sugar and honey. This must have had a lovely, sweet taste and encouraged people to clean their teeth but it undoubtedly contributed to decay. Another highly recommended tooth-powder was made of the "calcined branches and tops of Rosemary" mixed with an equal amount of burnt alum. It was applied by licking the finger, dipping it into the powder and rubbing the teeth, taking care not to "gall the gums". After cleaning, the mouth was rinsed with water or wine and then dried with a towel. Mistress Twist, the court laundress, one New Year's Day presented Elizabeth with "four tooth-cloths of coarse Holland wrought with black silk and edged with bone lace". The bone lace must have been a curious edging for coarse Holland, as it was a very elaborate and delicate netting made of black, white or multi-coloured silks often interwoven with gold and silver thread.

Of Cosmetics and Perfumes

Less tedious to use than tooth-powder, but infinitely more harmful, were small, pencil-like rolls, about four or five inches long, made of powdered alabaster and "gum dragonet". With these the teeth could be rubbed without wetting the finger—and rubbed much harder, too. Let the barber remove the scales, Platt advises, but keep your teeth clean by constant rubbing. He also cautions, very particularly, against allowing the barber to use aqua fortis on the gums "or you may be forced to borrow a rank of teeth to eat dinner". It seems fantastic that aqua fortis* was not to be used on teeth or gums although sublimate of mercury was used on the skin; and even more fantastic to learn that stubborn stains on the teeth should be removed by rubbing with a mixture of powdered pumice, brick and coral. This, in time, removed the enamel as well as the stain.

Everyday care of the teeth included washing them three times a day and a stern injunction never to pick them with an iron toothpick. Wood, only, was to be used. But a wooden toothpick was hardly suitable to the rank and style of a rich Elizabethan, so toothpicks were made of gold or silver and carried about in jewelled cases. The Queen was given several sets of gold toothpicks on several occasions (she also had a gold earpick garnished with rubies).

Such toothpicks must have been a very good in-between kind of present to give, neither too personal nor impersonal and useful as well as ornamental—rather like a book token. Certainly, Lady Lisle seems to have thought so . . . for it is recorded that when Philip of Bavaria—known as the "Palsgrave"—came to England as a possible suitor for Mary Tudor's hand (Elizabeth was about six at the time) he returned home via Calais, and

---

* It is difficult to believe that by *aqua fortis* Platt meant nitric acid although this had been discovered by Geber (Abū Mūsā Jābir ibn Hayyān), the most famous alchemist of medieval times, in the eighth century. It is more likely that Platt's *aqua fortis* was a supersaturated solution of salt or soda which, either plain or mixed, had Platt known it, would have been excellent for teeth and gums.

stayed with the governor, Lord Lisle. While there, Lady Lisle sent her husband a "tooth picker" to be given to the Palsgrave because, as she wrote, "when he was here (in England)' I did see him wear a pin to pick his teeth withal". This gift was a trifle on the personal side. The tooth picker was Lady Lisle's own and she had used it, herself, for seven years before sending it on to the Palsgrave. The English might be barbarous by Italian standards but, at least, they had elegance enough not to pick the teeth with a pin—Bavarian fashion.

Yet, after all the washing, drying, and picking, nothing really saved the Elizabethans' teeth—perhaps because of the quantities of sugar they ate. Even foreigners commented on the bad teeth of the English—as they continued to do until a few years ago. So, when the condition of the teeth had deteriorated too far, the wretched beauty was advised, "if the teeth are badly eaten away, lacking or too large, the best thing is to lisp and simper rather than laugh or smile broadly".[3] This counsel of despair was also enjoined upon those who suffered from unpleasant breath. It is a horrid thought that bad teeth or halitosis may lie behind the Mona Lisa smile.

Then there was the problem of hair. Although a rich gold or red-gold was far easier to obtain than either good teeth or a white skin, it could—and often was—a very dangerous business. And here, men seem to have been just as eager as women to achieve the right colour. Men, no doubt, wanted that sanguine look—even if they were by nature melancholy, choleric or phlegmatic. Sanguine man was, by definition, lusty, hopeful and amorous—and obviously had the best time. A good bleach for hair or beard was made of calcined lead and sulphur mixed with quick lime. This rubbed on, left for a quarter of an hour, rinsed and then washed out turned hair a lovely red. It did not in any way, so it was said, discolour or injure the skin, and the colour lasted a very long time. A less drastic, if less lasting, method of making the hair golden was to brush on the final water drawn from honey "being a deep red colour which performeth the same

Of Cosmetics and Perfumes

excellently, but the same hath a strong smell and therefore must be sweetened with some aromatical body".[2]

Or one could crouch in front of a fire repeatedly moistening the hair with alum-water, or sponge it with a decoction of turmerick, rhubarb, barberry-tree bark or dogberry. All these were probably quite adequate to brighten the mousey, or to make the nearly fair more golden; particularly as the golden illusion could be further heightened by sprinkling the hair with a red or yellow powder or, if really rich, with gold-dust—a hair brightener much favoured by Henry VIII.

Unfortunately, Celtic or Iberian types were beyond the aid of such innocent preparations as alum, honey-water, coloured powders or gold-dust. There was nothing for it, if the hair were black or dark brown, but oil of vitriol. This produced a glorious chestnut beard or a splendid red-gold head of hair though the risk was that if the user weren't exceptionally careful, he would emerge badly scarred and without any hair at all. But baldness in men was not so noticeable then, as men rarely went hatless even indoors. Besides, anointing the bald patch with onion juice and exposing it to the sun speedily produced a fine crop of hair. If this failed, those up in their Pliny knew that myrtle berries were an antidote to baldness; while a mixture of oil, ashes, and earthworms prevented the hair turning white (we have no record that the Elizabethans dyed the hair blue as some affected ancient Romans did).

Baldness in women simply didn't matter. They took to wigs when the hair fell out, turned grey or when they tired of trying to keep pace with the elaborate and constantly changing hairstyles of the day. One contemporary writer tells us, with a certain ponderous surprise, that hair can fall out in two ways—either naturally or by the use of too many bleaches or dyes; and then ladies had to cover their heads with wigs, perukes, periwigs or "gregorians". The latter was a variety of wig fashionable late in the reign and was named after a barber, Gregory, who carried on his business in the Strand. Wigs were all right for the bald, said the moralizers, but if they were used by women who were too lazy to trouble about attending to the hair which Providence had provided, then wigs and wig-wearers were wicked. This is just a trifle unfair. Hair-styles were so complicated, bleaching so dangerous, that a wig was often the safest way of being a golden rather than a scarred and bald beauty.

The Queen wore a wig—or a variety of wigs—until the day she died. But, as her hair had fallen out naturally, this could not be condemned. (Mary Stuart wore one, too, to cover her grey hair.) Many rich and fashionable women enticed children with a shilling to part with their hair—if it were golden—and there was a brisk trade in hair selling.* We don't know whose hair the Queen wore, or whether all her wigs were made of real hair, but there is a warrant dated April 19th 1602, from Greenwich

---

* Shakespeare in *The Merchant of Venice* (iii. 2) satirizes the fashion for wearing wigs.

> . . . Look on beauty,
> And you shall see 'tis purchased by the weight;
> Which therein works a miracle in nature,
> Making them lightest that wear most of it:
> So are those crisped snaky golden locks
> Which make such wanton gambols with the wind,
> Upon supposed fairness, often known
> To be the dowry of a second head,
> The skull that bred them, in the sepulchre.

Of Cosmetics and Perfumes

and signed by the Queen's hand, which reads, "To Dorothy Spekarde, our silke woman for 6 heades of heare, 12 yards of heare curle, 100 devises made of heare". [5] It is probable that silk was used in addition to hair certainly fine gold and silver wire was, but it seems an enormous quantity of false hair to order at one time. On the other hand, it would be a great time-saver to have a large number of wigs and false bits. Fashionable and idle women could, and did, spend a whole morning "trimming and tricking" their heads. Elizabeth was more than fashionable—she set the style for the whole of her long reign—but she was far from idle.

Hair was curled, frizzled, crisped, "laid out on wreaths and borders from one ear to the other". To keep it from falling down it was "underpropped with forks and wires", ensnared in a crippen (hairnet) or a caul (snood). Lord Russell gave the Queen a beautiful caul of hair in 1578 garnished with gold buttons and set with pearls. Hair, like hips, was probably padded out, too, for one contemporary observer says "On the edges of their bolstered hair . . . there is laid great wreaths of gold and silver curiously wrought and cunningly applied to the temples" and "hanged with bugles, ouches, rings, gold, silver, glass and such other gee-gaws and trinkets." [6] The writer was male but if he exaggerated he did so very slightly. Portraits, particularly of the Queen, show that the elaborate and fantastic styles in hairdressing almost rival that of the eighteenth century. The perfectly simple hair-styles of Anne Boleyn and Mary Tudor were dead as a door-nail. Only Puritan women affected this fashion now, and left their hair in the state it had been given them—even if it was as straight as string and colourless as moleskin. Non-Puritans took to curling and frizzling with the iron or, if they feared this—and it is difficult to understand how any woman willing to submit to Soliman for spots, and oil of vitriol for a bleach, could fear such a triviality as a brand from a curling-iron —there was a sort of "home permanent" made of burned and powdered sheep's horn mixed with oil which seems to have done

the trick; though it must have been exceedingly messy and boring to apply. Yet, the Elizabethan equivalent of brilliantine or
hair fixative must have been even messier. One of the most
favoured was made from the apple pressings left over from cider-
making and mixed with hog's grease. With unaccustomed logic
it was called "pomatum".

Men, almost as much as women, were given to the use of
cosmetics, and were as vain about the cut and colour of a
beard as they were about the cut and colour of doublet and hose.
Harrison, in the middle of a "dry mock" on fashions in dress,
drops in a "bitter taunt" or two about masculine beard- and hair-
styles. "I say nothing of our heads" he remarks—with paralipsis
worthy of Mark Antony—"which sometimes are polled, sometimes curled or suffered to grow at length like woman's locks,
many times cut off, above or under the ears, round as by a wooden
dish. Neither", says he, "will I meddle with our variety of
beards" and then meddles delightfully. Some were "shaven from
the chin like those of Turks"; others were cut short like that of
Marquess Otto, or rounded like a "rubbing brush". Some had
the "pique de vant", others were allowed to grow long. Barbers,
on the whole, the parson says, were as cunning as tailors when
it came to making a beard alter the shape of a face or cover some
fancied facial defect. The long, lean, straight face could be made
to look broad and large by a Marquess Otto cut. The owner of
a "platter-like" face need not be too unhappy, as a long narrow
beard quite altered the flat, plate-like look. For the "weasel-
becked", much hair left on the cheeks would make the owner
look "big like a bowdled-hen and as grim as a goose". These
seem singularly unattractive alternatives; there can be little to
choose between resembling a stoat or a barnyard fowl. Harrison,
too, strikes the note that all this—and all this included the
wearing of earrings of gold set with stones and pearls—is an
offence to the Lord since men were attempting to amend the
faces God gave them.

Shakespeare's Hotspur was as impatient of this type of man as

Of Cosmetics and Perfumes

Harrison. "Popinjays" he calls them and describes, for the benefit of Henry IV, how, after the battle of Holmedon when he was
himself breathless, faint, dry with rage and toil

> Came there a certain lord, neat, and trimly dress'd,
> Fresh as a bridegroom; and his chin, new reap'd
> Showed like a stubble-land at harvest home;
> He was perfumed like a milliner,
> And 'twixt his finger and his thumb he held
> A pouncet-box which ever and anon
> He gave his nose . . .

Young Henry Percy meant to be—and was—insulting in describing the "certain lord" as "perfumed like a milliner". But a
milliner was not a hat maker. He was a dealer in, or a seller of,
sundry small wares, articles of adornment and apparel, especially
those which came from Milan—gloves, ribbons, ornaments,
perfumes. Milliners (Milaners) and perfume sellers did a roaring
business up and down the country.

The age was as highly perfumed as it was spiced. Elizabeth's
nose "rising somewhat in the middest"[7] was, we are told, a good
one and "nothing offended her more than an unpleasant smell".[8]
This is an exaggeration. She was often far more offended by
people, events, and not getting her own way. But to be born
with a peculiarly sensitive sense of smell in those days must have
had all the drawbacks of a severe physical disability—a wooden
leg would be preferable—unless one knew how to counteract a
bad odour with a good one. Furthermore, it was a received
opinion that evil odours bred diseases, hence it was a wise pre-
caution to surround oneself with a cordon sanitaire of perfume
at all times. In times of plague specially concocted perfumes
were thought to be a preventive and, in London, every householder was required to put out wood to keep the great fumigating
fires going.

Some hundred years before Elizabeth's birth, Thomas Norton,
a Bristol alchemist, wrote a book called *The Ordinall of*

Alkimy. In it there is a long and extraordinary passage in Ogden Nash style relating the value of odours.

> When substance shall putrifie,
> Horrible odours are engendered thereby
> as of dragons, and of men that long dead be,
> their stinke may cause mortalitie.
> It is not holesome to smell to some soules
> for quenching some snuff a mare will cast her foals.
> Fishes love sweet smells also it is true
> they love not old kettles as they do newe.
> All things that is of good odour hath naturall heate
> though Camphire, Roses and things cold
> have sweet odors, as Authors have soules.
> No good odor is contrary to another but it is so of
>   stinkinge smelle
> For stinke of garlick avoideth stinke of dung-hill.

Leaving aside the miscellaneous information concerning mares, fish, and authors; the ancient doctrine that "stinke may cause mortalitie" and the equally ancient doctrine of "degrees" in relation to perfume is clearly set forth. It is also interesting to note the true observation that good odours blend rather than cancel each other out, while bad odours don't. There seems small choice between the evil odour and its "contrarie". In view of this, Hotspur's "milliner" was really taking the right precautions in appearing perfumed on a battlefield and sniffing his pouncet-box; particularly as the soldiers brought

> a slovenly and unhandsome corpse
> Betwixt the wind and his nobility.

This pseudo-scientific and medical background on the value of odours may have been a basis, or an excuse, for the sudden enormous increase in the use of perfumes during the period, but a contributing factor was the great increase in trade with other countries. Just as the extravagant and luxurious use of perfumed oils

Of Cosmetics and Perfumes

and unguents followed on Rome's conquest of the Middle East and the African shore of the Mediterranean, so the opening up of new, Eastern trade-routes and the girdling of the globe brought to England great quantities of spices and aromatic gums, ambergris, civet, and musk. The Italians were, as they had been for centuries, the great perfumers of Europe yet the English, too, must have gained fame abroad for their skill in the art. It seems a strange paradox to find that when the Sultana Valide, mother of Sultan Amurath III, sent the Queen a present of a robe, a girdle, two kerchiefs of Oriental design wrought in gold, three in silk, a necklace of pearls and rubies, and a wreath of diamonds she asked, in return, for cloth of silk or wool of English manufacture, for English cosmetics and particularly for distilled waters of every kind for the face, and perfumed oil for the hands.

English women had, of course, been distilling perfumed water from their own native flowers and herbs for centuries. Every grand house had a still room where aromatic waters, conserves, and remedies were made from recipes kept and handed down from generation to generation. The Queen's maids were required to be skilful in the art of distillation. They must have produced hundreds of gallons of rose water each season as rose water was used in, on and for everything from cookery to cosmetics. It was sprinkled all over rooms, furniture, face, hair and hands from bottles with perforated lids called casting bottles. The Queen had a beautiful one carved of agate, and such bottles, as well as the boxes of alabaster, wood, silver or gold in which perfumes and cosmetics were kept (they were called sweet coffers), were as plain or as ornamented as the wealth or religious scruples of the owner permitted.

Naturally, there were those who purported to have discovered new kinds of distilled waters possessing a variety of virtues. One, Ralph Rabbards, who calls himself a "gentleman studious and expert in Archemical Arts" sent the Queen some notes on the "most pleasant serviceable and rare inventions, as I have by long studdie and chargeable practice found out, and am ready to put in execution at a smalle charge".⁹ Among these rare inventions "waters of purest substance from odors flowers, fruites and herbes wholesomest, perfitest and of greatest vertue are first distilled by desensory, depured and rectified, clere as crystall, with his owne onlie proper virtue, taste and odor contynuing many years. One spoonful is better than a gallon for any prynce or noble person, or any that love their healthe. . . ." What Rabbards' secrets were he does not say, other than to warn against other waters which were "inaptly distilled" and "invenomed by the evill quallitie of mettalyne stilles" and so "do much more hurte than good". But he does recommend his own water of violets, "jilly-flower and pinckes" not only for their perfume and their medicinal qualities but also "to clense and keepe brighte the skynne and fleshe and preserve it in his perfitt state."

These pleasant, perfumed waters which were in such demand, represented, as toilet waters do today, the simple unsophisticated perfumes. They were the delicate, the light, the refreshing scents which almost anyone with a garden and a handful of spices could make up at home. The heavier kinds of perfume were far more complicated to make and must have been overpowering when freshly made. Since the use of alcohol or spirits of wine for the extraction of essential oils, and as a fixative, seems to have been virtually unknown perfumes were either in the form of a dry powder or a thick syrupy liquid. Henry VIII's favourite perfume must have been of the syrupy kind. It was made of six spoonfuls each of rose oil and rose water; a quarter of an ounce of fine sugar to which was added two grains of musk and one ounce of ambergris. This was boiled "softly" for five or six hours and was then ready for use. It must have smelled very strongly of amber-gris. Elizabeth is said to have preferred a syrup perfume made of musk, rose water, Damask-water and sugar. Her favourite dry-perfume is reputed to have been made of sweet marjoram and benjamin (benzoin), boiled, dried and powdered. But the plain truth is, Elizabeth loved perfumes of every kind. She was so delighted with perfumed gloves, a fashion the Earl of Oxford

brought from Italy, that she had a pair trimmed with four roses of silk and had her picture painted wearing them. The perfume was known for years as the Earl of Oxford's perfume. The Queen, also, had at least one cloak of perfumed Spanish leather and even her shoes were perfumed. One may be perfectly sure that every courtier or lady at court followed the Queen's example and the custom spread rapidly throughout the country.

Master Alexis of Piedmont was not to be outdone in the matter of perfumes either, and offers his followers many "secret" recipes. His formula for Damask perfume—and Damask was a great favourite—contains musk, ambergris, sugar, benjamin, storax, calamus and aloes wood. "Beat them well into a powder", he directs, "and put together in a little perfume pan, pour in as much Rose water as will be two fingers high and make under it a small fire that it may not boil, and when the water is consumed you shall pour in another and continue this doing a certain number of days." He also gives a recipe for making "Little cushions of perfumed roses" as well as a "perfume for the chamber". This was really an incense made of storax, calamint, benjamin, aloes wood and ashes of willow, beaten to a powder and then bound together in a paste with aqua vitae. The paste was then pressed into little cakes and laid on a coal to be consumed slowly and perfume the air.

A paste perfume was also the first step in making perfumed necklaces and girdles—great favourites with women. The paste was rolled into shape, pierced with a bodkin and the beads strung while the paste was still warm. In addition to all the perfume worn on clothes, beaten into hair pomade and cosmetics, oiled into leather and wood, or floating in the air, there were also the pouncet-box and the pomander. Sir Thomas Gresham in Moro's portrait holds a pomander in his hand, and jewelled pomanders— as opposed to those made from an orange stuffed with a sponge steeped in aromatic vinegar—were as common as ropes of pearls. To renew the strength of an old pomander, or to double the strength of a new one, a grain of civet and two of musk ground on a stone with a little rose water and then worked into the pomander was recommended by Sir Hugh Platt. "This" he re-remarks "is a sleight to passe away an old Pomander, but my intent is honest." So, indeed, was his intent when he invented the mirror-set ring so that card players could see if their opponents were cheating. And, almost in the same breath, he tells us of a sure method of attracting flies which otherwise "would flie upon pictures and hangings" and so deface them. This was a "cowcumber" pricked full of holes with a wooden or bone bodkin; into each hole was inserted a grain of barley, small end out. When the cowcumber was covered with barley sprouts it was to be hung in the middle of a room as a fly attracter. Flies must have been a plague in those days and though no one seems to have realized that they spread disease, all complained of the mess they made of oil paintings and rich hangings.

Hangings were perfumed, bed linen was perfumed. "Now are the lawn sheets fumed with violets" says Marston. Writing paper was perfumed; "letter after letter, gift after gift; smelling so sweetly—all musk."[10] Sachets or sweet-bags were laid away in clothing and in chests stored with tapestries and hangings. Rooms were "aired" with a perfuming-pan and perfumed powders were probably puffed about rooms with a miniature bellows as they were in France.

Cannon puffed sweet powders, too. On that famous occasion in 1581–2 when Elizabeth entertained the Duke of Anjou who, although half her age, was a suitor for her hand, a great tylt cum military tournament was held in his honour and cannons of wood shot off clouds of sweet powder and sweet water "very odoriferous and pleasant".[11] But the thought of the Duke of Anjou as king of England—which he would have been—was odoriferous in the wrong way, and far from pleasant to the members of Elizabeth's Council and to the people of England. Normally so anxious that the Queen should marry or at least name her heir, they wisely forbade this particular match.

How deeply Elizabeth's emotions were involved with her "Little Frog", as she called him, is not easy to determine. She was forty-six; a great and brilliant Sovereign, *politique* to her finger-tips . . . but she was also a woman who was already lying about her age, and painting to look younger. Anjou was twenty-three; an ill-favoured, cowardly, double-minded and malicious little man, according to contemporary accounts, which we have no reason to disbelieve.

It is just possible that Elizabeth was in love with Anjou. Certainly she wept and seemed scarce able to bear to let him depart. Perhaps she was in love with the idea of love, or his youth may have deceived her into believing that age had not withered her . . . . and had no power to do so. Or perhaps she was just acting a part.

The Elizabethans at Home

Did she say what she really felt in the poem *On Mount Zeur's Departure* written in her own hand and signed Eliz. Regina? Or is it just the record of a transient passion; is it an exercise in self-deception or one in the writing of stanzas in the Spenserian or the Petrarchan manner? Whether the sentiment is genuine or not, the stanzas are most graceful

I

I grieve, yet dare not show my discontent
I love, and yet am forced to seem to hate,
I dote, but dare not what I ever meant;
I seem stark mute, yet inwardly do prate;
I am and am not—freeze, and yet I burn,
Since from myself my other self I turn.

II

My care is like my shadow in the sun—
Follows me flying—flies when I pursue it,
Stands and lives by me—does what I have done
This too familiar care doth make me rue it.
No means I find to rid him from my breast,
Till by the end of things it be suppressed.

III

Some gentler passion steal into my mind,
(For I am soft and made of melting snow)
Or be more cruel, Love, or be more kind,
Or let me float or sink be high or low,
Or let me live with some more sweet content,
Or die, and so forget what love e'er meant.[12]

But it was Anjou who died, some two years later, possibly of poison. Elizabeth, hearing the news, shut herself up for days to grieve and refused to transact state business or consult with her ministers.

Of Cosmetics and Perfumes

It was fortunate for everyone concerned that sometime in the two years between the arrival, departure, and death of Anjou, Elizabeth had begun to take notice of a handsome, adventurous young man who hailed from the West Country and who spoke with a broad Devonshire accent. The young Ralegh, perhaps, helped to diminish her grief. He dressed bravely, wore a pearl earring and a pointed beard which must have scandalized William Harrison. But Ralegh was also a poet of no small distinction, "Silence in love bewrays more woe than words" he writes in *The Silent Lover*. It may be, at this crisis, he understood Elizabeth better than anyone else did.

Elizabeth recovered to face the greatest days of her reign—ageing, yet ageless and certainly not beautiful for all Richard Puttenham's Partheniad. Once in these later years—and for a moment fixed in time—the pink and white and golden mask was dropped. In the wonderful Ermine Portrait now at Hatfield House, we see her as she must have looked, with her strange, hooded eyes; her hawk-like nose above a mouth, soft yet well-defined and no longer tight-lipped as in her other pictures, it is a strong face. Aloof, wise—and uncommonly sad.

There is a better word portrait than Puttenham's, by Sir John Hayward. "She was a Lady", he says, "upon whom nature had bestowed and well placed many of her fairest favours; of stature mean (medium) slender, straight, and amiably composed; of such state in her carriage, as every motion of her seemed to bear majesty; her hair was inclined to pale yellow, her forehead, large and fair; a seeming set for princely grace; her eyes lively and sweet but short-sighted; her nose somewhat rising in the middest; the whole compass of her countenance somewhat long but yet of admirable beauty."

This description of the Queen, written some years after her death by a man who also comments that "her virtues were such as might suffice to make an Aethopian beautiful", is undoubtedly a portrait produced by a memory and a devotion both of which were kind, but not too kind, to the sitter.

CHAPTER TEN

Of a Lady Surprised by Time

WE are a curious race. On the fifth of November each year we publicly rejoice that, in 1605, the Houses of Parliament were NOT blown up. Yet, were we as logical as the French or as tradition-minded as we believe ourselves to be, there is another day in November of greater significance and of far more importance than that which records the failure of the Gunpowder Plot. It is November the seventeenth. On that date, four hundred years ago, Elizabeth the First became Queen of England.

Unlike us, our ancestors for two hundred years afterwards had grace, gratitude, and appreciation enough to realize that this date was truly worthy of commemoration. They kept November the seventeenth as the Great Anniversary of English History. It is true they did not understand, until after the Northern Rebellion of 1569, that, in Elizabeth, England had been blessed among nations; but from then on the conviction grew steadily, strongly and justifiably. In the eyes of her people there was no one to equal—or who ever could equal—Elizabeth. They loved her with such passion and such pride that the fire of it warms us even now. And she, in return, loved them—fiercely and protectively.

Once, in conversation, she asked Sir John Harington's wife—perhaps idly or perhaps out of curiosity because the Haringtons were notoriously happy—how she kept her husband's goodwill and love. The answer Lady Harington gave was that she had confidence in her husband's understanding and courage, well-founded

on her own steadfastness not to offend or thwart but to cherish
and obey, and hereby she persuaded her husband of her own
affection and in so doing commanded his.

"You are wisely bent, I find," Elizabeth told her, "after such
sort do I keep the good will of all my husbands—my good people
—for if they did not rest assured of some special love toward
them, they would not readily yield me such good obedience."

There is no cant, no hypocrisy, no play-acting about this.
Elizabeth's one great love, the overriding passion of her life,
was England; and to this she subordinated everything else. Listen
to her as she speaks to her Members of Parliament on another
November day at the end of a reign which had made England
great. "Though God has raised me high," she tells them—and
the tired old voice echoes down the centuries—"yet this I count
the glory of my crown, that I have reigned with your loves . . .
and though you have had, and may have, many mightier and wiser
princes sitting in this seat, yet you never had, nor shall have, any
that will love you better."

Although she was unnecessarily modest in believing—if indeed, she did believe—that we might have mightier and wiser

princes after her, the speech was profoundly true. It was also her valediction. Less than two years later, on March 24th 1603, she was dead. Reluctant and stubborn, she had kept death waiting for days, like some obscure petitioner in an anteroom.

In a small cabinet beside her bed—perhaps the same cabinet in which she kept the likeness in little of "my Lord" which long, long ago she had shown to Sir James Melvil—was the last letter Robert Dudley, Earl of Leicester ever wrote her. Across it in her own hand was written "His last letter". Dudley, "my eyes", as she always called him had died in the September of Armada year. Walsingham, "my faithful Moor", who had given her once a night-gown and who organized, at his own expense, the secret service, had followed Dudley two years later. That "faithful Spirit", William Cecil, had left the world and its cares to his clever, intriguing son, Robert. Lightfooted and handsome Christopher Hatton had died a dozen years before. The great privateer—Admiral Drake, had left his bones to be picked clean by fish off Portobello. Hawkins, who redesigned her ships, left his off Porto Rico. Humphrey Gilbert had never returned after setting up the first colony in North America in 1583. Frobisher who, it was said, brought back two tons of gold from Kodlunarn died of wounds in 1592 (there was a time when she had had to borrow a gold chain "24 ounces and 22 karretts" from Mr. Rogers to give Captain "Frubisher" when he set out on one of his expeditions). Even Parson Harrison, one-time rector of Radwinter had died, a Canon of Windsor, in 1593. The great, the adventurous, the adventuring, the Renaissance Elizabethans were gone.

All but one. On November 17th in the year of her death—the date which marked the forty-fifth anniversary of her accession—the last of the great Elizabethans, facing a charge of treason, spoke of the dead Queen as, "a Lady whom time had surprised".

When young, he had been gallant enough to spread his cloak in the mud so that she might not soil her shoe. Now he dismissed her in six words.

Of a Lady Surprised by Time

"A Lady whom Time had surprised. . . ." Had she heard the phrase she would have thrown her shoe at Ralegh as she had once thrown it at Walsingham, or banished him from court as she had once banished "that saucy poet" her godson. But Time, which she so hated, was both her enemy and her friend. It overtook her but it also immortalized her.

SEMPER EADEM

R

SELECTED BIBLIOGRAPHY

English Social History. G. M. Trevelyan.

History of England. G. M. Trevelyan.

Tudor England. S. T. Bindoff.

Oxford History of England, Vol. VIII. J. B. Black.

A Description of England (Elizabethan England). William Harrison (ed. L. Withington).

Progresses of Queen Elizabeth. John Nichols.

England as Seen by Foreigners (in the Days of Elizabeth and James I). Compiled by W. B. Rye.

A Survey of London. John Stow.

The Age of Shakespeare. Boris Ford.

Life in Shakespeare's England. J. Dover Wilson.

Memoirs. Sir James Melvil.

A Journal of all that was accomplished by M. de Maisse, Ambassador in England from King Henry IV to Queen Elizabeth. Translated and edited by G. B. Harrison and R. A. Jones.

The Age of Elizabeth. Andrew Browning.

Elizabethan and Jacobean Prose. Ed. Kenneth Muir.

Memoirs of the Court of Queen Elizabeth. Lucy Aikin.

Queen Elizabeth (Lives of the Queens of England). Agnes Strickland.

Mary Tudor. H. M. Prescott.

Elizabethan Life in Town and Country. M. St. Claire Byrne.

Middle Class Culture in Elizabethan England. L. B. Wright.

Memoirs of the Reign of Queen Elizabeth. Thomas Birch.

The England of Elizabeth. A. L. Rowse.

Elizabeth and her Parliaments. Sir J. E. Neale.

Architecture in England. John Summerson.

Essays: or Counsels Civill and Moral. Francis Bacon.

Family Papers and Accounts of the Cavendish Family. Chatsworth Settlement.

Calendar of the MS. of Maj.-Gen. Lord Sackville. Vol. 1, Cranford Papers, 1557–1612. H.M.S.O.

A History of Hampton Court Palace. E. Law.

The English Farm House. Martin S. Briggs.

Selected Bibliography

English Furniture Styles. Ralph Fastnedge.
The English Chair. Moss Harris and Sons.
Old English Furniture. Moss Harris and Sons.
The English Interior. Ralph Dutton.
English Interior Decoration (1550–1880). Margaret Jourdain.
English Decoration and Furniture in the Early Renaissance. Margaret Jourdain.
Silver. Gerald Taylor.
Three Centuries of English Silver. B. and T. Hughes.
The Great Herbal. John Gerard (1597 edition).
The Englishman's Food. Drummond and Wilbraham.
The English Housewife. Gervase Markham.
Itinerary. Fynes Moryson.
British Herbs. Florence Ransom.
The Jewel House of Art and Nature. Sir Hugh Platt.
Delights for Ladies to Adorn Their Persons. Sir Hugh Platt.
The Anatomy of Melancholy. Robert Burton.
Man on his Nature. Sir Charles Sherrington.
A Short History of Medicine. C. Singer.
A History of Medicine. Douglas Guthrie.
Journal of the Medical Women's Federation. Vol. 38, No. 3.
A Dietary of Health and Introduction of Knowledge. Andrew Boorde (ed.
    F. J. Furnivall).
The Secrets of Rev. Master Alexis Piedmont. Trans. Wm. Ward, 1595.
The Story of the Garden. E. S. Rhode.
A History of Gardening in England. Alicia Amherst.
Five Hundred Points of Good Husbandry. Thomas Tusser.
The Profitable Art of Gardening. Thomas Hill.
Country Contentments. Gervase Markham.
A Cristal Glass for Christian Women. Philip Stubbs.
The Anatomie of Abuses. Philip Stubbs.
The Diary of Henry Machyn. Camden Soc., No. 42, 1848.
The Elizabethan Woman. Carrol Camden.
Crudities. Thomas Coryat.
The Mystery and Lure of Perfumes. C. J. S. Thompson.
The Book of Perfumes. Eugene Rimmel.
The Art of Perfumery. G. W. S. Piessé.
Various relevant articles in *History Today*; *Country Life* and *The Encyclopaedia Britannica*.

SOURCES

CHAPTER I

1. John Strype: Harleian and Lansdowne MSS., Br. Mus.
2. G. M. Trevelyan: *History of England*.
3. William Harrison: *A Description of England*.
4. G. M. Trevelyan: *English Social History*.
5. Agnes Strickland: *Lives of the Queens of England*, Vol. IV.
6. S. T. Bindoff: *Tudor England*.
7. *England as Seen by Foreigners in the Days of Elizabeth and James I*, compiled by W. B. Rye.
8. Richard Hakluyt: dedication to his *Voyages*.
9. W. B. Rye: op. cit., quoting Samuel Kiechel.
10. Etienne Perlin: *Antiquarian Repertory*.
11. Henry Machyn: *Diary*, Camden Soc., 42, 1848.
12. and 13. John Earle: *Micro-cosmographie*.
14. John Nichols: *The Progresses of Queen Elizabeth*.
15. Sir John Hayward: *Annals*, written 1612, edited, J. Bruce, 1840.
16. De Maisse: *A Journal of all that was Accomplished by M. de Maisse, Ambassador in England from King Henry IV to Queen Elizabeth*.
17. Ashmolean MS. Lib.

CHAPTER II

1. Thomas Fuller: *Worthies* (1661).
2. Andrew Boorde: *A Dietary of Health and Introduction of Knowledge*, edited by F. J. Furnivall.
3. John Nichols: op. cit.
4. John Nichols: op. cit.
5. E. Law: *History of Hampton Court Palace*.
6. Andrew Boorde: *A Dietary of Health*.
7. *England as Seen by Foreigners*, compiled by W. B. Rye.
8. Francis Bacon: *Of Building*.
9. William Harrison: *A Description of England*.

Sources

CHAPTER III

1. Margaret Jourdain: *English Decoration and Furniture of the Early Renaissance*.
2. *England as Seen by Foreigners*, compiled by W. B. Rye.
3. John Nichols: op. cit. There was a Dr. Dale at Court and Mrs. Dale was probably his wife.
4. John Nichols, Agnes Strickland and others: All gifts recorded in this chapter and the next are, for the most part, taken from the list included in Nichols's *Progresses*.
5. W. B. Rye: op. cit.
6. W. B. Rye: op. cit.

CHAPTER IV

1. Thomas Birch: *Memoirs of the Reign of Queen Elizabeth*.
2. Thomas Birch: op. cit.
3. John Nichols: *The Progresses of Queen Elizabeth*.
4. Inventory of effects of Robert Dudley, Earl of Leicester.
5. B. and T. Hughes: *Three Centuries of English Silver*.
6. John Nichols: op. cit.
7. William Harrison: *A Description of England*.
8. William Vaughan: *The Golden Grove* (1600).
9. *England as Seen by Foreigners*, compiled by W. B. Rye.
10. W. B. Rye: op. cit. The relevant passage reads:
    Zwey lang Einhörner seind daselben auch ver wahrt
    Das ein war gar glat, und eins gewundner
    Fast au vier ellen lang . . .

CHAPTER V

1. John Nichols: *The Progresses of Queen Elizabeth*, which record details of visit to Sandwich and Kenilworth.
2. William Harrison: *A Description of England*.
3. William Harrison: op. cit.
4. William Harrison: op. cit.
5. William Harrison: op. cit.
6. Family Papers and Accounts of the Cavendish Family.

Sources

7. Ancaster MS. Accounts: as quoted by M. St. Clair Byrne.
8. William Harrison: op. cit.
9. William Shakespeare: *The Merry Wives of Windsor*, i. 1.
10. William Harrison: op. cit.
11 and 12. William Harrison: op. cit.
13 and 14. John Nichols: op. cit. Agnes Strickland: *Lives of the Queens of England*, Vol. IV.
15. John Gerard: *The Great Herbal* (1597 edition).
16. John Gerard: op. cit.
17. John Gerard: op. cit.

CHAPTER VI

1. John Nichols: *The Progresses of Queen Elizabeth*.
2. John Nichols: op. cit.
3. Robert Burton: *The Anatomy of Melancholy*.
4. A proverb which crops up in many forms. Burton quotes it and George Herbert included it in his collection of *Outlandish (Foreign) Proverbs*, 1640.
5. Robert Burton: op. cit.
6. Andrew Boorde: *A Dietary of Health*.
7. Andrew Boorde: op. cit.
8. Douglas Guthrie, M.D., F.R.C.S.: *A History of Medicine*.
9. Sir Hugh Platt.
10. J. B. Black: *Oxford History of England*, Vol. VIII.

CHAPTER VII

1. Philip Stubbs: *The Anatomie of Abuses*.
2. Gervase Markham: *Country Contentments*.
3. Agnes Strickland: *Lives of the Queens of England*, Vol. III (Mary Tudor).

CHAPTER VIII

1. John Nichols: *The Progresses of Queen Elizabeth*.
2. *England as Seen by Foreigners*, compiled by W. B. Rye.
3. Francis Peck: *Desiderata Curiosa*, but note this was published in 1732–35 and although Peck had a remarkable facility for finding out odd

Sources

facts Theobalds had by then disappeared. John Thorpe made a plan for the park at the request of James I when James exchanged Theobalds for Hatfield in 1607.

4. W. B. Rye: op. cit., quoting Paul Hentzner.
5. W. B. Rye: op. cit., quoting Paul Hentzner.
6. William Bullein: *Book of Simples* (1562).

CHAPTER IX

1. John Donne: *Paradox II.*
2. Sir Hugh Platt: *Delights for Ladies.*
3. Sir Hugh Platt: op. cit.
4. Sir Hugh Platt: op. cit.
5. Musgrave MS., Br. Mus.
6. Stubbs: *Anatomie of Abuses*, edited F. J. Furnivall.
7. Sir John Hayward: *Annals*, written 1612, edited J. Bruce, 1840.
8. Agnes Strickland: *Lives of the Queens of England.*
9. Lansdowne MS.
10. William Shakespeare: *The Merry Wives of Windsor*, ii. 2.
11. John Nichols: *The Progresses of Queen Elizabeth.*
12. Ashmolean MS. Lib.

INDEX

Index

Index

Dudley, Robert, Earl of Leicester, 12, 28, 30, 41–2, 81, 95, 106, 109, 112, 117–18, 127, 132, 135–6, 190, 260

Dyes, 237–8

Edward VI, 16

Elizabeth I: procession to the Tower, 11–12; characteristics, 13–14; choice of ministers, 14; financial acumen, 15; and the Navy, 16; Anglicanism, 17–19; and her seamen, 22–3, 25; at Woodstock, 27; and Dudley, 28, 117; on the Thames, 30–1; idolized, 31–2, 35–6; Sir J. Hayward on, 32–3, 257; her Court, 33–4; ability in languages, 35; her progresses, 40–2; at Theobalds, 42–3; 59–60; at Osterley Park, 43; at Longleat, 46; at Mrs. Fisher's, 52; at Croydon, 61–2; instals water-closet, 64; coronation procession, 72–4; and Mr. Fuller's book, 88–9; as needlewoman, 89; and the French ambassador, 89–90; loves clothes and finery, 90–2, 94–5, 120–3, 131–2; loves furnishings, 98; at Ditchley, 99; angry with Harington, 107–108; her spice-box, 111; her chandelier, 113; her clocks, 116; exchange of gifts with her subjects, 117–18; loss of jewellery, etc., 124–5; her letter-writing, 125; gift from Haring-ton, 126; her miniatures, 127–128; fond of indoor games and music, 130–1, 193–4, 196–8; her earrings and looking-glasses, 131; her old age, 132–3; at Sandwich, 134–5; at Kenilworth, 135–6; and the fish laws, 149; her daily menu, 152–3; ritual observed for serving food, 153–4; attempts to poison her, 153; receives gifts of sweets, 161; her toothache, 164–5; healthiest of the Tudors, 165–6; her illnesses, 166; at Burghley's death-bed, 171–2; her astrologer, Dr. Dee, 176–7; fond of tylts, 189; good horsewoman, and skill with crossbow, 190; her lapdogs, 192; at Earl of Hertford's garden-party, 211–12; at Cobham Hall, 219–21; her heraldic beasts, 222; at Gorhambury, 226; and Dr. Cox, 228–9; colour of her face, 238; her toothpicks, 243; her wigs, 246–7; love of perfumes, 251–253; and the Duke of Anjou, 255–6; and Ralegh, 257; Ermine portrait of, 257; a great queen, 258–61

Ely Place, Holborn, 228–9

Embroidery, 87

Essex, Earl of, 132, 133

Ewers, 107

Fairs, 195–6

Farmhouses, 51–3

Index

Index

Index

Index

Index